THE HANDBOOK OF
SURVIVAL AT SEA

THE HANDBOOK OF
SURVIVAL AT SEA

CHRIS BEESON

LEWIS
INTERNATIONAL, INC.

First published in 2003 by Lewis International, Inc.
2201 N.W. 102 Place, #1
Miami, Fl 33172 USA

Tel: 305-436-7984 / 800-259-5962
Fax: 305-436-7985 / 800-664-5095

Library of Congress Cataloging-in-Publication Data available.

ISBN 1-930983-21-2

Editorial and design by
Amber Books Ltd
Bradley's Close
74–77 White Lion Street
London N1 9PF
www.amberbooks.co.uk

Project Editor: Michael Spilling
Design: Graham Curd
Illustrations: Tony Randell and Kevin Jones Associates

PICTURE CREDITS
Front cover: Courtesy US Coast Guard

Publisher's note
Neither the author nor the publishers can accept any responsibility for any
loss, injury or damage, caused as a result of the use of techniques described
in this book. Nor for any prosecutions or proceedings brought or instigated
against any person or body that may result from using these techniques.

Printed in Italy by Eurolitho S.p.A.

Contents

Introduction 6

1
Preparing to Survive 8

2
Coastal Survival 42

3
Offshore Survival 62

4
Navigation 92

5
Water Supply 114

6
Food Supply 132

7
Attracting Rescue 156

8
Making Landfall 172

Glossary 188

Index 190

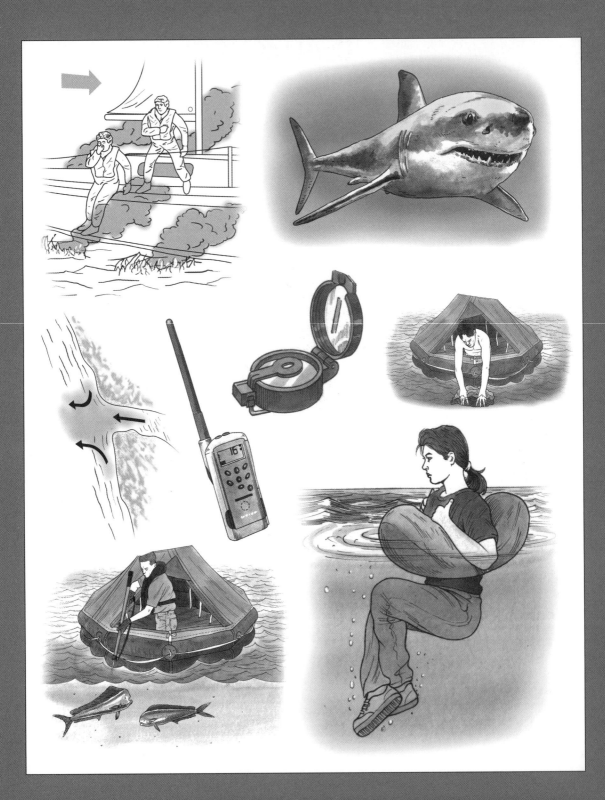

Introduction

The difficulties of survival at sea have made legends of several individuals. The five members of the family Robertson and one friend survived for 38 days, first in a life raft and then in a dinghy, before being rescued by a deep sea trawler. Steve Callahan lasted 76 days in a life raft before being taken to safety by fishermen. The Baileys, husband and wife, lasted 117 days in a life raft before fishermen rescued them. And merchant seaman Poon Lim survived an astonishing 130 days before fishermen plucked him from his wooden raft.

The most inspiring of all these remarkable feats of endurance is, for two reasons, that of Poon Lim. He survived at sea for longer than anyone else - his record still stands - and, except for the life jacket he grabbed before abandoning ship, he had no equipment at all, not even clothes.

That he managed to stay alive for so long is a tribute to human innovation and an inspiration to those who, through fault or fate, find themselves in a sea survival situation. That drive to survive is first and foremost in the list of requirements for survival at sea. We are all born with it and it will be the last urge we lose. Using that drive, we can focus the power of human ingenuity to innovate the means to the end of survival using whatever we have to hand.

Everything else is preparation. This book helps you to learn the techniques required to survive: how to recognize the main threats to survival, how to overcome them, and how to attract rescue at sea.

It also helps you to ensure that, if you do find yourself in a sea survival situation, you have the right equipment for survival, or at least the knowledge to improvise the equipment you lack.

People go to sea for many reasons: to ply their trade; to get away from it all; or to pass some personal milestone of achievement. Some never return. With knowledge and equipment, and powered by the drive to survive, you can give yourself and your crew the best chance of beating the capricious odds of nature, should the purpose of your voyage change, for whatever reason, to survival.

CHAPTER ONE

Preparing to survive

Survival at sea is about staying alive long enough to reach safety. To do so, you will need to know not only the main factors that endanger your survival and the techniques and equipment needed to overcome them, but also, most importantly, to maintain the right attitude and keep the will to survive.

The evolutionary process began in the primordial soup of the ocean that covered the earth 3500 million years ago. From those single-celled origins evolved all the species that swim the oceans, fly the skies and walk the earth today. Each of them is adapted to survive in its own natural habitat and occupies its own unique position in the food chain. Some species have proved so successful at exploiting their natural habitat that they have not needed to evolve any

further. The shark, for instance, can be considered a dinosaur of the seas: fossilized remains dating back 370 million years show that it has evolved little. At that stage, skeletons made from bone had yet to develop, and the shark's skeleton is made from cartilage and gristle. Rather than the scales that protect more evolved species of fish, the shark has dermal denticles, small toothlike structures that are very rough and can easily tear human skin if contact is made.

Even its jaw is made of compacted mineral deposits rather than bone. The shark is the perfect predator – further adaptation has been unnecessary.

Other species did not have such an easy ride. The reptiles from which humanity eventually developed left the ocean around 200 million years ago and adapted to live on land, growing legs, developing lungs that extracted oxygen from air rather than water, and evolving into the first warm-blooded mammals. Later, some of these mammalian species took to the trees to escape terrestrial predators and to exploit the plentiful food resources of the forest canopy. Eventually, some of these species returned to the ground while others remained aloft. The latter developed, about 40 million years ago, into monkeys, while the former began the long quadrupedal, then bipedal march to become modern man. Fossils show that our earliest ancestor, Ramapithecus, first walked upright some 14 million years ago, but it was not until five million years ago that Australopithecus first used tools for hunting and killing.

Homo sapiens, modern man, has existed for just 35,000 years, but in that time he has

The perfect predator

The shark is such an effective predator that it has evolved very little in some 370 million years. It has neither bones nor scales as it was already an extremely successful predator long before these adaptations evolved in other species of fish.

evolved into the most adaptable species on the planet. This is testament to the rigours that our ancestors had to endure, the adaptations the species has had to make in order to survive and procreate, and the indomitable will to survive. Our ancestors' ability to hunt and kill in packs, using basic language for operational coordination, shows an ability to plan, to share learning and information, and to execute complex routines as a team – all indicative of a higher form of intelligence that is unique to our species. The manufacture and use of tools shows the ability to innovate and improvise using available materials to find and exploit sources of food, water and protection.

In short, *Homo sapiens* stands in this exalted position today because of evolutionary pressure. Having overcome his comparative physical weakness and fragility by using his intelligence, guile and survival instinct, *Homo sapiens* sits at the top of every food chain.

Man has evolved to live very successfully by farming the land, extracting and using the earth's mineral resources and exploiting the food sources of coastal waters. At sea, however, we are in a completely alien habitat. Once we are away from our industrial infrastructure, shelter and utilities, we are forced to rely on our evolutionary legacy: intelligence, learning, innovation, improvisation and the awesome drive to survive. These faculties have kept our species alive for 14 million years and even in an unnatural habitat such as the ocean, we are capable of extracting what we need from what we find around us. Equipped with basic knowledge and equipment, we can innovate techniques and adapt equipment to improvise the means of survival. In every sea survival situation, we will rely on the hard-earned skills handed down to us. They have kept us alive for 14 million years and, if confidence is placed in them, they will keep a survivor at sea alive until safety is reached.

PREPARATION

Arguably the most important of these faculties is learning, the ability to share acquired knowledge rather than having to start from scratch every time. Our evolutionary legacy is powerful indeed, and if the sea survivor is thoroughly prepared for his ordeal, knows what to expect and how to deal with it, he will not be beaten. Preparation for a sea survival situation has three aspects: these are knowledge, equipment and attitude.

KNOWLEDGE

Survival at sea is about staying alive until safety can be reached or until rescue arrives. In order to stay alive, we must be aware of the four main enemies to survival, how potent they are and how we can defeat them. They are, in order of priority, drowning, exposure, thirst, and hunger.

Drowning

This is the ocean's number one killer. The body cannot function without oxygen being transported by the blood to the vital organs, but since emerging onto the land some 200 million years ago, our lungs have lost the ability to extract oxygen from water. We need to breathe air. So great is our need for oxygen that the body's entire blood supply, about 4 litres (8 pints), passes through the lung's 300,000 million tiny blood vessels – some 2400 kilometres (1500 miles) in length – about once a minute. The brain, although only three percent of our bodyweight, uses 20 per cent of all the oxygen we breathe. Without sufficiently oxygenated blood, the brain will become hypoxic, causing unconsciousness, brain damage, then finally coma within a matter of minutes.

However, when we are immersed in water, our lungs help to keep us afloat. The lungs are easy to inflate, 100 times easier than a child's balloon thanks to their extreme elasticity, and if the head, or at least the face, is kept above the surface of the water, we can inflate our lungs easily and stay afloat. The average breath replaces just 14 per cent of the air in the lungs so it is important to breathe deeply, to maximize the buoyancy provided by the lungs and to increase the supply of oxygen.

Above all, it is essential that the immersed survivor stays calm. Panic will increase the body's demand for oxygen, which is used in the chemical reactions that convert stored energy into expended energy. It will also reduce the oxygen intake as breathing quickens but becomes shallower, reducing the exchange of oxygen and the waste product of its chemical activity, carbon dioxide. As the panicking survivor becomes exhausted, she will lose the energy to remain afloat, and drown.

Exposure

The normal human body maintains a core temperature of 36.8°C (98.4°F) and under normal circumstances this varies little more than 0.6–1.1°C (1–2°F) above or below the norm. There are records of survival after sustained core temperature drops of as much as 11°C (20°F), but core temperature increases of as little as 4°C (7°F) for extended periods have proved fatal.

It is essential therefore that the body's core temperature be kept as close to normal as is possible in the survival environment.

Cold

When the body is immersed in water, it loses heat up to 25 times faster than it does in air. This is because water is a more effective conductor of heat than air, and also because the majority of body heat is lost through the skin – there are about 1.8 square metres (20 square feet) of it on the average man. Remember, too, that the greater the difference between body temperature and water temperature, the greater the rate of heat loss.

The body's temperature-regulating centre is based in the hypothalamus, at the base of the brain. As soon as a drop in blood temperature is noted, the hypothalamus triggers its defence mechanisms. First the body shivers, an automatic reflex intended to restore the body to its normal temperature. By contracting muscles, large amounts of heat are produced as stored energy is converted into expended energy.

If the temperature drops to below 35°C (95°F), the body becomes hypothermic. The survivor will be numb with cold and shiver intensely, thereby impairing motor function and coordination; his speech will be slurred and slow; and mental function will be impaired, so his decision-making ability will be poor and he will find it difficult to concentrate. All this is owing to the hypothalamus triggering its next defence mechanism – vasoconstriction. The diameter of the blood vessels constricts to the point that blood vessels in the extremities of the body – the hands and feet, followed by the legs and arms – will no longer receive an adequate supply of blood, and these will turn white as blood vessels near the skin close off completely. This is intended to restrict the loss of heat from blood circulating in those more exposed extremities and also to concentrate the blood around the vital organs in the abdomen and the skull.

Extended vasoconstriction leads to frostbite. Without an adequate supply of blood, body tissue begins to die, starting with the skin. Frostbite appears as grey or yellow blotches, accompanied by a numb sensation. At this stage, the affected area can be warmed against the abdomen of a fellow survivor without any long-term damage to the affected area. If the area is not warmed, it will gradually turn grey and hard, darkening eventually to blackness as the water in the cell tissue freezes and the tissue dies. Once this occurs, it is unlikely that the affected area will ever recover.

If core temperature continues to drop, survival becomes increasingly unlikely. At 32°C (89.6°F), the body's defence mechanisms will begin to fail. Shivering will be replaced by muscle rigidity and cramping but, very much more dangerously, vasoconstriction fails. This allows the blood to return to the extremities - hands, feet, legs and arms - lowering blood pressure and slowing the pulse and the rate of respiration. It also means that the blood loses more heat as it passes through the cold extremities and this colder blood will circulate around the vital organs, impairing their function still further. The survivor will become confused, disorientated, apathetic and, eventually, unconscious. Death occurs if the core body temperature drops below 25°C (77°F). Apathy is the most important and worrying sign, as it indicates that the will to survive has been extinguished. Without the will to survive, we die.

Heat

In a sea survival situation, exposure to heat is potentially more dangerous than exposure to cold because this involves sweating - the loss of fluid. Slight rises in core temperature will cause the veins near the surface of the skin to expand, increasing the amount of blood near the surface of the skin. By the processes of convection, conduction and radiation, heat will be lost from the blood to the surrounding air in an attempt to return core temperature to normal. Core temperature rises of between 0.25-0.5°C (0.5 to 1°F) will be registered by the hypothalamus, which will trigger the sweat glands to secrete sweat, essentially water and salt. Sweat appears on the surface of the skin, and heat from the body makes the water in the sweat evaporate, leaving the body cooler. If sweat can be seen on the skin, this is because heat production is exceeding evaporation, which usually occurs when humidity is high.

Exposure to the sun

To avoid losing water and salt through sweating, the survivor must rest in the shade during the heat of the day. Wear light clothing that covers the skin and, if necessary, dampen the clothing.

If sweating fails to return core temperature to normal, the effects of the loss of water and salt will begin to manifest themselves. After sweating for some time, the survivor will experience cramping in the body's extremities and also in the abdomen, although her temperature appears to be normal. This is as a result of salt deficiency and you can prevent the situation becoming worse by taking a salt tablet and water, or mixing ¼ teaspoon of salt with 1 litre (about 2 pints) water and then drinking it. The survivor should also be placed in the shade to rest – erect a canopy if you do not already have one.

If salt is not replaced and exposure to heat and direct sunlight continues, the survivor will suffer from heat exhaustion, which is a form of shock. As water and salt are lost, the blood begins to thicken and blood pressure drops. The effect of this drop in pressure is reduced blood flow to the vital organs, including the brain. The survivor's skin will feel cool and clammy as the blood supply to the skin is reduced, and she may report headache and dizziness, confusion and drowsiness as the lack of oxygenated blood to the brain brings on hypoxia. Another effect of reduced blood flow is that reserves of energy are not converted effectively, leaving the survivor feeling weak. Once again, to reverse this decline, both salt and fluid must be replaced and the survivor placed in shade with her feet, arms, and head raised to concentrate the blood around the vital organs.

If corrective action is not taken, heat stroke will eventually follow. To counter the drop in blood pressure, the blood vessels widen – a phenomenon known as vasodilation – and heart rate increases to restore blood flow. However, as fluid and salt levels decrease, the blood thickens further and sweating, the body's primary method of lowering core temperature, fails. The skin feels dry and hot as the heart beats faster and

faster in an attempt to raise blood pressure. Lack of oxygen to the brain brings on unconsciousness, hypoxic brain damage and, eventually, death. Cooling the body as rapidly as possible can prevent death. Immerse the survivor in water or soak her clothing, and keep her in the shade with her feet and arms up. Administer fluids and salt only if the survivor is conscious.

If the survivor takes precautions to avoid exposure, the body will adjust to the new environment within a week. Sweat will still be produced, but its salt content will be greatly reduced as the body protects it mineral reserves.

Heat exposure often involves exposure to the sun's ultraviolet (UV) radiation and if the survivor is not protected by clothing or sunblock, sunburn will result. Sunburn is categorized as a first-degree burn because it affects only the skin, but it is at best uncomfortable and at worst extremely painful, proving debilitating and sapping morale. What's more, the body's water is attracted to the burned area beneath blisters. These may then burst, which means that the water is lost and the open wound may become infected. If the burns are serious, the body's temperature regulation mechanism can be damaged and the symptoms of shock may also be seen.

The first response, if you do suffer sunburn, is to get out of the sun and cool the area, either by immersing it in water or putting on clothes dampened with sea water. The evaporation of the sea water will draw heat away from the body. If the burns are serious, you should pat them dry and place sterile gauze over the area, then bandage or tape it in place.

Another potential risk of exposure to the sun's ultraviolet radiation is sunblindness. In strong sunlight, the sun's UV radiation hits the eye directly and between 3 and 30 per cent can be reflected by the water, depending on the incident angle of the light. After as little as six hours' exposure to UV radiation, the cornea will burn, just as the skin does. The survivor with sunblindness will complain of a gritty sensation, as if sand is in the eye, and possibly deterioration of vision. To solve this, you should move into the shade, then place a damp cloth, thick enough to block out all light, over the eyes for 18 hours - in cold climates, the cloth need not be damp. This will relieve the symptoms of sunblindness, but just as burned skin is more sensitive to sunlight, so too are your eyes. If you have no sunglasses, improvise a pair in the way that the Inuit do: cut eye slits in a strap of soft leather and tie that around the head to cover the eyes but allow a degree of vision. As you are unlikely to have soft leather, use thick fabric or two equal lengths of duct tape stuck to each other in a double layer.

Despite the survivor's effort to keep the interior of the life raft dry and free of sea water, some will inevitably enter. Saltwater sores will occur first on the areas in regular contact with sea water - feet, knees, buttocks, elbows and hands - and then spread to the rest of the body. The application of waterproof sunscreen will provide some relief, but this will be temporary as it will inevitably be rubbed off through contact with the life raft. Resist the urge to tamper with or drain the resulting boils, because they will become open sores and ulcerate.

Dealing with sun blindness

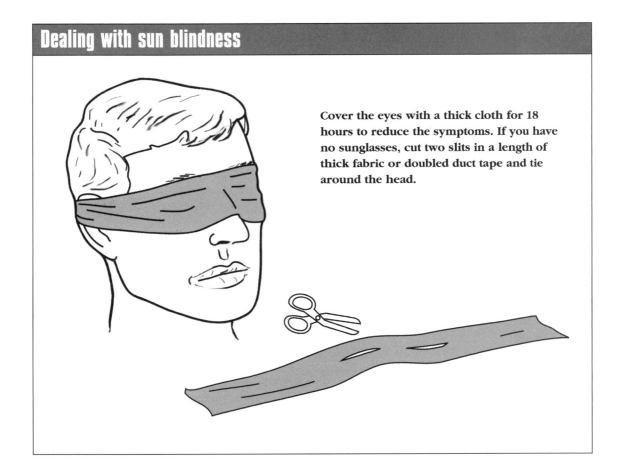

Cover the eyes with a thick cloth for 18 hours to reduce the symptoms. If you have no sunglasses, cut two slits in a length of thick fabric or doubled duct tape and tie around the head.

If broken skin is exposed to saltwater, the wound will not heal, rather it will become infected, scabrous and filled with pus. These scabs should not be broken, but those on the legs and arms will almost inevitably be damaged by abrasion from movement around the life raft. This will eventually lead to ulceration. Antiseptic ointment should be applied to the wound and sea water should be kept away from it. Petroleum jelly can be used for this purpose, but abrasion is again likely to remove this protective coating. Saltwater sores are likely to be a problem in any case, but if the life raft is not kept as dry and free of salt as possible, they will sap morale sooner.

Saltwater sores

These are an inevitable result of the prolonged exposure of skin to saltwater. Apply any protective oils or creams you have, otherwise leave them alone.

If immersed for long periods in cold water, you will begin to suffer from a mild form of frostbite. First the feet will become numb, prickling and tingling occasionally, and then they will become red and begin to swell and develop blisters. Resist the urge to rub warmth into feet in this condition, as the skin is especially delicate at this stage. Pat them dry if possible and place them against a fellow survivor's abdomen to warm them. Wiggle your toes to ensure blood flow and put your feet up whenever possible.

In warm water, prolonged immersion will turn the skin dull, pale and wrinkled. There is little that can be done about this other than, once again, attempting to keep the skin dry. Pat the affected area dry, but again do not rub it – it will be sensitive and prone to tearing. Ensure that any watertight seals around the wrists and ankles are loosened to ensure there is a good supply of blood to the area. If you have any waterproof sunscreen, smooth that on. It will be rubbed off quickly through contact with the life raft, but will provide some protection.

Thirst

During a prolonged survival period at sea, sources of fresh water to replace lost fluids may not be readily available. As your reserve supplies are unlikely to be adequate for normal human function, you must limit the amount of water your body is losing. On abandoning ship, your nervous system will have reacted automatically by triggering its 'fight or flight' mechanism. This is perhaps the most significant part of our evolutionary legacy, where the body responds to potential threats by shutting down processes not immediately related to survival.

In stressful situations, your body will increase its production of the hormones adrenaline and noradrenaline. As a result, the pupils dilate to increase visual acuity and the sense of hearing sharpens, heart rate rises, and vasodilation increases the blood supply to the heart, brain and lungs. Blood flow to the skin, however, is reduced by vasoconstriction to prevent excessive bleeding in the event of injury and to concentrate blood around the vital organs. The increased amount of oxygen absorbed into the blood through the lungs converts larger amounts of stored carbohydrates into available energy and raises metabolism. Critically, digestion shuts down, saving water, and water in urine is reabsorbed into body tissue, darkening its colour.

This response cannot be maintained for long periods, however. To survive we must conserve water by limiting its loss. First, the survivor must take medication to prevent seasickness. A huge amount of fluid is lost through vomiting, and the apathy that accompanies seasickness reduces the drive to survive. The sight and smell of vomit may also stimulate others to vomit as well, increasing the fluid requirements of the survival unit. If a survivor is about to vomit, it should be into a seasickness bag that can be sealed – vomiting overboard will attract sharks. If a bag is not available, the vomit should be cleared up as soon as possible. In these circumstances, rubbing some aromatic ointment under the nose of the other survivors will mask the smell and prevent the urge to vomit in other survivors.

In the medium term, you are likely to become constipated, possibly for several weeks, owing to your lowered consumption of water and food, which in turn reduces water loss. You should resist the urge to urinate, but if you have to, do so into a container inside the life raft and expect to find it very dark in colour; any excess water has been recycled in the body. Urinating overboard increases the risk of falling out of the life raft and also attracts sharks. Once you've finished urinating, check for sharks and if none are present, throw the waste – but not the container – as far from the raft as possible, again to avoid attracting sharks.

Preserve your energy

To save water in the longer term, you must reduce water loss, the primary source of which is sweating. Reduce activities to the bare minimum – those that are essential to survival – and carry them out during the cooler parts of the day only (around sunrise and sunset) or at night. Dampen your clothing if you are working for extended periods, and never work between 1000 and 1700 in tropical climates. You should stop working when you feel yourself begin to sweat, and lie in the shade, dampen your clothing if necessary, and rest with your mouth closed to prevent loss of moisture in exhaled breath.

As a survivor at sea, water will be the single most important factor in your life. You will dream about water and your every waking hour will be spent waiting for the chance to exploit sources of fresh water, rationing your supply, ensuring its purity and protecting its storage. For you, water and life will become synonymous. That is not to say you cannot survive without it for fairly long periods, however.

The normally hydrated human body can retain most of its essential functions for five to seven days, and remain alive after 10-12 days without water. With 560 ml (1 pint) of water per day, the same survivor can retain essential function for 10-14 days and remain alive for 20- 24 days.

Collecting rainwater

Water collection equipment should be kept salt-free and ready for deployment at very short notice. Don't forget the stomach is an excellent collection vessel and that rain offers the survivor a chance to rinse encrusted salt from both body and clothes.

Hunger

In terms of importance, hunger comes a very distant second behind thirst. The healthy human body can survive without food for up to 30 days before becoming dysfunctional – even more if there are considerable deposits of fat. Hunger is painful, but it is malnutrition that kills. Once the survivor's stores of fat are burned to produce energy, his body will then draw energy from breaking down the proteins in the muscles, leading to muscle wastage and physical weakness. Coordination will be affected and movements will slow, decreasing the chances of successfully hunting or gathering food. Standing up suddenly will leave the survivor feeling light-headed, with dizziness and possibly fainting following, because blood pressure lowers as the heart pumps more weakly and slowly to conserve energy.

Without reserves of insulating fat or the capacity to generate heat by shivering, the body is more susceptible to the effects of cold. The sensation of thirst will increase, along with a craving for salt. For evolutionary reasons, the eyes will remain sharp and hearing will actually improve as the survival urge to hunt adapts the body to its immediate purpose. Feelings of hunger will last no more than five to seven days, although the survivor will become irritable, aggressive and depressed thereafter.

Provided the survivor has adequate supplies of water however, malnutrition is unlikely. The area beneath a life raft is up to 200 times richer in food than the same area on land. Your life raft will, quite literally, attract food, and provided you have the means to harvest those sources, you will not go hungry at sea. What you should eat, though, is a different matter.

The majority of the ocean's food sources are rich in protein, and protein requires water for digestion – water that your body supplies. If you lack an adequate water supply (more than 560 ml/1 pint per day), do not eat protein. Carbohydrates are much more useful foodstuffs in a sea survival situation. When packing your emergency supplies, make sure you have a plentiful supply of carbohydrate snacks, such as chocolate, a resealable tin of boiled sweets with glucose powder, and biscuits. These require less water to digest than proteins and are more easily converted into energy for short- to medium-term needs. If you have 280 ml (½ pint) per day or less, do not eat at all because all digestion requires some water.

EQUIPMENT

With the main enemies of survival now identified, the survivor needs to make sure that she has the right equipment to avoid them. The following list is exhaustive, outlining every item you could conceivably need in a sea survival situation; some of these will provide back-up systems should the primary survival systems fail. When

deciding what equipment to take, expense may tempt you to leave some out – don't! You will succeed only in making yourself vulnerable; the thought of how much money you saved will be of no comfort as you are drowning, or trying to fight through the mental fog of hypothermia.

Water is essential. Since you cannot rely on being rescued before your supply of bottled water runs out, you must must make certain that you have other options available. It is true that your drive to survive will spur you on to remarkable feats of endurance, but failing to provide adequate means to promote your own survival is not intelligent. In any case, you will inevitably be forced to improvise and innovate as your equipment becomes less efficient or fails, but your survival chances will be significantly reduced if you have to improvise from the start.

The equipment you take with you is intended to keep you alive, and its value should be considered in those terms. Every item of equipment used outside the raft should be attached to you by a lanyard. And it will be too late to realize the importance of this when you watch your last knife, or your signal mirror, spiral down into the depths of the ocean. Inside the raft, all equipment should be stored securely in pockets and grab bags, and fastened to the inside grab lines of the life raft. In the event of capsize, the sudden and aggressive ingress of water will inevitably snatch some of your equipment. Your equipment is as important as your life because it will sustain your life. Treat it with the respect it deserves.

Personal equipment

A PFD (Personal Flotation Device) is the most important thing you can pack. This single piece of equipment will defeat the ocean's biggest killer, so leaving port without one is not an option. It should be in good condition, within its reinspection date, and you should know how to fasten it securely

Personal Flotation Device (PFD)

and both full-sleeved and full-legged. Much of the body's heat is lost through the extremities (the hands, feet and head), so the inner layer should include thermal gloves, socks and a hat.

The middle layer should be made of modern synthetic fleece material, tight-weave wool or thick cotton. Again it should be full-sleeved and full-legged, and you should include socks and gloves in the middle layer too. Choose a polo neck (known as a turtleneck in the United States), as the carotid arteries and jugular veins are close to the surface at the neck, and heat will be lost through them.

The outer layer is foul-weather gear, thick and waterproof (unless the survivor is immersed). Sea boots should be worn, as should waterproof hard-wearing gloves to protect and insulate the hands. The hood of the jacket should be used to help prevent heat loss through the head. Also take sunglasses to protect against sunblindness.

The principle of layering is to prevent the air or water immediately surrounding the body from escaping. It will be warmed by the body and the multiple layers will make sure that heat energy stays next to the body rather than being lost and replaced by water at ambient temperature. Layering reduces the temperature gradient between the body and its immediate environment, reducing heat transfer as a direct result. Several light layers will always prove more effective than a single heavy layer.

Again, store all your foul weather gear and in the wet locker so that it can be collected quickly by one of the crew in an emergency.

and in a hurry. It should include automatic CO_2 self-inflation and a manual top-up tube in case the automatic system fails; a whistle; and a strobe light to aid your relocation at night. When not being worn, all PFDs should be stored in the wet locker, close to the hatch, so that they can be collected quickly by one of the crew in an emergency.

Clothing
This should provide you with the means to avoid exposure to cold and heat.

Cold
Clothing should be layered. In cold climates, the survivor should be wearing inner, middle and outer layers.

The inner layer should be thermal, made from tight-weave materials that retain heat,

Heat
To protect against overheating and the effects of the sun, you need full-legged trousers and a full-sleeved top with a collar. You should also have a sunhat and sunglasses to protect the head and eyes, soft shoes to protect the feet, and sunscreen

to apply to any exposed areas, such as the neck, the ears, the hands and the nose. This will ensure that the sun's UV radiation is not in direct contact with your skin. Also, if you feel yourself warming up, or you begin to sweat, douse your clothing in sea water, then put it on again and get into shade in order to lower your body temperature.

In tropical climates, where skies are generally cloudless, the temperature difference between day and night is often great. You will need some warm clothing to protect yourself from the cold at night.

Pocket kit

There are certain items that a mariner – a potential survivor – should never be without:

Multitool

This is always useful and should be securely attached to your belt or your jacket by a lanyard. The knife should be kept sharp at all times because you may need to cut something in a hurry – for example, a fishing line if you catch a shark or a fish that is too large and heavy and so threatens to capsize the life raft.

Whistle

Attached to your jacket by a lanyard, this is a back-up should the one on your PFD be torn off during abandon ship.

Sunscreen

For daily use to prevent the debilitating effects of sunburn.

Dye marker

Should you go overboard during the day, you can use this to help your relocation or attract SAR (Search And Rescue) services.

Chemical light stick

These last between five and 30 minutes, depending on intensity, and are visible

Warm weather clothing

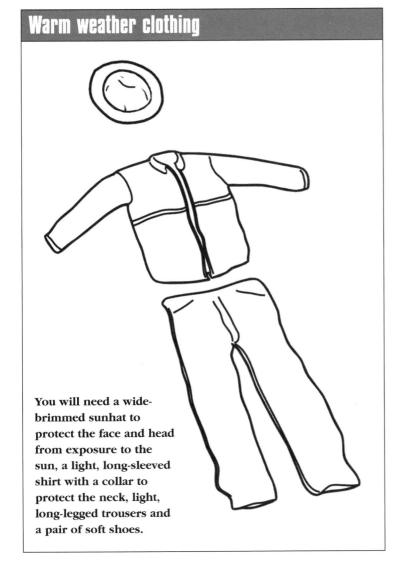

You will need a wide-brimmed sunhat to protect the face and head from exposure to the sun, a light, long-sleeved shirt with a collar to protect the neck, light, long-legged trousers and a pair of soft shoes.

Cold weather clothing

A. Waterproof jacket

B. Thermal gloves

C. Waterproof leggings

D. Harsh weather gear,
   including sea boots

from up to 1.6km (1 mile) away. Always attach a lanyard because their visibility increases when swung above the head in a larger circle than the arm can manage.

Life raft

There are many options on the market, from one-man life rafts to 24-man life rafts or those designed for airliners. Their design concept is governed by the IMO's (International Maritime Organization) SOLAS (Safety Of Life At Sea) regulations, first drawn up after the *Titanic* disaster and regularly updated. These specify that the life raft must be made of at least two separate buoyancy chambers, either of which can support the weight of the number of crew for which it is designed. It must have a canopy to protect its occupants against the worst onslaught of the elements; a double-skinned inflatable floor, usually manually inflated, to protect the

occupants from the cold of the ocean; and, below that floor, self-deploying ballast bags to help prevent capsize.

The regulations also specify that the design should allow 0.36 square metres (4 square feet) of space per survivor. However, this is inadequate. In cold climates, the survivors will all be wearing bulky clothing and there will be a great deal of extra survival equipment brought into the life raft too. The space specified is not enough to co-exist in any degree of comfort for extended periods. It's handy for sharing heat, but you will not be able to rest effectively or stretch out if suffering from cramps. A solo sailer should buy a two- or four-man life raft; two crew members need a four- or six-man life raft; and four crew, a six- to eight-man life raft. This will allow a moderate degree of comfort for the survivors and also cut down on contact that

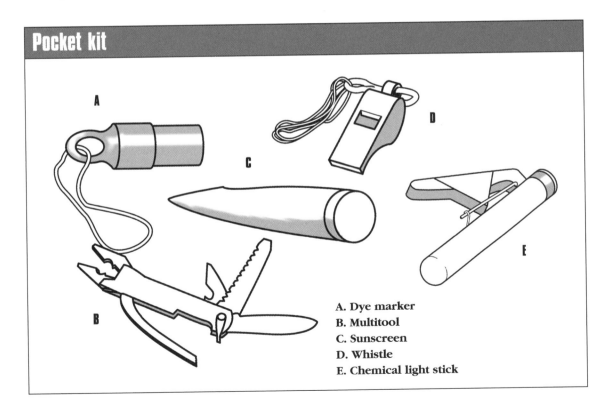

Pocket kit

A. Dye marker
B. Multitool
C. Sunscreen
D. Whistle
E. Chemical light stick

Life raft

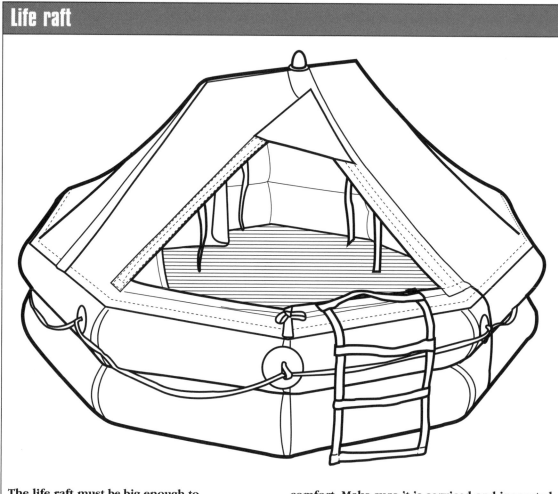

The life raft must be big enough to accommodate you, your crew and your survival equipment with some degree of comfort. Make sure it is serviced and inspected regularly and stowed somewhere easily accessible in the event of emergency.

might aggravate saltwater sores. In cold climates, you can still huddle together to share warmth, but the option of a little personal space is one you will certainly appreciate.

All life rafts come with basic survival kit. Although contents may vary between manufacturers, these will include:

Life raft kit

Drinking water – 560 ml
(1 pint) per person sealed in plastic, foil, or can containers

1 x Life raft knife, blunt-tipped, to cut the static line

1 x First aid kit

1 x Flashlight with spare battery and bulb

2 x Paddles, wooden or aluminium

2 x Parachute flares

3 x   Hand flares
1 x   Signalling mirror
1 x   Distress signal guide
1 x   Bailer
1 x   Sponge
1 x   Sea anchor with 30m (100ft) of line
1 x   Rescue quoit with 3m (10ft) of line
1 x   Manual inflation pump
1 x   Life raft repair kit (including bungs, patches and adhesive)
1 x   Whistle
1 x   Fishing kit
       Seasickness pills
       Emergency
       procedures handbook

You should acquaint yourself with the safety equipment stored in your life raft – bitter experience has shown that some of it is inadequate in certain circumstances. For instance, the adhesive supplied in the repair kit specifies that the patches and area to be repaired should be clean and dry. In reality, this is seldom possible. The bungs themselves are useful for small tears, but for anything larger, they are inadequate and the effort required to keep a semi-repaired tube inflated is considerable.

There are other much more reliable raft repair options on the market and you should investigate these. One such option is the raft repair clamp, a pair of contoured metal ovals, one of which is placed inside the tear and the other outside. They are drawn together with a connecting bolt, and rubber seals on the contact surfaces ensure an airtight repair. They come in three sizes and will save you a huge amount of effort both in repair and constant reinflation.

You should also ensure that you have a spare sea anchor. These are essential to help prevent the life raft capsizing in rough weather and also to take advantage of favourable currents to increase speed. The sea anchor will be deployed for much of

Life raft repair clamps

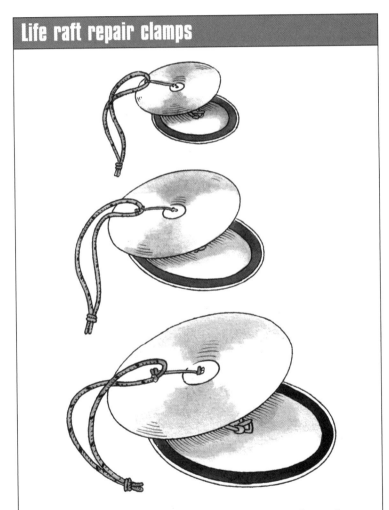

As the life raft's repair kit is seldom adequate, explore other options. The repair clamps shown are an easy-to-use, reliable and effective solution for repairing tears in your life raft.

Life raft kit

A. Water, can openers, sea sickness pills
B. Repair kit, flares, stopper, sponge, knife
C. Sea anchor
D. Paddles
E. First aid kit
F. Bailer
G. Fishing line and hooks
H. Survival leaflets

I. Quoit and line
J. Bellows
K. Flashlight and spare batteries
L. Resealing lids

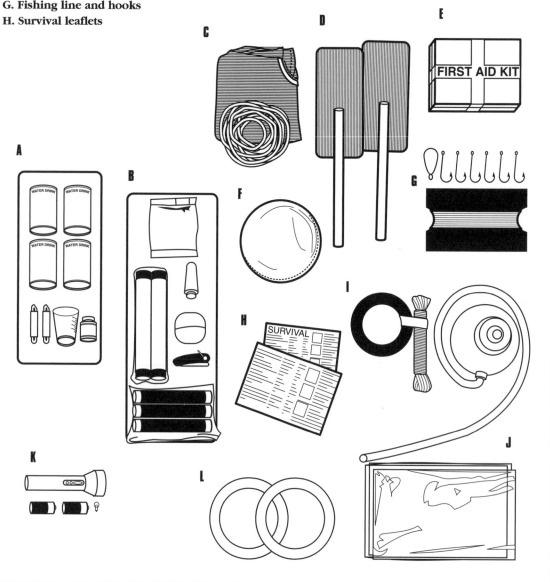

your time in the raft. Wear and tear will stress the equipment, and after extended survival periods, these are often lost.

Having a life raft gives you a sense of security. In the event that your parent craft is lost, you will be able to get into your life raft and survive for long enough to reach safety. A life raft that does not work as it should, when it should is a liability – it will severely damage morale and reduce your potential for survival from weeks or months to hours or days. To ensure that it works, you should have it serviced as regularly as the manufacturer recommends. You should also ensure that the company servicing it is reputable, endorsed and approved by the manufacturer. One blue water cruiser took his life raft for a service while well away from his home port. Several weeks later, he decided to check his life raft and opened the canister to find a neatly stacked pile of bricks. Fortunately it wasn't required on that voyage, but if it had been, survival prospects would have been extremely slim.

Having acquainted yourself with the survival equipment supplied, you will probably want to customize some of its contents. Ask your service agency about including extra equipment in the life raft canister itself. Your comprehensive fishing kit could be packed into a small resealable plastic box and included. Laminated route charts and laminated charts that show oceanic currents, shipping lanes and major flight paths, would be very useful in a sea survival situation; ensure that both feature compass roses. A waterproof logbook and waterproof pen could be included. Reasonable service agencies will understand your concerns and take your point.

Grab bag

Also known as an 'abandon ship bag', 'ditch bag" or 'flee bag', this is the bag that contains the equipment that you will need to survive at sea for any length of time. It should be clearly marked as the grab bag and stored in a cockpit locker so that it can be grabbed quickly should the parent craft become holed and flooded rapidly. There are a variety of options on the market, but very few will meet all your requirements. The bag should be completely waterproof, even when immersed, and this generally indicates a dry bag. It should also be brightly coloured to make it easier to see at night and to help relocation should the bag be lost during abandon ship.

The most essential quality in a grab bag is that it should float. It would be a major setback to say the least if, while scrambling at night across the wave-slicked, pitching deck to the life raft, you dropped your grab bag and watched it slide over the side and sink without trace. Manufacturers often make inflated claims regarding flotation and you should always check their claims before finally deciding on which bag to buy, remembering to replace the valuable contents with an equal weight before testing. Most bags are padded with closed cell foam to offer a degree of protection to the contents and improve flotation, but when packed with your essential survival kit, this buoyancy is easily overcome.

If your fully loaded grab bag is too heavy to be carried in one hand by someone of average build and strength, it is too heavy. It will almost certainly exceed the bag's buoyancy. You should split the contents into two bags to make the abandon ship procedure more manageable.

The fully waterproof cockpit grab bag should contain the vital equipment – in other words, those essentials associated with fresh water, fishing and rescue – while the rest should be contained in another grab bag kept near the first aid kit, in an easily accessible location near the wet locker below. The bag should be equipped with strong webbing handles, stitched securely around the bottom of the bag.

Keep your grab bag secure

Your grab bag contains life-sustaining equipment and must always be secured: in the cockpit before you abandon; to your personal flotation device (PFD) while you abandon; and inside the life raft after you've abandoned.

Given the essential nature of the contents, it would also be wise to attach a lanyard, or a spare safety harness to the handles and a spring clip to the other end so that the bag can be secured in the cockpit prior to abandon ship. During abandon ship, it can be attached to your PFD to guarantee it goes with you and also secured to the inside of the life raft on boarding.

To make your grab bag stand upright and add some extra buoyancy, cut some marine plywood to fit into the bottom of the bag. Sand the edges smooth and coat it with marine varnish and you will have an extra chopping board in the life raft.

The life raft and grab bag should be stored in the abandon ship locker in the cockpit, along with the two 36–45-litre (8–10-gallon) screw-top containers three-quarters full with fresh water, both tied together. Stow the water in the locker first, as that will be the last item to load, then the grab bag and, finally, the life raft. Remember the grab bag contains expensive life-sustaining equipment, so don't compress it – you risk damaging its contents and your chances of survival.

You must be disciplined about not using your abandon ship locker for anything else. When you give the order to prepare to abandon ship, you will not want one of your crew digging his way through boom covers, biminis and buckets to get at the life raft and grab bag. The only other items you should store in there are the inflatable tender and your large water containers, because you will be taking these with you.

Water collection kit

Fresh water is essential to sustain life for a prolonged period at sea. There are several methods of production and collection and all require particular equipment.

Production

Reverse osmosis pump
Chemical desalting kit

Collection

You will need impermeable plastic sheeting to collect rainwater. Remember that the covering of the life raft canopy, useful for rainwater collection in the short term, will invariably be covered with salt and will degrade in the sun's UV radiation, thereby contaminating your collected rainwater. You will also need resealable containers for storage, screw-top preferably.

Testing your grab bag

Replace the contents of your grab bag with an equal weight to ensure that the bag has enough buoyancy to float fully loaded.

Distillation

Again, impermeable plastic sheeting is required, preferably transparent or at least translucent, one large and one small watertight container.

Bottled water

Adding tightly sealed bottles of fresh water with a flotation air gap to your grab bag will not harm its buoyancy as fresh water is less dense than sea water. The two large

Using a reverse osmosis pump

It's hard work on the hands but a well-maintained reverse osmosis pump can produce fresh water from sea water on demand (almost 1 litre/1¾ pints per hour at 40 cycles per minute) making it an essential part of your survival kit.

containers in the abandon ship locker will be your main reserve source of fresh water. Remember to replace the water whenever you reach port.

Measuring jug or cup

This takes the guesswork out of rationing and ensures that all survivors in the life raft get the same ration. Dehydrated and hungry survivors can become irritable and a small perceived slight will start an argument.

Ration kit

Water is the critical factor here too. Your emergency rations should be carbohydrate-based because carbohydrates require less of your extracellular water supply for digestion than other foodstuffs, particularly proteins. Carbohydrates are quickly converted into monosaccharides and absorbed into the blood stream as sugar to provide for short- to medium-term energy requirements.

Fishing kit

The fishing kit included with the life raft is not comprehensive and you will need to bring your own complete kit if you are to survive for an extended period. When line fishing, the survivor never knows what will bite. If the catch is too big for you to fight, you will have to cut it loose to protect your hands, to avoid being dragged overboard and

Ration kit

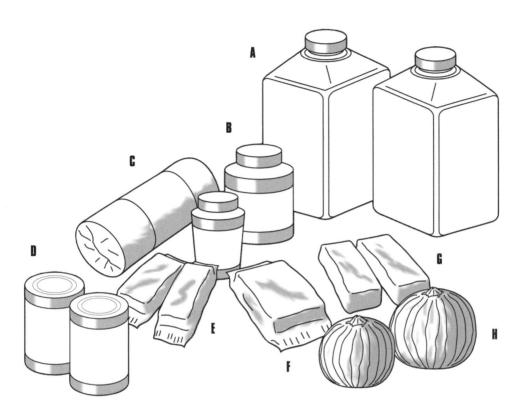

A. Jar of powdered yeast – a good source of Vitamin B complex

B. Boiled sweets – fruit flavour in a resealable tin, with glucose powder

C. Ginger biscuits – ginger in any form helps to ward off seasickness

D. Canned fruit

E. Chocolate bars – these are degradable, so replace regularly

F. Kendal mint cake

G. Muesli bars – these are degradable, so replace regularly

H. Onions – the most vitamin-rich vegetable, but degradable, so replace regularly

to prevent the raft capsizing. For this reason, the survivor will need a plentiful supply of hooks and line. The items on page 32 will provide the survivor with the means to catch fish for extended periods.

First aid kit

Sickness and injury will damage the survivor's capacity to survive – and if left untreated, they may even kill. At the least, you as a survivor will be physically incapacitated to some extent and therefore unable to concentrate your efforts on survival.

The body needs water to repair tissue, remove toxins from the system and fight infection, all of which depletes the

Fishing kit

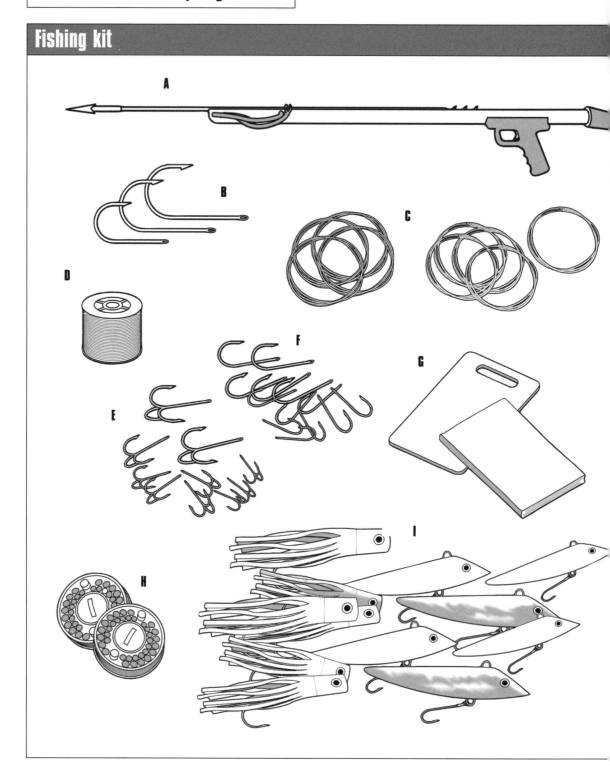

A. 1 x Spear gun (with spare power bands, shafts and tips)
B. 3 x Large stainless steel straight shank barbed hooks (for gaff fishing)
C. 180m (600ft) monofilament fishing line (good for weights of 18kg/40lb)
D. 2 x Reels
E. 12 x Stainless steel treble-barbed hooks of various sizes
F. 36 x Stainless steel barbed hooks of various sizes
G. 24 x Swivels
H. and I. 24 x Assorted sinkers
J. 2 x Industrial gloves
K. and L. 18 x Various lures
M. 1 x Chopping board
N. 1 x Fishing handbook with details of knots

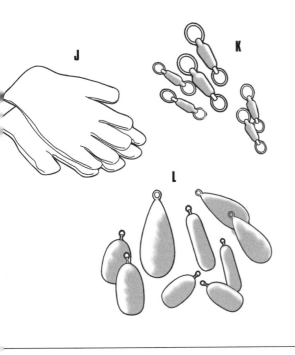

extracellular water supply. Sickness is also damaging to morale. It is extremely important that a survivor is able to react at a moment's notice, in order to catch rainwater, land fish or signal to passing traffic, so to keep yourself as healthy and responsive as possible, you will need a comprehensive first aid kit (see page 34).

This equipment should be kept in a sturdy, waterproof resealable plastic box and stored in an area that is easily accessible and close to the hull to keep it cool. Some of this equipment, primarily the drugs and ointments, will degrade with time, so it is important to keep a record of expiry dates on a sticker on top of the box and replace the supplies as they become out of date.

Navigational kit

The survivor will need to know where he is and in which direction he is drifting or sailing to estimate a time of arrival and, if possible, to alter the direction of travel to reach safety quicker. Also, if the life raft is drifting through shipping lanes or under major flight paths, the survivor should keep a regular lookout and attempt to make contact using the VHF (Very High Frequency) handheld radio, signal mirror, handheld and rocket flares. For these reasons, a navigational kit is required. All this equipment – in particular the sextant, timepieces, handheld GPS (Global Positioning System), all batteries, compass, non-laminated charts and sight reduction tables – must be kept dry. Keep them in a resealable plastic box inside the waterproof grab bag to ensure they do not degrade or corrode in damp, salty conditions. Include the following:

1 x Waterproof logbook
2 x Waterproof pens
1 x Sextant and tables
1 x Handheld GPS with spare batteries

First aid kit

A. First aid handbook (you should also take a recognized first aid course)

B. Seasickness pills; Aspirin

C. Salt tablets (preferably suppository)

D. Scissors

E. Suture kit with iodine

F. Petroleum jelly

G. Waterproof sticking plasters

H. Antiseptic ointment

I. General purpose antiseptic ointment

J. Scalpel

K. Surgical tape

L. Surgical gauze

M. Elastic bandages

N. Antiseptic wipes

O. General purpose antibiotic pills

Using a sea anchor

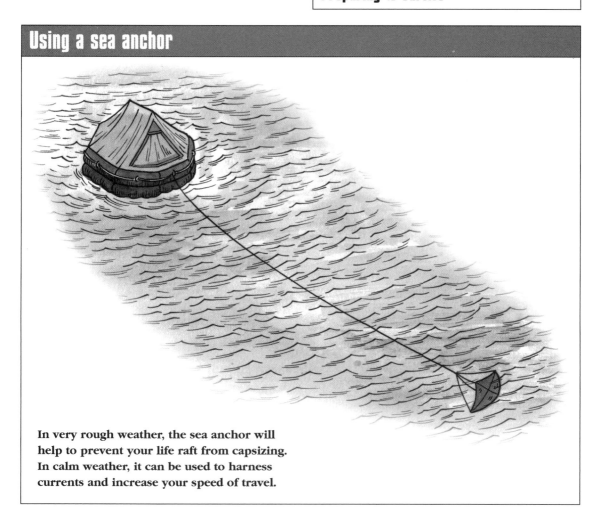

In very rough weather, the sea anchor will help to prevent your life raft from capsizing. In calm weather, it can be used to harness currents and increase your speed of travel.

1 x   Handheld compass
1 x   Laminated global chart
1 x   Laminated routeing charts showing winds, current, flight paths and shipping lanes
3 x   Chinagraph pencils
1 x   Reliable waterproof watch (GMT)
1 x   Reliable waterproof watch

Rescue kit

Survival at sea is about staying alive until safety can be reached. The survivor will be equipped mentally and physically to stay alive, but if safety can be attracted before landfall is made, your survival is all the more successful – unnecessary or prolonged discomfort is pointless. To attract potential rescuers or to raise the alarm, the survivor will need a variety of electronic, pyrotechnic and general equipment:

1 x   406MHz (or L-band) Cat. 2 (Manual) EPIRB
1 x   Handheld EPIRB (PLB) with built-in GPS
1 x   Handheld VHF with spare batteries
1 x   Portable solar panel for recharging GPS and VHF

1 x Binoculars
1 x Signal mirror
2 x Flashlight with spare batteries and bulbs
1 x Foghorn with spare air canister
1 x Whistle
6 x Yellow or orange smoke canisters
12 x Rocket flares
12 x Parachute flares
12 x Handheld red flares
6 x Dye markers or streamers

Utility kit

Survival means that every item in the life raft will have at least two purposes. As equipment breaks or becomes less efficient, the survivor will need to innovate repairs and improvise replacement equipment. For this reason, a utility kit is essential. This will comprise a variety of specific and general utility items, including:

6 x Raft repair clamps
Emergency plugs for Pressure Release Valves (one per valve)
1 x Spare manual life raft inflation pump
1 x Sea anchor with 30m (100ft) of line
1 x Toolkit –
hacksaw with spare blade; metal file; sheathed marlinspike; flat-head and cross-head screwdrivers; variety of hose clips and stainless steel U-bolts
2 x Rolls duct tape
24 x Plastic cable ties
24 x Resealable plastic zipper bags
12 x Black plastic garbage bags
Various bungees/shock cords
6 x Knives –
serrated, survival, straight, all sharpened and in a resealable plastic box
1 x Whetstone
Rubber tubing
1 x Funnel
1 x Collapsible bucket

1 x Head-mounted flashlight
1 x Sewing kit
Large pack condoms
Inspirational reading

Extras

Depending on the nature of the parent craft's distress, you will be able to salvage a considerable amount of equipment before she dips beneath the waves. Once the parent craft has sunk, buoyant equipment will continue to surface as it escapes the hull and you will still be close enough to the scene to gather this flotsam. Anything and everything will be useful, but you should prioritize the following:

Bottled fresh water (leave enough air in the top for the bottle to float)
Dinghy or tender (with paddles)
Fruit and vegetables
Tinned fruit
Watertight storage containers
Ropes and lines
Sail (bagged jib preferably)
Sleeping bags
Fenders

ATTITUDE

With knowledge of the main killers and the equipment to combat them, the final and most critical part of your sea survival preparation is attitude. We have already looked at our evolutionary legacy and we know we have the mental capacity to learn and to plan, and the physical capacity to innovate and improvise the means to the end of survival.

It is hard-wired in every cell of our bodies and has been stress-tested and refined over millions of years by the principle of the survival of the fittest – those best able to adapt. With bottomless confidence in those faculties, with the bulletproof belief in our ability to endure and adapt, we are fully equipped to survive.

No episode of endurance at sea better illustrates this than the experience of Poon Lim. In November 1942, at the age of 25, Second Steward Poon Lim was part of a crew of 55 onboard the British merchant vessel *Ben Lomond* when she left Cape Town bound for Paramaribo in French Guyana (now Surinam) on the northeastern coast of South America. The *Ben Lomond* was off the coast of Brazil when she was spotted and fatally torpedoed by a U-boat on 23 November. The order to abandon ship was given and Poon Lim dived overboard, naked save for the life jacket he had grabbed, and swam away from the foundering vessel. The Atlantic water soon found the boilers and the *Ben Lomond* exploded, then sank.

On the crests of the Atlantic swell, Poon Lim searched for signs of other survivors. He spotted a lifeboat with a few survivors onboard, but failed to attract their attention (this boat contained five of the 12 survivors from the *Ben Lomond*). He was floating alone when he received the luckiest break of his life. He spotted a wooden life raft that had drifted off the deck of the *Ben Lomond* as she was going down. It was just 0.7 square metres (8 square feet), but he scrambled onboard to find a 45-litre (10-gallon) container of water, canned ship's biscuits, flares and a flashlight. Poon Lim figured he had enough to survive for a month, by which time he must surely be rescued. He saw several ships and air patrols, even a U-boat,

Using a sextant

A sextant and sight reduction tables will allow you to calculate your position from sun and star sights – vital information if you're nearing shipping lanes, flight paths or land. Daily changes in position will reveal how fast you're travelling and in which direction.

GMDSS – Global Maritime Distress and Safety System

EPIRB
There are currently two different types of EPIRB (Emergency Position Indicating Radio Beacon):

406MHz and L-Band. Both of them use different satellite constellations: COSPAS-SARSAT and INMARSAT respectively. When an EPIRB is switched

on, it sends a Distress Alert, via one of these constellations, to an MRCC (Marine Rescue and Coordination Centre) and the alarm is raised.

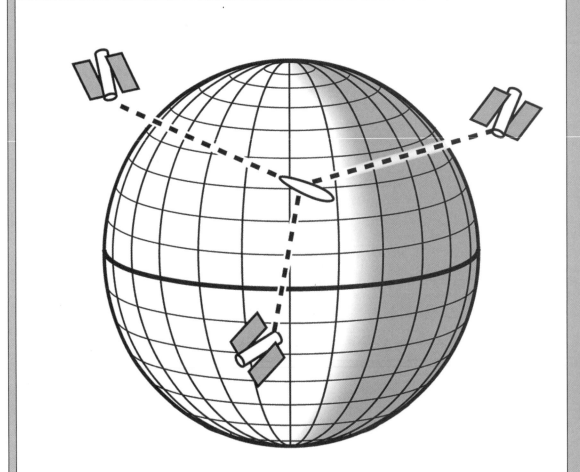

GMDSS is the greatest single advance in maritime safety since Marconi invented radio communication in 1895. The system uses a complex system of satellite

constellations to relay distress signals from almost anywhere on any ocean or sea to a Maritime Rescue and Coordination Centre within five minutes.

COSPAS-SARSAT

This constellation is comprised of geostationary satellites (Geos, orbiting over a fixed point on the earth's surface) over the equator, giving this system a far-ranging footprint that stretches from 76 degrees North to 76 degrees South.

When your EPIRB is switched on, it sends a Distress Alert containing your UIN (Unique Identification Number) on the 406MHz frequency to the satellites and these relay the Alert to an MRCC in less than five minutes, quite possibly in three.

Your UIN informs the MRCC of the vessel's and owner's details, but only 406MHz EPIRBs with built-in GPS transmitters can inform the MRCC of your exact position, accurate to within 30m (98ft). Without a built-in GPS, details of the vessel's voyage and whereabouts must be tracked down before SAR (Search And Rescue) begins, delaying your rescue.

When it does, SAR services will use the 121.5MHz homing signal also transmitted by the EPIRB to find the source of the signal.

As EPIRBs with built-in GPS become the norm, the 121.5MHz signal will no longer be monitored.

INMARSAT

This is also a constellation of Geos and again, there will be less than three minutes between the sending of a Distress Alert from an L-Band EPIRB and its reception by the MRCC. The L-Band EPIRB Alert is sent on the 1.6GHz frequency and informs the MRCC of the EPIRB's system code, containing vessel and owner details, position from its built-in GPS, the time of the last position update, speed, course and the type of distress.

DSC VHF

Digital Selective Calling (DSC) VHFs operate like pagers. Normally, VHF broadcasts to any receivers on the same channel in the area using an analog signal. DSC units broadcast a clearer digital signal on Channel 70 and, when registered on purchase, receive an MMSI (Mobile Maritime Service Identity) number.

If you need to contact an individual boat, or fleet or boats, you can do so by programming in their MMSI numbers and calling them specifically rather than broadcasting to everyone.

The DSC VHF is also equipped with a red Distress button. When pressed, this will transmit your MMSI number and your location if the VHF is linked up to your GPS unit. Otherwise, the location must be programmed in by hand.

This information is broadcast digitally on Channel 70 to all DSC receivers in the area, and will keep transmitting every three or four minutes until an acknowledgement is received, along with the MMSI of the acknowledging vessel. Voice contact can then be made if the acknowledging vessel is near enough to receive your analog voice signal.

Until recently, all emergency traffic would take place on Channel 16 (156.8MHz), but with DSC now compulsory on all large ships, most do not monitor Channel 16. To contact shipping without using DSC Distress Alert, you will need to use Channel 13, allocated for bridge-to-bridge communication.

but all his flares went unseen. As his supplies ran low, he realized that he had already had one life-saving piece of luck and that he neither could nor should count on another. His survival lay in his own hands. He began to think like a survivor.

He estimated his position using the moon and the stars and kept a rudimentary log by carving notches into the raft, one for each day adrift. To avoid the worst of the heat and sun, he slid into the water and swam round his raft, first checking to make sure he had no sharks for company. This stopped him losing fluid and salt through sweating and also gave his legs a little exercise. As the water ran low, he tore the canvas from his life jacket and used the material for collecting rainwater. As his stores dwindled, he pulled the battery spring from inside the flashlight and fashioned a crude fishing hook. He pounded out a few nails from his raft and battered them into hooks, then removed some of the hemp line round the raft and replaited it into a fishing line.

Using biscuits as bait, he caught his first fish and gutted it using a lid from one of the cans. Rather than eat the fish whole, he ate half and saved the other half for bait. With every survival success, every fish he caught, every pint of water he collected, his drive to

Fighting for survival

survive grew stronger. By the end of the second month, he decided to catch one of the seabirds that occasionally circled overhead. Using seaweed, he built a nest for the weary bird and added some rotten fish as an incentive to land. His ruse worked, a bird landed and Poon Lim lunged. It proved to be a surprisingly close fight, but Lim won.

Once again he banked some of his catch as bait and, with growing confidence, decided to catch a small shark. Using the canvas life jacket cover to protect his arms from abrasions from the shark skin, he hooked in and was soon hauling his catch onto the raft and beating it to death with the

water container. As the sun set on another day, Poon Lim realized he was surviving, succeeding one day at a time, improvising with the little equipment he had to exploit sources of food and water.

Finally on 23 April 1943, after 130 days alone on his raft, Poon Lim spotted a sail on the horizon and attracted it by using his canvas as a flag. The Brazilian fishermen brought Poon Lim onboard, but fished on for three days before landing him in the then British colonial town of Belém in Brazil. Poon Lim had survived at sea for 133 days in total, a record that stands to this day. He had lost 14kg (30lb) and could eat very little, but he could walk unaided. After four weeks in hospital, he emerged fit and healthy.

This is the most inspiring example of the power of the drive to survive. True, Poon Lim had the good fortune of finding the raft. You should not count on such luck. When you go to sea, be aware of and prepared for the worst case scenario.

If you are set adrift, you must also be humble enough to realize that the sea's moods do not change for you. Success for you is no longer about a better salary, it is about seeing the next sunrise. Life doesn't get any simpler than survival.

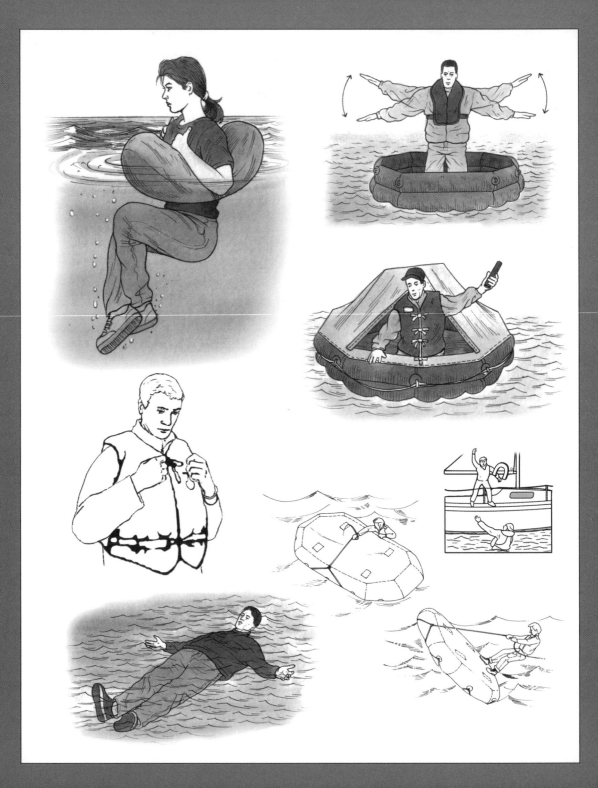

CHAPTER TWO

Coastal survival

Statistically, coastal waters are more dangerous than deep ocean. There are two reasons for this: they are used for leisure by those unaware of and unprepared for the potential risks, and they are protected by reefs and submerged rocks

More people die within sight of land than offshore. Even highly experienced mariners have found themselves unable to stand-off a lee shore in a gale and been forced to abandon ship and watch as the parent craft is pounded to matchwood on the rocks, possibly following shortly after themselves. But experienced mariners are not the main source of Coastguard statistics around coastlines. The majority of the victims claimed in coastal waters are those unaware of the potential dangers the sea presents, those unequipped to deal with danger when it does arise, and those unprepared for survival, even for the shortest period.

First we need to define the degrees of risk of coastal waters. If you are sailing, swimming or using an inflatable within sight of a busy beach,= and you find yourself in danger, your chances of rescue are very high. To maximize those chances, however, you must know how to attract attention, have the equipment to do so, know the techniques to remain buoyant, and have enough confidence in your knowledge and equipment to avoid panic. That is not to say you should ignore the risks or be willing to leave yourself vulnerable to them. Drowning, the sea's number one killer, can occur within a couple of minutes in water less than 30cm (12in) deep. Exposure, the number two killer, can sap vital heat energy from the body and threaten life well within an hour. Between them, these two killers are responsible for nearly every coastal fatality.

If, however, you are well away from civilization – at sea during the night, out of season, or off a deserted coastline – the chances of being seen from shore are greatly reduced. You should prepare yourself for an extended survival period by ensuring that you know what dangers you may encounter, that you have the equipment to survive them, and that you are mentally prepared and have the right attitude to survive at sea until you can reach safety. Your preparation should be along the lines outlined later in this and the following chapter.

Relaxed floating technique

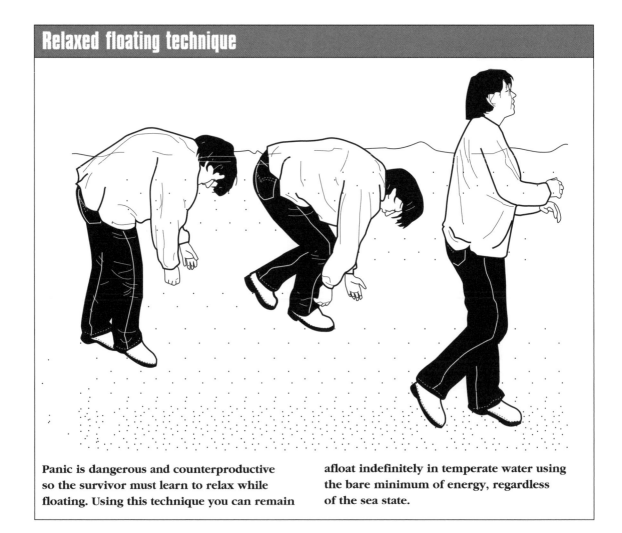

Panic is dangerous and counterproductive so the survivor must learn to relax while floating. Using this technique you can remain afloat indefinitely in temperate water using the bare minimum of energy, regardless of the sea state.

Floating without a PFD

The easiest way to float is on your back with you arms out at your sides and your lungs fully inflated. However, this method is only useful in calm water.

Whether as a bather or coastal sailor, you should not be deterred from enjoying the many pleasures of the coastline. Just be aware of the potential risks and know both how to avoid them and what equipment and techniques will keep you alive long enough to reach safety or attract rescue by raising the alarm.

The two primary risks inherent in using coastal waters in any capacity are, as already noted, drowning and exposure. The extent of the risk, and the techniques involved in coping successfully with them, will vary, depending on whether you are swimming, using an inflatable dinghy, or coastal sailing.

SWIMMING OR USING AN INFLATABLE DINGHY

Staying afloat

Swimmers who find themselves too far from shore, or swept away from shore by strong currents, often panic and thrash frantically for the safety of shore. They soon become exhausted and, if their efforts show no results, despondent, and are then susceptible to drowning. Even strong swimmers can exhaust themselves swimming against a riptide or an estuarine current while attempting to reach the shore. And once exhausted, cramped and breathing hard, it is very difficult to stay afloat. Indeed, the sea

Fastening your PFD

Your PFD must be sufficiently buoyant to support your weight and adjusted to fit securely and comfortably.

distress to those onshore or at sea in other craft. Above all, you must be aware that panic is entirely counter-productive to survival.

If you are wearing a PFD, as you should be, you will float either on your back or vertically in the water without any effort. Unfortunately, as Coastguard statistics confirm, few people wear PFDs while swimming for pleasure. But even without a PFD, it is possible to float calmly – and the importance of learning to do so cannot be overstated. It allows you to conserve energy, and therefore heat and strength, for the longest possible period. Remember, survival is about staying alive long enough to reach safety.

Should you find yourself in distress without a PFD, your clothing can offer a limited amount of buoyancy:

If you are wearing a shirt or T-shirt, you can blow into the neck or between the second and third buttons down to inflate the garment. Most of the air will automatically move to the back of the shirt, enabling you to float on your front. The air will leak through the material and out of the neck so you will need to reinflate regularly, but it will assist your buoyancy and save vital energy.

If you are wearing long trousers, remove them, then tie knots at the bottom of each leg and fasten the fly. By pulling the trousers, waistband first, above your head you can trap air in the trousers legs and use these to

claims most of its victims inshore from those who cannot stay afloat calmly while simultaneously signalling distress.

A modern Personal Flotation Device (PFD) will prevent you drowning, whether you are conscious or unconscious, alert or lethargic, strong or exhausted. Everyone operating in water deeper than chest level should be issued with a PFD, or some other effective means of securable and reliable buoyancy. Coastal water users must also learn the hand signals required to signal

Signalling distress

A. To signal distress using hand signals at sea on an inflatable or coastal sailing boat, place your arms straight out from your sides and move them slowly up and down, from the ten-to-two to the twenty-to-four positions on a clock face.

B. If you are in an immersion situation, you can signal distress by placing one arm straight up in the air and moving it slowly from side to side, from the five-to to the five-past positions on a clock face.

assist your buoyancy. Again, the air will gradually leak out from the fabric.

Without a PFD, the best way to remain afloat in calm water is to float on your back (see page 45). Take a deep breath and hold it to keep the lungs inflated and retain maximum buoyancy. Place your arms out from your sides and arch your back. Your face will stay above water, allowing you to breathe, and this position requires the absolute minimum of effort. Remember to check regularly all around you for opportunities to signal your distress.

If the water is too rough to adopt this position without swallowing sea water as waves wash over your face, use the relaxed floating technique (see page 44). Tread water and quickly but carefully look overhead and all around you (360°) for opportunities to

signal distress. Then take a deep breath, shut your mouth and eyes and place your head below water. Stretch your arms out ahead of you and allow your legs to find their own relaxed position. Stay in this position until you need to draw another breath, then repeat the procedure.

If you feel yourself cramping, massage the affected muscle after taking a deep breath and keep it immobile. Remember, the aim is to stay calm, and you should not be exercising strenuously enough or sweating severely enough for cramp to be an issue.

You should never swim in rough weather. A PFD will keep your head above water, but if you are swept onto rocks or over a reef, you will suffer major incapacitating injuries. Even close to the beach, body surfing in heavy surf can leave you with sprains, broken bones and abrasions as you are slammed onto the beach. You could also become winded, even unconscious, and drowning is a definite possibility if you are bundled to the sea bed and caught in an undertow. There may also be submerged rocks, and these may inflict traumatic injuries. In rough weather, stay on the beach and enjoy the power of nature from a respectful distance.

Monitoring your position

If you are in an inflatable dinghy and you find yourself too far from shore, stay calm. If you stay with the inflatable dinghy, you will not drown. Take transits on the shore: pick out fixed objects such as trees, telegraph poles or

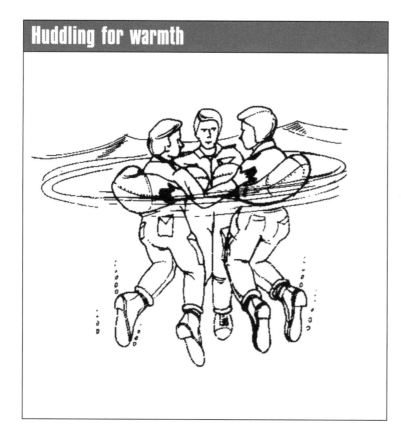

Huddling for warmth

Using transits

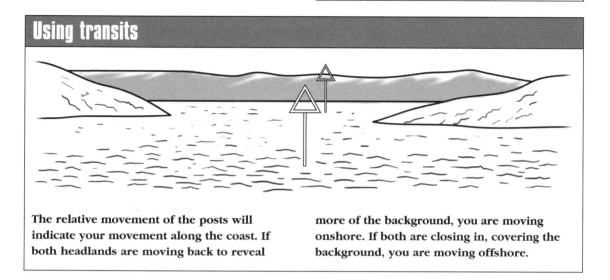

The relative movement of the posts will indicate your movement along the coast. If both headlands are moving back to reveal more of the background, you are moving onshore. If both are closing in, covering the background, you are moving offshore.

headlands and watch their movement relative to their background to see which way you are drifting. Then paddle calmly towards shore, using regular strokes and not thrashing, for thirty seconds. If your transits do not indicate you are any nearer, signal distress by using the hand signals shown, by blowing the whistle attached to your PFD or by shouting.

If you are swimming, tread water briefly while you check your transits in the way shown above to find out which way you are drifting. Then swim calmly towards shore for thirty seconds, again using regular strokes. Thrashing is a fairly effective way of signalling distress and may get you noticed, but it consumes huge amounts of energy and will attract the attention of sharks, making a bad situation considerably worse. If you are not making any discernable progress, stay calm and signal distress by using the hand signals shown for swimmers, by blowing the PFD's whistle or by shouting.

Once attention is attracted and the alarm raised, or once it is clear that attention cannot be attracted, you should float calmly in the water until rescue arrives or there is another opportunity to signal distress.

Coping with Exposure

Cold

At night, or in colder climates, you should never swim without a PFD and a wetsuit or, preferably, a drysuit. Without a wetsuit, immersion or survival suit, your life expectancy in waters of 10°C (50°F) or less will be an hour at most. Even with protection, you should not exercise in an attempt to keep warm. Shivering is a reflex response to a drop in core temperature, but do not start to exercise. This will simply expend your energy faster; you will lose heat and your blood will become cooler as the flow returns to your colder extremities. In short, the net effect will be to reduce your life expectancy. Instead, you should adopt the HELP (Heat Escape Lessening Posture) position to minimize your heat loss (see page 50).

If you are immersed in cold water for long enough, the blood flow to your hands and feet, then to your legs and arms, will be restricted by vasoconstriction to limit heat loss from these extremities. This is why your hands and feet will begin to feel numb and become a grey-blue colour.

The HELP position

This position works in two ways. First, it decreases the exposed surface area of the body through which heat can be lost, thus decreasing the rate of loss. Second, it traps water close to the body, particularly around the chest and abdomen where the vital organs are located. Cross your legs below the knee and bring your knees up as far as your PFD will allow. Cross your arms around the front of your PFD or around your knees if you can reach that far.

This position works well with a PFD. If you do not have one, combine the HELP position with the relaxed floating technique. First take a deep breath while looking all around for opportunities to signal distress. Then shut your mouth and eyes and place your head below water. Bring your knees up to your chest, cross your ankles and hug your shins with your arms. Stay in this position until you need to draw another breath, then repeat the procedure.

Heat

During daylight, swimmers will be highly unlikely to suffer from heat exposure. If you are not wearing a wetsuit or clothing, you should at the very least be wearing waterproof sunscreen to protect against skin cancers that can be caused by the sun's ultra-violet radiation.

If using an inflatable dinghy without a wetsuit, wear a T-shirt, sunglasses and a cap in addition to waterproof sunscreen to guard against the effects of the sun. The sunglasses will protect your eyes from the glare of the sun and its reflection off the water, thus protecting against sun blindness.

The cap will give protection against heat-induced headaches, if you are afloat for extended periods. If you are in distress on an inflatable dinghy, get into the water for three minutes every 20 minutes to cool the body and to wet your T-shirt and cap. As the water on your skin evaporates, it will draw heat from your body. Never let go of the dinghy; best, attach yourself to it.

COASTAL SAILING

Coastal sailors should ensure they have the right pocket kit: multitool and whistle, both on lanyards; sunscreen; a chemical light stick; and dye marker - all in a zipped pocket. The PLB (Personal Locator Beacon) is a handheld EPIRB, preferably with a built-in GPS, designed to be carried as pocket kit and always attached to you by a lanyard. This is an expensive option, but it could be the one that saves your life, particularly if you are sailing well away from other craft and popular beaches.

Unless you are familiar with the area, you will need to check your position regularly using the handheld compass or GPS and a chart. This will allow you to avoid endangering your crew by sailing near rocks, reefs and shoals.

MOB - man over board

Even the most experienced coastal sailor can be caught out by capsize in a sudden gust, a swinging boom during an accidental gybe or a flailing sail. A PFD will save your life if you go overboard unconscious. Experienced sailors know that if conditions require the wearing of jackets or other foul weather gear, they also require the wearing of PFDs and harnesses. Not to do so places you at risk of falling victim to the sea's number one killer - not a smart move for such an experienced sailor.

Inexperienced crew members should wear PFDs in all conditions - their ignorance of the boat's performance and motion makes them particularly susceptible to the risk of becoming yet another MOB.

Sailing dinghies are generally equipped with a centreboard instead of a keel and are therefore more prone to capsize. They rely on a precise balance between the capsizing moment - the force of wind in the sails - and the righting moment - the crew hiked out over the windward side. Often this fine balance is lost and for this reason, PFDs should be considered mandatory for all crew at all times in sailing dinghies.

If one of your crew goes overboard, it is essential that the drill to recover a MOB is carried out quickly, efficiently and without panic. Unnecessary shouting will obscure instructions and could delay recovery. Every coastal skipper must be qualified, and well practised, in this drill and all members of the crew should know their roles.

Practise using a fender with a bucket attached as a substitute MOB. In emergencies, only an efficient drill will ensure a smooth performance and swift recovery.

If you go overboard while conscious, use the whistle on your PFD to alert your crew and keep one arm aloft to increase your visibility. And if you are not wearing a PFD, it's a mistake you will vow never to make again as you watch the stern of your craft dipping behind the swell. Start shouting to attract the attention of your crew and again, keep one arm aloft until you are seen.

Once you have been located, tread water or use the relaxed floating technique, but avoid the urge to swim towards the boat. Your skipper will find it more difficult to manoeuvre the boat to recover a moving target and you will be losing energy and heat - both of which you will need if the skipper needs to take a second or third run to recover you.

Man Over Board

After attracting your crew's attention by shouting and using your whistle, tread water with your arm waving side-to-side and await recovery.

Coping with exposure

Cold

In cold climates or at night, sailors should be wearing inner, middle and outer layers: gloves, boots and a cap; wet or dry suits; and thermal clothing. Should you go overboard, these layers will trap water, which will be warmed by the body. This reduces heat loss and increases your survival time. Such insulation will be increased if you adopt the HELP position (see page 50).

As stated above, a PFD – equipped with at least a whistle and preferably a strobe light too – will greatly increase your chances of survival, relocation and rescue. In very cold climates, when there is a possibility of frost or ice on deck, a PFD is an essential piece of equipment. You should not be on deck without one and you should also harness yourself to the boat to eliminate the possibility of going overboard. Immersed in cold water, your life expectancy could be reduced to just a few minutes.

Heat

Coastal sailors should also guard against the effects of exposure to heat. With the wind cooling the skin, the effects of extended exposure to the sun often go unnoticed, but

Floating together

If your dinghy sinks leaving you and your crew afloat in rough weather, harness yourselves and your grab bag together and stay close to share warmth and raise visibility.

Righting a dinghy

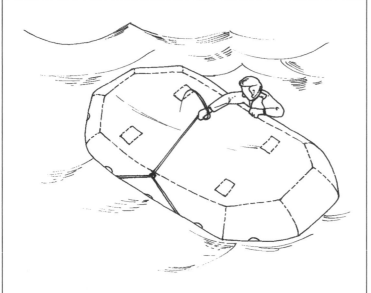

This procedure requires more effort in heavy seas and high winds. Grab the righting line from the opposite side.

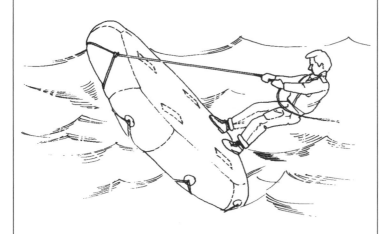

Brace your feet against the dinghy and pull. The dinghy should rise up and over, and will pull you temporarily out of the water.

sweating dehydrates the body and bottles of fresh water and salt tablets should always be carried to replace lost fluids and salt.

In a sailing dinghy, the crew will be exposed to the sun for the entire duration of the voyage. After extended exposure, particularly without a cap, you may suffer headaches and feel your limbs and stomach begin to cramp. Take a salt tablet and drink plenty of fresh water (or add a large pinch of salt to one of the bottles of water before setting out). Rest in the centre of the cockpit, shaded by a sail or a jacket, gently massaging any cramps.

Check on your crew members regularly. If one of the crew has been inactive in the sun for extended periods and begins to feel light headed, gets a cold sweat, becomes clumsy and unable to complete basic tasks, she is showing symptoms of heat exhaustion. Stop sailing at once. Soak her clothing by splashing her with water, and get her into the shade immediately.

Give her a salt tablet with some fresh water and instruct her to rest, with her legs and head raised if possible. Make sure a competent crew member is assigned to check her pulse and temperature regularly to check for any deterioration in condition. Alter course for the nearest port off the wind. Sailing upwind produces more violent motion than sailing off the wind and increases the risk of capsize.

Without a PFD, the heat-exhausted crew may then drown in the confusion, and even with one, she will be poorly coordinated and difficult to get back onboard.

Capsize

Every effort should be made to avoid capsize. As you feel a gust, hike out further and ease the sheets, dumping them completely if the angle of heel keeps increasing. If possible, try to stay on the boat by climbing over the windward side and standing on the centreboard, but if you realize you are going to end up in the water, jump clear of the mast, sails and running rigging to avoid injury and entanglement.

Once in the water, make sure that all members of the crew are present, conscious and calm. If one crew member is missing, call for him. If there is no answer, climb onto the hull using the centreboard and look around; he may have been knocked unconscious or trapped beneath the sail and require help.

Next, attempt to right the dinghy. If the mast is horizontal in the water, one crew member should swim towards the cockpit (carefully avoiding becoming tangled in the maze of lines), to ensure that all the sheets are released and thus prevent the boat sailing away once righted. (Actually, these should have been released already in an effort to prevent capsize.) Climb onto the centreboard and use your weight to lift the mast out of the water. If your weight is not sufficient, work with another member of the crew. As the dinghy rights, watch the hull and boom to make sure you are not hit by them.

Any crew not directly involved in the righting of the vessel should hang onto the stern, to avoid obstructing the mast and

sail; to prevent the dinghy sailing away once righted if a sheet jams in the righting process; and to avoid being covered by the sail or hit by the mast should the boat capsize in the other direction. Once the dinghy is righted, one crew member should climb into the cockpit and begin bailing while the others hang onto the gunwales and stern, keeping the dinghy head to wind.

Once sufficient buoyancy has been restored, other crew members can climb in and assist with the bailing, or begin sailing if the dinghy has self-bailers. Remember, though, that the dinghy may still have too much water in it, meaning that you will not be able to sail fast enough for the self-bailers to operate properly. If so, continue bailing.

If the dinghy is inverted, make sure none of the crew is trapped below, and that all are present, conscious and calm. If one is missing, call her name, then climb onto the dinghy and look around. If there is no sign, check under the boat. If the missing crew member is tangled in lines and trapped below the dinghy, use your multitool to cut her loose and bring her to the surface. Check she is conscious and breathing. If not, get her onto the upturned hull as fast as possible. Lay her on her front to clear water from the air passages, then on her back to perform artificial respiration.

Once you have ensured that your crew is complete and safe, swim to the mast. Then, without swimming under the upturned hull where you may become entangled and trapped, feel for one of the halyards. Climb onto the upturned hull with it. Use the halyard as a righting line by leaning over the opposite side of the hull, making sure the wind is in your face (this will help you to right the boat once the mast is clear of the water). As before, if your weight is not sufficient, add another crew member to the righting effort. Again, make sure you are not struck by the hull, boom or mast on righting. And then start to bail.

If you are unable to right the boat after several attempts using the maximum righting moment, find as many bottles of water as you can; cut free the grab bag if you have one; and get yourself and your crew onto the upturned hull – the strongest crew member should climb up first to help the others onto the hull. Then follow the procedure for raising the alarm.

Sinking

Most modern sailing dinghies are equipped with sealed internal bulkheads and should stay afloat even when holed. Older dinghies, however, will not have this safety feature.

However, regardless of whether your dinghy has this feature, you should have reserve buoyancy. Attach blocks of closed

cell foam to the boat, under the thwarts, gunwales and at the bow, to help the dinghy stay afloat.

If your dinghy is still floating, it is essential that you remain with it. There are three reasons for this:

– To save energy
Climb onto the hull. This will save you the physical energy required to stay afloat, the heat energy lost to the water during immersion, and avoid expending the energy required to deter sharks in warm climates.

– To stay together
Tie yourselves onto the centreboard or rudder in rough weather.

– To raise your visibility for SAR (Search And Rescue) services
If the vessel is about to go down, collect all the fresh water bottles you can find and cut free the grab bag if you have one. Tether yourselves together to increase your visibility, to share heat if one of you begins to show signs of exposure in cold climates, and to reassure each other of the strength of your will to survive.

REMOTE COASTAL CRUISING

As a coastal sailor, you will have a greater range than swimmers or inflatable dinghy users, and you may be exploring remote coastlines where opportunities for attracting attention are limited. Should you find yourself in distress some way off the coast, you cannot rely on hand signals to attract rescue. There are several options open to you:

- Mobile phone/cellphone: waterproof, and with the Coastguard number programmed in
- VHF handheld radio
- GPS handheld receiver

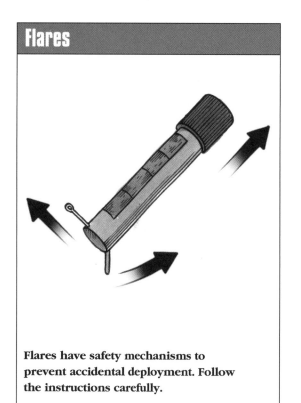

Flares

Flares have safety mechanisms to prevent accidental deployment. Follow the instructions carefully.

Safety first

The golden rule is, preparation. The most effective method of staying alive is to avoid an emergency in the first place:

- When swimming, check first that the beach is safe to swim. If there is no briefing or chart information available, observe the beach. Look for flotsam on the water, or throw in a piece of wood, and watch how it moves. Look for disturbances other than waves on the water surface; these may indicate undercurrents, riptides or reefs. These areas should be avoided.

- When wading in unknown waters, always wear soled footwear to avoid stepping on sea urchins, stingrays or venomous fish, and use a stick to disturb the area ahead of you.
- It is safest not to go into water deeper than chest level. If swimming through deeper water, swim out for ten seconds, then stop and tread water while taking transits on fixed objects on the shore, or headlands, to discover if there is any current across the area. If there is no discernable change in the orientation of your transits, repeat the

procedure. A sudden change in water temperature indicates a sharp increase in water depth. This is another potential indicator of stronger currents.
- If using an inflatable dinghy, use the same procedures. Check your transits every minute to ensure you are not drifting further out to sea or too far down the coast. Never fall asleep on an inflatable dinghy. You will not be able to keep track of your position; and, during the day, you run the risk of first-degree burns from the sun and heat stroke.

– Pyrotechnics: handheld flares, rocket flares, parachute flares, smoke canisters
– EPIRB: Emergency Position Indicating Radio Beacon

All this equipment should be stored in a watertight grab bag that floats when loaded with all your survival gear. Also include a good store of carbohydrate rations and more bottled water.

Make sure the grab bag is attached to the dinghy inside the stern so that it cannot drift off in the event of capsize, but can be cut free with your multitool should the dinghy begin to sink. Storing the bag further forward will keep it drier but will also make the bag difficult to remove, meaning that you run the risk of becoming tangled in the lines dangling beneath the capsized dinghy – which could be very dangerous.

After removing any equipment from the grab bag, close it as soon as possible. The bag contains equipment that is vital to your survival and you should not risk damaging it with sea water, losing it, or flooding the bag so that it sinks.

RAISING THE ALARM

Step 1

If you are within sight of land during daylight and can see people on the shore or other craft nearby, blow SOS on your whistle, or foghorn if you carry one. This SOS signal is three short blasts, three long blasts, three short blasts. A single long blast is also a recognized signal of distress, but it will exhaust you quicker if you are using a whistle, or your air canister if using the foghorn. Once you have attracted attention,

Coastal sailing

The golden rule is, preparation. As skipper, the boat and crew are your responsibility.

- If you are sailing anywhere other than immediately off the beach, you will need a range of survival equipment. Check that your phone is fully charged and operational and that your GPS and VHF are both in working order and fully charged. Check the marina's position on GPS tallies with its chart position and conduct a VHF radio check on the marina frequency before setting sail. Also ensure that you have spare, fully charged replacement batteries for the GPS, VHF and, if possible, for the EPIRB. There are portable solar panels that can be used to power the GPS and VHF. All your survival equipment should be kept in the grab bag.
- Inspect your flares for any sign of water or corrosion, and check they are within their inspection dates before placing them back in their watertight canister, then into the grab bag.
- Carry a foghorn with a spare air canister; a flashlight with spare batteries; duct tape or sail repair tape; and a basic First Aid kit in the grab bag.
- Carry carbohydrate snacks, in the grab bag.

- Always take a laminated chart of the sailing area, taped to the boat's deck or stored in the grab bag if you know the sailing area well. Also take a handheld compass on a lanyard to triangulate position. The handheld compass is vital for navigation, so consider carrying a spare.
- Make sure that water bottles contain enough air to stay afloat. In warm climates, make sure that one has a pinch of salt mixed into it.
- Every crew should be carrying the required pocket kit.
- Make sure that PFDs are within their inspection dates, fitted with a whistle and preferably a strobe light. Make sure they fit your crew and that everyone is aware of how to put on the PFD and of the procedure for manual inflation should the PFD not inflate automatically.
- Before setting sail, ensure that the hull is seaworthy from stem to stern; that the mast, running and standing rigging and sails are in good condition; that your outboard, if carried, is fully functioning; and that there is extra fuel, oil and a set of spares and tools stored securely onboard. Make sure there is sufficient reserve buoyancy (closed cell foam

blocks, fenders) secured under each thwart to prevent the dinghy from foundering.
- Always take seasick medication at least 30 minutes before setting sail. Seasickness causes physical and mental weakness and turns a survivor into a casualty, significantly reducing the drive to survive. Repeated vomiting is a major source of water loss.
- Check the weather forecast before setting sail. If there is the slightest question in your mind that the conditions expected might exceed your abilities and those of your crew and craft, stay in the club bar.
- Make sure that accurate details of your voyage – estimated time of departure (ETD); estimated time of arrival (ETA); destination; ports of call, boat name and type; and number and names of crew – are logged with a responsible party on land. If you're not believed to be missing, nobody will look for you.
- Check with every member of your crew for any special medical requirements. Use their experience of their condition to brief the crew on what procedures to follow should they succumb in a survival situation.

Using a GPS device

You will need a position fix (using your GPS or by triangulating your position with a **handheld compass) before beginning to send your Mayday call.**

use the recognized hand signals to indicate that you are in distress.

If your attempts to attract attention fail, or if it is night, move on to Step 2.

Step 2

Open the grab bag and remove your waterproof phone (a phone that is not waterproof will be of little use). Or take out your handheld VHF, and the handheld GPS unit, which should be switched on to obtain a position fix as soon as it is removed from the bag. If you have no GPS, remove the handheld compass from the grab bag, take a bearing off a known landmark and estimate

your distance from it. If your distance judgement is unreliable, take at least three bearings on known landmarks to enable the SAR services to triangulate your position.

If using the mobile phone, contact the Coastguard using the programmed number. A phone should not be considered a cheap alternative for a handheld marine VHF; it has several drawbacks.

Firstly, you will be contacting only the Coastguard, but it is quite possible that just out of sight are vessels that could receive your VHF call and offer assistance. Secondly, the cell network is not designed for marine use and coverage at sea will be poor.

Thirdly, if you are at the edge of a cell, your call may be dropped before you have given sufficient location information. Finally, SAR services are unable to obtain a bearing from cellular signals.

If transmitting by VHF, switch to Channel 16 (156.8MHz). Make sure the device is switched to high power and press the transmit button. (Note that shipping will no longer be required to maintain a listening watch on Channel 16 after February 2005, by which time DSC VHF will have

replaced all VHF units.) Then follow this exact procedure:

Using a flare

Always hold the flare as far downwind as possible to prevent damage to the life raft.

- Mayday Mayday Mayday
- This is: *repeat the boat's name three times*
- Mayday
- This is: *the boat's name*
- My position is: *give your exact latitude and longitude from the GPS unit; or distance and bearing, using the hand compass, from a known landmark or headland. If you don't know, say you don't know.*
- I am: *describe your problem briefly*
- I have: *give your total crew number and any other useful SAR information, such as direction of drift; what pyrotechnics you have; how many flares you have used*
- I require immediate assistance
- Over.

Await acknowledgement on Channel 16. If none comes after 20 seconds, repeat the procedure until acknowledgement is received, then follow the instructions you receive. However, VHF range will be restricted to 3.2km (2 miles) at most if you are immersed in water because your aerial is lower. If you receive no acknowledgement after 10 minutes in cold water, or 30 minutes in warm, move to Step 3.

Step 3

Open the bag and unscrew the lid of the pyrotechnics canister. During daylight, remove an orange or yellow smoke canister. At night, choose a handheld red flare. Take care at all times to ensure that no water gets into the canister or into the bag.

Daylight

Use a smoke canister. Follow the instructions for activation and place the canister in the water downwind of you. The dense orange or yellow smoke will indicate your position to those onshore and the alarm will be raised.

Night

Use a red handheld flare. Follow the instructions for activation and hold the flare above head level but downwind of yourself. Those onshore will raise the alarm.

If neither of these measures works, use a parachute flare. Remember to fire it slightly downwind – it will turn into the wind once deployed. If the wind is strong, fire the flare downwind at an angle of 15° to ensure that the flare returns to your position. If there is low cloud, you should fire the flare downwind at an angle of 45° to ensure that the flare burns below the cloud base.

If you are still unnoticed, move to Step 4.

Step 4

Open the Grab bag, remove the EPIRB and close the bag. If the EPIRB is automatic, it should operate as soon as it is placed in water. If it is manual, open the switch cover and switch on the EPIRB. Most are equipped with a strobe light to indicate activation and aid relocation.

Ensure that the aerial is deployed and that the unit and the aerial are vertical, otherwise the EPIRB will not function properly.

CHAPTER THREE

Offshore survival

Survival offshore can involve complete self-sufficiency for days, weeks, even months. Abandoning ship is a major step that should be taken only to increase your chances of survival. Remember, you and your crew must be fully equipped and prepared for what lies ahead.

Disastrous modern maritime experiences, such as the storm-lashed 1979 Fastnet Race, have shown that there is one golden rule in the event of abandoning ship: if it's still afloat, stay on the boat. But like every rule, it has exceptions.

Of the 24 boats abandoned during the race, 19 were salvaged afloat. The obvious conclusion seems to be that many of those who abandoned their boats in favour of their life rafts took unnecessary risks and placed

the lives of their crew in unnecessary danger. Abandoning ship is a last resort. If you're not prepared to place your trust in several tons of floating wood, GRP, aluminium or steel, why place it in a few pounds of rubber?

However, those who chose to abandon told a different story. Their boats had been rolled several times by breaking waves as they lay a-hull or hove-to. Yes, the boats were still floating, but the rolls left the crew who

Capsized

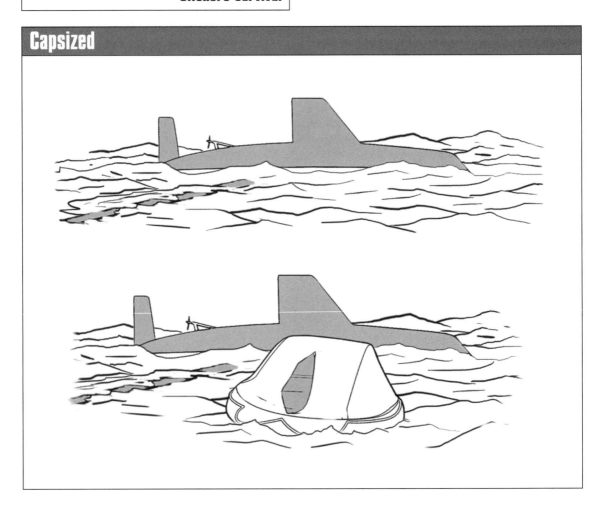

were harnessed on deck trapped and injured below the upturned hull. Some crew members were lost as their harnesses parted under the shock loads. Crew members in the partially flooded cabin below were flipped about like rag dolls, targets for flying stores, cutlery and sections of cabin sole (floorboards); broken bones and head injuries were the result.

Any boat that inverts in such a violent way will usually right itself but lose its mast in the process, leaving it crumpled over the side, but still attached by rigging. Use bolt croppers to cut away the broken spar as soon as possible to prevent it punching a

hole in the hull and sinking the boat. However, this means going on deck and running the risks described above. And once the mast is cut away, the boat capsizes more violently because there is nothing above deck to dampen the speed of the roll. Life below deck is hazardous in the extreme and many crews took to their life rafts in desperation, to escape the danger of staying on their boats.

Still, most of the boats survived. Had they provided a bearable refuge, crews could have stayed with them rather than taking to their life rafts. An obvious measure to make existence below decks during a major storm more bearable is to ensure that all lockers and drawers can be fastened securely with latches that do not rely on gravity, and that they are also strong enough to contain their contents shifting violently. The boat should not have any glass onboard. The cabin sole and any stores or equipment stowed beneath should also be firmly secured to prevent movement, and there should be harness points to which the crew can attach themselves to prevent being hurled around. Seeking refuge in a smaller cabin will also reduce impact injuries. If anything does break free, secure it or get it out of the cabin as soon as possible. Crash hats will help to prevent head injuries and unconsciousness.

STAY OR GO?

In reality, there is no hard and fast rule about when you should abandon a holed vessel. If the boat is going down, you obviously need to abandon ship and take to your life raft. But in any other scenario, it is a matter of judgement, dependent upon the climate and your assessment of the weather conditions.

Often the abandon ship order is given as the parent craft is filling rapidly with water. The life raft is launched and the crew boards it with all the survival gear. Once on the life raft, the crew is ready with the knife to cut the static line as the parent craft slips beneath the waves – except it doesn't. Most modern boats have sufficient reserve buoyancy built into their structure to remain afloat for some time, even when completely waterlogged. If you stay onboard, you will at least present the SAR services with a bigger target to find; likewise, passing ships. You may even be able to sail the waterlogged hull in calm waters.

However, there is always the risk that one of the watertight compartments will fail, at which point the boat will sink very quickly, possibly before the crew can escape. This risk increases in heavy weather.

If your boat is holed in tropical waters,

still afloat but waterlogged, the decision to stay onboard will mean you are sheltered from the sun and at less risk of shark attack. You will be able to use the coachroof to escape from continual immersion and to sleep at night, harnessed on. The vessel's fresh water supply cannot be relied upon because the tanks will probably be contaminated, but you will have the capacity to collect and generate fresh water using the equipment in your grab bag. You will also have the capacity to fish – essential because the vessel's stores will be spoiled by seawater. Once again, however, the boat could sink without warning.

In cold climates, continual immersion in cold water presents a significant risk of hypothermia so you will be forced to spend much of your time on the coachroof. You can create a degree of shelter by slinging a sail or tarpaulin over the boom and securing it to each guardrail, but the life raft would offer more shelter. That said, rough weather is also more likely in colder climates, and this is easier to endure inside the waterlogged hull than in a life raft. However, the risk of capsize and sudden sinking will be increased.

You must consider too what happens to the life raft itself. Having launched it, you cannot then deflate and repack it – in the event that the parent craft sinks, there will not be enough time to inflate it manually. You could leave it inflated and tethered by the static line to the parent craft as you return to the parent craft. You will need to take a second line to the life raft – remember, the static line is designed to break under a certain strain. You do not want to begin your morning watch searching the horizon for a lost life raft.

With the second line to ensure that the life raft will not be lost, the safety equipment can be kept onboard the comparatively dry life raft rather than in the waterlogged boat. The problem here is that, even without the weight of the crew, the weight of the safety

Prepare to abandon ship

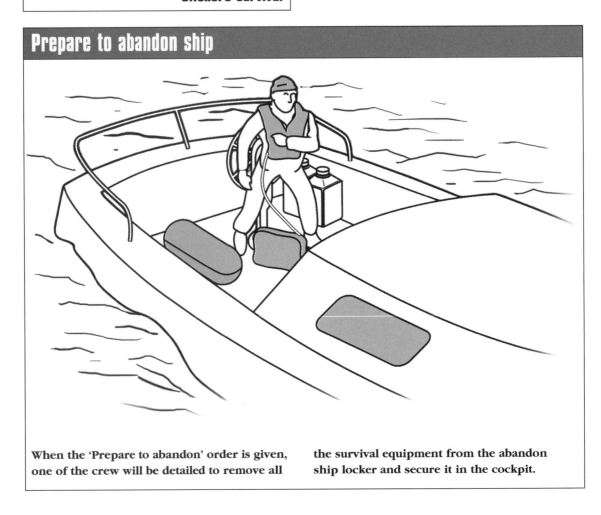

When the 'Prepare to abandon' order is given, one of the crew will be detailed to remove all the survival equipment from the abandon ship locker and secure it in the cockpit.

equipment will place extra strain not only on the static line and second line, but also on the grab lines to which the second line is attached. In rough weather, while you are sheltering in the waterlogged hull, the life raft's grab line could pull free and the static line snap, leaving you without life raft or safety equipment. You cannot stow the life raft closer to the hull, or on the deck of the parent craft, because the many contact points will chafe through the buoyancy chambers and leave you with a useless life raft.

A possible solution is to keep the essential survival equipment - water kit, fishing kit and rescue kit - in the waterproof grab bag near the hatchway in the parent craft and to leave the rest of the equipment in the life raft. Make sure that all watchkeepers are briefed to take an extra line to the life raft if the weather looks like becoming rough.

The above has described just one possible scenario. You need to consider all potential emergency situations and work on potential solutions. In an emergency, there is right and there is wrong - and there is the need to make a call. By thinking yourself into and out of these situations, you are mentally preparing for survival at sea. Preparation is the foundation of survival, and you need to be able to make these calls with confidence; there will be precious little time to weigh up the pros and cons when the cabin sole is rising at a rate of 30cm (12in) every ten seconds.

There are many different factors to consider before ultimately deciding to abandon ship and the final decision will depend on the individual circumstances. Whatever decision you make, you know that you have everything you need to survive until you reach safety.

HULL TRAUMA – THE FIRST RESPONSE

Sadly, the oceans are littered with objects that can fatally damage the hulls of most boats. Drifting logs and cargo containers floating just below the surface are the major culprits; growler ice is a problem in extreme latitudes; and marine life also poses a threat – accidental collisions with great whales and deliberate attacks by killer whales have both been known to sink boats.

At the moment of impact, it is possible that one or more of your crew members will be thrown overboard. Delegate one of your crew on deck to make sure everyone is still on board, to drop all sail and to start pumping the bilge using the manual pump. Detail another crew member to operate the electrical bilge pump, if fitted and operable, and to bail by hand using buckets and basins.

Emergency hull repair

Locate the hole, fill it and brace your internal repair to hold it in place. Then fill the hole externally and hold that repair in place using a sail strapped around the hull like a bandage.

Meanwhile, take another crew member with you and locate the impact area by looking for water ingress. If the hole is on or only just below the waterline, get your crew to shift both themselves and heavy equipment to the opposite side to heel the boat and get the hole out of the water.

Try to plug the hole using cushions, blankets, sleeping bags, sailbags, kitbags –

indeed, anything soft and shapeless. Hold these in place by hand or foot while your assistant locates something hard to place over the repair, such as a chopping board or a torn-off locker door. Then you will need a brace to hold the repair in place. Spinnaker poles sawn to the right length are ideal, but also suitable is anything sturdy and long enough to cross the cabin or reach another suitable bracing point, such as an oar. There are devices, similar to umbrellas, which can be pushed through the hole and opened outside the hull to stem the ingress of water, and these may buy you some time.

If the ingress of water has been slowed to a rate that can be handled by the pumps, you will have time to improve your repair. Take your stormjib, or your strongest available jib, and a bagged spinnaker, cushion, or sleeping bag on deck. Attach the foot of the jib to one toerail or handrail and send a suitably dressed crew overboard, checking for sharks first, to pass the head of the sail under the hull. Take the head from him and pass him the sailbag, cushion, or sleeping bag to place against your repair, then tighten the sail under the hull to hold the external repair in place, as you would hold sterile gauze in place with a bandage. If your boat is long-keeled, consider different orientations of the sail, fore and aft even, to plug the gap.

When making your immediate assessment, based on the visible rate of water ingress into the cabin, you must decide quickly whether attempting repair is a reasonable course of action. If the hole is too big to plug - bigger than 0.37 square metres (4 square feet), say - or the impact area is not directly accessible, you would be wasting the little time that remains and jeopardizing the lives of your crew by attempting repair. In the time it takes you to strip out the joinery or fittings that obscure the impact area, the water level in the cabin could be too high to work on any repair. Make snap judgements; there is no time to

lose. Always err on the side of caution - your Mayday message can be downgraded or cancelled later, and the life raft and grab bag returned to their locker.

PREPARE TO ABANDON SHIP

There are various actions that need to be carried out to abandon ship successfully. Depending on the number of your crew, many of these can be conducted at the same time as other members of the crew attempt to save the vessel. All your survival equipment must be tied or clipped to the parent craft so that it is not lost if the boat starts to roll or capsize. Spare time can be used to salvage equipment from the hull, but the main priorities are as follows:

1. Your entire crew should make sure they are wearing their PFDs and the appropriate personal kit. Wearing the PFD is essential, and you must have your multitool with you at all times.

When not in use, your PFD should be stored with all the foul weather gear in the wet locker, close to the hatch, so that one crew member can collect it all in a hurry and throw it into the cockpit. There will not be enough time to search cabins.

2. If the life raft is stowed on the coachroof, take the life raft's static line and tie it securely to the boat on the leeward side near the cockpit. Next unlash the life raft and move it into the cockpit. If your life raft is stored in the cockpit, attach its static line to the leeward side and then move the life raft into the cockpit. Never move the life raft if the static line is not tied on to the boat - you cannot afford to lose it. Life rafts are heavy, so consider delegating two people to this task.

3. Take the grab bag from its locker. Place it next to the life raft and attach it to the boat's leeward side using its spring clip. If there is a second grab bag below, remember to put the ship's first aid kit, sextant and any other navigational equipment not

Hull trauma

Hundreds of containers are washed off the decks of cargo ships every year. These float just below the surface and represent a huge danger to small craft users offshore.

duplicated in your navigation kit into the bag. Then pass the bag up into the cockpit and make sure it is clipped on to the leeward side. You should also have at least two 36–45-litre (8–10-gallon) screw-top containers of water, three-quarters full, tied together in the abandon ship locker. Remove and secure them also.

4. Send out a DSC Distress Alert using your DSC VHF. This will alert all shipping, and other DSC units in the area on VHF Channel 70. The alert will be transmitted automatically until acknowledgement is received. When it is, the recipient will contact you on the distress working channel (Channel 16) or listen on 16 for your Mayday.

Having sent your DSC VHF alert, send a Mayday message on VHF Channel 16 to alert non-DSC receivers in the area and to clarify your DSC Distress Alert for DSC users. Remember, the DSC Distress Alert is a digital signal, which means that it is possible that the recipient will have received the message but be unable to contact you, nor you him, using analog voice transmission. So, even if you get a garbled voice response on Channel 16, you can be sure that your Distress Alert has been received. Make sure you are on high power and attempt to make contact.

These are the essential duties and a well-drilled crew of as few as two should take no more than two minutes to complete this. Everything you need to survive is now in the cockpit, ready for launching and loading. Abandoning ship in mid-ocean however, is a traumatic process and you are unlikely to be able to think and plan clearly. This is why preparation is so important. By completing your preparation in advance, when you can think clearly, by and establishing and rehearsing an abandon ship routine, the actions become automatic and you can be sure that nothing is left behind in the confusion.

With the essential kit now in the cockpit, your crew should use the remaining time onboard – if there is any – to concentrate on salvaging anything from the parent craft that will improve their chances of survival:

5. Inflatable tender or dinghy. If your tender is inflatable and uninflated, move it into the cockpit, making sure it is tied on. Should anything happen to your life raft, you now have a back-up. If you have a rigid dinghy tied to the stern, move it round to the leeward side and secure its painter there. If it is stored on the coachroof, launch it, then move it to leeward and tie its painter within reach of the life raft static line. Owing to their hexagonal shape and ballast bags, life rafts do not sail well. The tender or dinghy, set with sail, can be used like a tug to tow you towards safety.

6. Take seasickness pills and drink as much water from the tap as you can manage. Fill to three-quarters full every screw-top bottle and resealable watertight container you can find.

7. Bag up useful stores, such as fresh fruit and vegetables, particularly onions; canned fruit; chocolate; biscuits; and honey. Place the bag in the cockpit.

8. While in the galley, place useful knives and cutlery into a resealable plastic box and bag those up too.

9. Collect the crew's sleeping bags. These will help to insulate the life raft floor against the cold and also protect against the battering you will receive from the ocean's more inquisitive fish.

10. Grab a sail in a sailbag. The sail itself will help to protect against the charging fish, and can also be used like a bib to protect the life raft tubes while fishing. Sections can be cut off to make sheaths for any sharp objects, to be used as a canopy and a sail, and for emergency water collection in rainstorms. In rough weather, it can be streamed in the water to increase your drag. It will also improve your visibility if SAR services are searching your area, and while in the water, the shade it creates attracts fish.

Launching the life raft

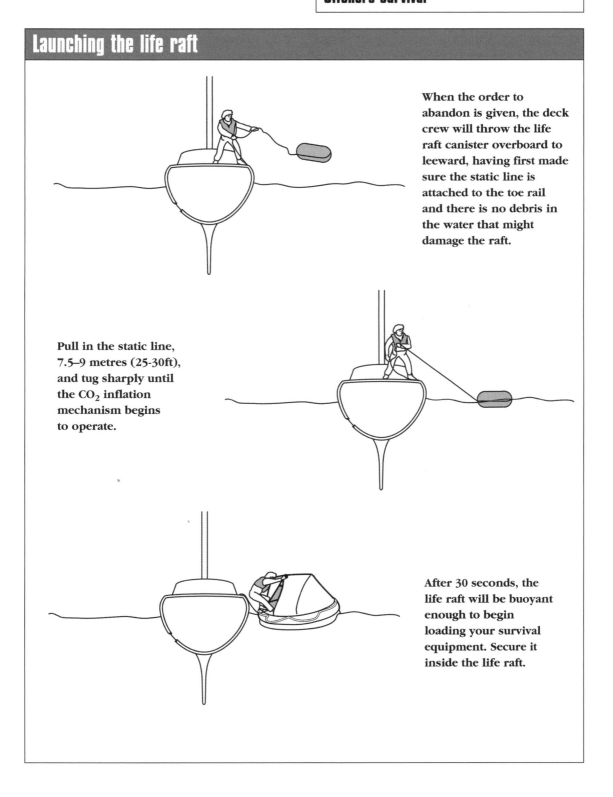

When the order to abandon is given, the deck crew will throw the life raft canister overboard to leeward, having first made sure the static line is attached to the toe rail and there is no debris in the water that might damage the raft.

Pull in the static line, 7.5–9 metres (25-30ft), and tug sharply until the CO_2 inflation mechanism begins to operate.

After 30 seconds, the life raft will be buoyant enough to begin loading your survival equipment. Secure it inside the life raft.

The sailbag can be used for general storage or converted for use as an emergency sea anchor.

11. Resealable plastic boxes for water collection and storage, and fish storage.

12. The sailmaking kit is full of general utility equipment.

13. Ropes and lines, particularly polypropylene, which floats.

14. Fenders, for extra buoyancy.

All this equipment will prove useful if you are to survive at sea for some time, and the tender or dinghy will provide you with more space to store this equipment; there will be precious little space left in the life raft. You and your crew are now prepared to abandon ship, confident in the knowledge that you have everything you need.

ABANDON SHIP – HOLED VESSEL

Your vessel is holed and sinking. Repair is not an option, or has proved unsuccessful, but your equipment is prepared in the cockpit and your crew is equipped with PFDs and wearing all their personal kit. You give the order to abandon ship:

1. Check the static line is firmly attached to the boat on the leeward side and that there is no debris in the water that could damage the life raft's tubes.

Throw the life raft overboard to leeward or, if it is too heavy, slide it into the water under the lower guardrail. Pull in on the static line until it stops paying out - expect 7.5-9 metres (25-30 feet) of static line - then tug sharply until the self-inflation mechanism operates, inflating the life raft. It may require several firm tugs before the self-inflation system activates. Thirty seconds after activation, the life raft will have taken shape and will be buoyant enough to start loading equipment, although full inflation will not occur for about two minutes.

2. Check the rest of the survival gear from the abandon ship locker is in the cockpit and secured to the leeward side.

3. Once the life raft is inflated, pull it alongside using the static line and delegate one able crew member to get into the life raft. Always step in by placing one foot on the upper tube, leaning forward and placing the other foot on the life raft floor while cushioning your landing by placing your hands on the inflated arch. Never jump into the life raft - this puts unnecessary stress on the structure and may cause damage. The life raft crew should take a second line to the boat doubled back to the life raft because the static line is designed to break if the vessel sinks before you cut the static line. Adding a second line will ensure that, should the static line break before all your equipment and crew have boarded, the life raft will remain alongside. The life raft crew should locate the life raft's survival equipment and keep it safe and available.

4. Pass the survival kit to the life raft crew, making sure the essential equipment is loaded first, starting with the grab bag (or bags) and water.

5. The life raft crew will first secure the grab bags and water to the interior grab lines to ensure they cannot be lost; next spread the sleeping bags over the floor of the life raft; and finally load the rest of the equipment.

6. The life raft crew will then untie or cut the dinghy painter and secure it to the outer grab rope of the life raft. If you have an inflatable dinghy and time to inflate it, do so and remember to bring the bellows with you. If there is no time, pass the inflatable and the bellows into the life raft for inflation later.

7. The life raft crew then helps the rest of the crew into the life raft by holding onto the parent craft with one hand and using the other to assist the boarding crew, ensuring that there are no heavy landings that might damage the life raft's structure. As each crew member enters, they should move to the far side of the life raft to make room for the

incoming crew and to reduce the risk of capsize. Remember that even though you have a larger life raft than is technically required, the space inside will be very limited. The final crew member to board should ensure that there is nothing left in the cockpit and that there are no other crew left on the boat before boarding. When the final crew has boarded, release the second line to the boat, but leave the static line attached until the parent craft founders.

8. Some life rafts have sea anchors that deploy automatically on inflation while others have theirs stored inside for manual deployment. If yours deploys automatically and can be recovered without your getting wet, do so. Otherwise, try to ensure it does not snag on the parent craft and become lost. Your sea anchor is essential to prevent capsize in rough weather.

9. When the parent craft sinks, cut the static line with your multitool or the life raft knife.

Again, a crew of two should be able to complete the abandon ship in two minutes. Added to the time taken to prepare to abandon ship, this makes a total of four minutes. Time will be very limited, so it is essential that your crew knows exactly what is required, where equipment is and what to do with it. Each should have a role allocated to them, on deck or below, and any problems will be highlighted in abandon ship rehearsal. Keep rehearsing until you hit the two-minute target.

RAPID ABANDON SHIP

If the parent craft is holed badly and sinking fast, you will not have even four minutes to complete the abandon ship procedure. The Robertsons' boat *Lucette* – a 19-ton, 13-metre (43-foot) wooden schooner – sank in just 60 seconds after being holed by a killer whale attack. In that brief time they salvaged their GRP dinghy, but very little else, and yet they still managed to last 38 days at sea

before being rescued.

Assuming there are at least two crew members, one should work on deck and the other below and the following should take no more than one minute.

- **On deck**:

1. Remove the life raft first, secure its static line and deploy it immediately.

2. Cut the dinghy painter and tie it near the life raft. If your PFD has arrived in the cockpit by this time, put it on.

3. Remove the grab bag and attach it to your PFD.

4. Remove the water and load it into the life raft, along with ropes, fenders, inflatable dinghy, etc., from other cockpit lockers.

5. Board the life raft with the grab bag.

- **Below deck**:

1. Remove the PFDs and personal kit from the wet locker, put on your PFD and pass the others and the rest of the personal kit into the cockpit.

2. Remove the second grab bag and clip it to your PFD.

3. Remove the first aid kit and any non-duplicated navigational equipment and place it in the grab bag.

4. If the vessel's electrical equipment is still operative, send a distress alert using your DSC VHF. If there is time, follow up with a Mayday message, or send a conventional Mayday on standard VHF.

5. Get on deck and board the life raft.

While you will leave much very useful gear on the parent craft, your preparation means you have covered every base and are equipped for sea survival.

FIRE – FIRST RESPONSE

Fire can present even greater problems than being holed. It spreads very quickly and can destroy the boat within minutes, preventing you carrying out vital areas of your abandon ship preparation. To avoid starting a fire:

- Don't take risks such as smoking while refuelling or while below;
- Make sure your refuelling pipe is earthed to prevent a spark of static igniting the fuel, and fit flame traps to your fuel tank vents;
- The gas locker must drain overboard. When using your gas system, always turn the gas bottle off and let the gas left in the pipe burn out before shutting down the burner;
- Make sure none of your lockers is stuffed full of waste paper or old rags because these will act as tinder for the slightest spark;
- Store any flammable maintenance liquids securely in an external locker.

Also make sure your boat is equipped with fire extinguishing equipment. A fire blanket should be installed in the galley, away from the stove, so that you can pull it out without burning yourself. Dry powder extinguishers (in blue canisters) can be used to extinguish all kinds of fire and prevent their reignition. Make sure your engine room is fitted with an automatic gas extinguisher or a fire-fighting hole so that you don't need to remove the engine cover to fight a fire.

It is vital that your regular boat maintenance includes checking for potential sources of fire:

- Check your electrical wiring to make sure there are no loose connections, frayed or exposed wires, and no signs of scorching (which may indicate a short circuit).
- Check your bilge to make sure there is no fuel or oil sluicing around. If there is, remove it and investigate the source. If there is fuel or oil present when you next check, there is a leak somewhere that you need to fix urgently.
- Your gas system should also be checked regularly. The gas bottles should be in

good condition. Replace them if they are dented or corroded and ensure that the valve is securely fastened to the bottle. The tubing should be securely attached to the bottle with hose clips, also in good condition. If there is any sign of perishing, replace the tubing at once or stop using the gas system until you have replaced it. Always check to ensure that your tubing is not chafing on anything along the length of its run and take corrective action if this is the case.

Firefighting

There are three elements fire needs to exist – heat, oxygen and fuel. If you can deprive the fire of just one of those, it will die. There are four potential sources of fire onboard your vessel: galley, electrical, fuel, and gas.

Galley – a fire in the galley could be caused by something as simple as a tea towel catching light or overheated cooking oil combusting. In the former case, simply move the tea towel into the sink and douse the fire with tap water to deprive the fire of heat. Don't take it to the hatchway to throw it overboard; you may set light to something else on the way. To counter burning oil, your galley should be equipped with a fire blanket. Pull this from its container and drape it over the burning pan, from the side nearest you to the side furthest away to ensure that you do not get burned. This deprives the fire of oxygen. Clothing fires should also be extinguished using the fire blanket to smother them.

Electrical – first shut off the batteries to prevent the supply of electricity. Then use the dry powder extinguisher, held upright so that the entire contents can be discharged, to stop the fire. Never use water on an electrical fire.

Fuel – if you have an automatic gas-type extinguisher fitted in your engine room, keep it serviced, and it will extinguish any engine room fires. Keeping your bilge free of fuel and oil will stop an engine room fire spreading outside the engine room itself and into the main cabin.

Gas – a gas explosion will blow your boat apart, so the utmost care must be taken when maintaining your gas system. Gas is denser than air and any leakage sinks into the bilge and the engine room. If the electric bilge pump switches on or the engine is turned over, the gas will explode – with catastrophic effects. Make sure you have a gas alarm fitted to detect any gas leakage.

If a fire shows any sign of becoming uncontrollable despite your fire-fighting efforts, you will need to abandon ship as fast

as possible. When abandoning ship because of fire, you must first remove the life raft and tether it to the windward rail, then launch it. Gather the survival gear and abandon ship from the windward side – not the leeward, as in the holed vessel scenario. This is to prevent the flames destroying the life raft.

Grab the rest of the equipment – grab bags and water – from the abandon ship locker, load the life raft, board quickly, cut the static line, and paddle to windward. In strong winds, use the paddles to avoid the flames as best you can. In this case, do not wait for other crew to board before pulling clear of the parent craft. Fires spread quickly on

Using a fire blanket

Remove the blanket from storage and hold it by two adjacent corners. Drape the blanket over the fire moving it away from you, and release the blanket once the fire is covered.

Engine room fire

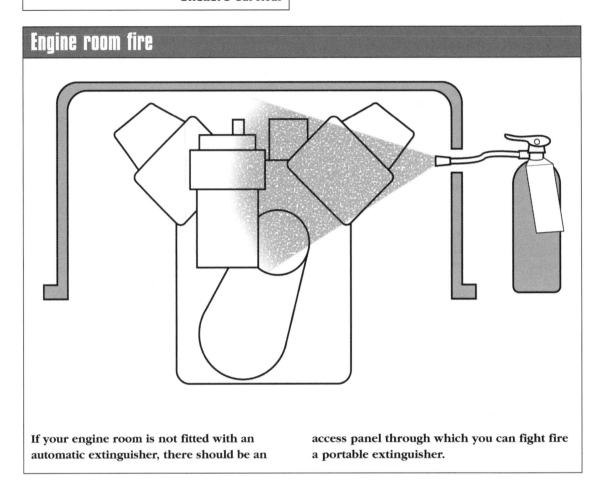

If your engine room is not fitted with an automatic extinguisher, there should be an **access panel through which you can fight fire a portable extinguisher.**

boats, and by waiting you may wreck everyone's chances of survival by damaging the life raft. Your crew will know that the life raft will be to windward of the boat and will rendezvous there as soon as possible.

There is a chance that the fire will prevent you from getting at some of your safety equipment. There is nothing you can do about this. Most fires start in the galley, navigation station and engine room – all clustered around the main hatchway, which means that you may not be able to get below to the wet locker, the second grab bag and first aid kit. This is certainly a setback, but you should never risk your life attempting to get equipment that might save your life – it

doesn't make sense. Remember that smoke is as much, if not more of a killer than fire.

If the parent craft sinks before the crew has boarded the life raft, the nearest crew member should cut the static line to guarantee the life raft does not sink with the parent craft. If the parent craft is on fire, get the life raft to windward or across the wind as fast as possible using the paddles. In both circumstances, the crew should all swim towards the life raft and hang on to the outer grab rope.

RIGHTING THE LIFE RAFT

In strong winds, the inflating life raft may be flipped over before its ballast bags –

designed to prevent capsize – have filled. In this case, your strongest crew member should swim to the life raft and locate the self-inflation CO_2 canister. The life raft should be turned around until the gas canister is to leeward. The crew member should then scramble onto the life raft tube above the canister using the righting strop, grab ropes and boarding ladder (it is important to avoid having to lift the extra weight of the canister and also to avoid being knocked unconscious by it as the life raft rights). This will not be easy, and rough

water will not help. Placing both feet on the tube above the canister, the crew member should grab the righting strop about 30cm (12in) in front of his feet and lean back, using his weight to exert a righting moment on the life raft. This will take some time because the water trapped in the canopy must drain before the life raft will right. As it does so, take a deep breath.

When the life raft does right, you will find yourself beneath it. Don't panic. Simply, pull yourself along the righting strop until you reach the other side of the life raft and

Launching a life raft to windward

If you are forced to abandon by an uncontrollable fire, do so from the boat's windward side to avoid the smoke, flames and embers to leeward.

surface and can breathe freely again. Turn the life raft so that the entrance is not facing to leeward; this will reduce the chances of the life raft capsizing as you are boarding it.

BOARDING FROM THE WATER

Again, you need your strongest crew member to board the life raft first in order to assist the others, who should hold on to the outer grab rope while waiting to board. Most modern life rafts are equipped with boarding ladders, but these vary in efficiency. Some are simply webbing strops that float away; others are weighted to stay in place and fitted with plastic spacers to keep the step open. Whichever you have, hold on to the life raft's outer grab rope with one hand while locating the ladder and holding the step open with the other. Place your foot in and climb. As soon as you are able, grab the handholds inside on the life raft floor to pull yourself onboard.

Once onboard, assist others to board, starting with the injured and the weak. If they are unable to use the ladder through exhaustion or unconsciousness, turn them round so that their back is to the life raft entrance. Grab them below their arms and lean back into the life raft so that they land on top of you. Once everyone is onboard (conduct a head count to make sure none of the crew is missing), secure the sea anchor's bitter end to the life raft's stern. Next, deploy the sea anchor (if it does not deploy automatically), which will help to prevent the life raft capsizing and also slow your drift. If your EPIRB, DSC or VHF Distress Alerts have been received, this is the place rescuers will look for you.

If there is more than one life raft carrying survivors from the wreck, use the rescue quoit and line to make sure the life rafts stay together. They should be tethered together using 6metres (20feet) of line. At the middle of the line, there should be a weight attached

to buffer the tether's strain at their attachment to the life raft grab lines. The life rafts should not come into contact with each other, as this could cause damage to the buoyancy chambers. In rough weather, shorten the tethers so that all the life rafts stay within the same wave pattern – again, this is to reduce the stress on the tethers.

RESCUING MISSING CREW

If you are missing crew, the sea anchor will also make sure you stay on location while you conduct a visual search of the area for them. At night, listen for their whistle and watch for the strobe light from their lifejacket or for their chemical light stick. During the day, listen for their whistle and watch for waving arms and dye markers. On no account should you leave the life raft to rescue them. A rescue quoit with 30m (100ft) of line is in the life raft survival kit. Throw the quoit and pull them back.

If you spot an unconscious crew member within swimming range, select the strongest swimmer, then attach the rescue line to her at the quoit end and to the life raft at the bitter end. If the unconscious survivor is beyond 30m (100ft) but the swimmer is confident that she can rescue the drifting crew, tie together more line so that when she reaches the survivor, or if exhaustion or cramp prevents her from being able to effect rescue, she can be hauled back.

ABANDONING SHIP THROUGH FUEL-COVERED OR BURNING WATER

If the parent craft's fuel tanks have been holed or ruptured, the surface of the water may be covered in fuel. Just as in a fire or potential fire situation, you should abandon ship to windward, but before entering the water, make sure your PFD is uninflated. If your PFD is self-inflating, pull the toggle until it inflates, then deflate it using the pressure release valve. Wearing your deflated PFD, remember which direction is windward,

Abandoning ship

With the life raft pulled alongside, the life raft crew should enter the raft (stepping on the upper tube and placing hands on the life raft's canopy tube) and prepare to receive and secure the survival equipment from the deck crew.

then jump feet first into the water, pinching your nose and keeping your eyes closed.

As soon as you are underwater, start swimming in the windward direction using the breaststroke. When you need to breathe, push water towards the surface with your arms above your head. This will keep you underwater while clearing a fuel- or flame-free space on the water's surface. Once the space has been cleared, surface quickly, take a deep breath and submerge again. Once you have escaped the fuel- or flame-covered area, surface and inflate your PFD manually while searching for other survivors and life rafts or anything buoyant

on which you can float. Blow your whistle to attract attention. If you see other survivors, you should gather together and stay together by tether or by linking arms. Remember to relax – you will need to conserve as much energy as possible until you find a buoyant refuge. If there was no time to launch the life raft, wait until the vessel sinks and salvage any buoyant debris.

SALVAGE

For several minutes after the parent craft sinks, buoyant equipment will float to the surface from the wreck. Anything buoyant is useful. This could include water bottles,

Inflating and boarding a life raft

A. If the raft is attached to you with a rope, pull the raft towards you. If it is upside down in the water, pull it the right way up by moving to the opposite side and grabbing the lanyard and pulling it over, so as to flip the life aft.

B & C. To board the raft, grab the handles on each side of the raft and pull yourself in, while kicking your legs in the water.

C. In tropical climates, the turmoil of abandon ship could well attract sharks. Most will simply be curious, searching for food. If they find none, they will be likely to search elsewhere.

D. Alternatively, get one knee inside the raft and pull yourself forward into the raft as shown here.

E. When you are inside the raft, make sure it is fully inflated and check for any leaks.

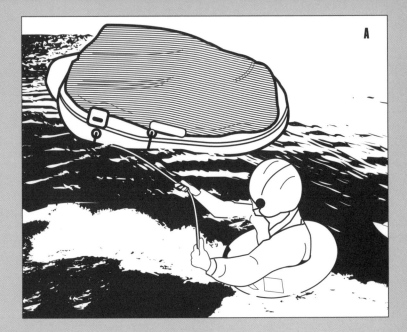

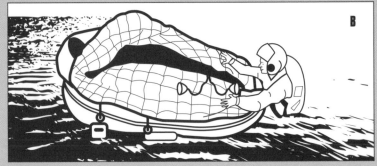

provided there is enough air in them to guarantee their buoyancy; fenders; lifebuoys; MOB markers; even, perhaps, the rigid dinghy if you managed to cut its painter. All this equipment will be useful to you in some way and at some stage, so collect it while you are still on the scene.

LIFE RAFT

Having ascertained that the entire crew is onboard the life raft, the sea anchor is properly deployed and everything useful has been salvaged from the wreck site, you can turn your attention to your new craft. The skipper of the parent craft should now become skipper of the life raft because leadership will be more important than ever. The skipper will ultimately be responsible for every aspect of the upkeep and welfare of the life raft, its equipment and its crew. This will include log-keeping and navigation; implementing a new watch system and briefing watchkeepers on their duties regarding sightings and contacts; routine maintenance of life raft, equipment and crew; rationing of supplies; discipline and morale. If the skipper is lost or injured, promote the next in the chain of command.

The first step is to ensure that the life raft is fully inflated, including the inflatable floor, and topped up when required. The manual bellows will be required for this; it will be stored in the life raft survival kit. The tubes should be firm, but not drum-tight. Remember that, as the air inside warms during the day and cools during the night, you will need to deflate and inflate to account for the air's expansion in heat and contraction in cold. If you are unable to inflate fully one of the tubes, search the tube and the valve for leaks. The life raft will include a repair kit, including bungs. These will come in several sizes and can be jammed into holes to stem the leaking of air. In the longer term, these will not be effective. Smaller repairs can be effected

using duct tape, a roll or two of which should feature in your utility kit. For larger repairs to be effective in the long term, raft repair clamps will be required.

In rough weather, make sure the sea anchor is streamed over the stern of the life raft and that the entrance is closed and facing downwind. Huddle in the middle of the life raft with the heaviest crew at the centre to prevent capsize. The heaviest crew member should also be tethered to the life raft with a line long enough to ensure that he can get onto the bottom of the life raft in the event of capsize. In such a case, it is likely that several crew will be swept out of the life raft – or perhaps all, in which case the life raft could be blown downwind and lost in seconds. If someone is tethered inside, the life raft will remain nearby, ready for righting by the heaviest crew and reboarding. Brief all the crew members on procedures following capsize and their individual responsibilities.

With the life raft now fully and securely inflated, bail out any seawater. Extended exposure to seawater causes morale-sapping salt water sores and corrodes any electrical equipment and even metal, including canned goods. Make sure all your survival equipment – both grab bags, the life raft survival kit, any extras – is securely stowed inside the life raft and tethered to the inside grab line.

Should the life raft capsize, this equipment will remain inside the life raft rather than falling through the entrance which will be torn open by water pressure. Use this example during your emergency drills to stress how critical it is that all equipment is attached to the life raft or yourselves at all times.

CREW

The first step to ensure your crew's health is to give each member seasickness pills to make sure they don't spend their first three days onboard vomiting away fluids and minerals. Anyone who has suffered from

Using a rescue quoit

If a survivor is struggling to make it to the raft, use the rescue quoit to haul them in.

If an unconscious survivor, or one too weak to swim, will need recovery, the strongest swimmer should swim out securely attached to the rescue quoit.

seasickness will know how debilitating it is for the sufferer under normal circumstances – and living in a life raft is very far from normal. When food and nutrition are at such a premium, you simply cannot afford to have one of your crew taking more than their ration and then hurling it into a bag that could be used for water storage, or over the side, attracting sharks.

For those not already seasick, the smell and sight of vomit is often enough to induce nausea, so bags are preferable for seasickness. You should consider carrying in the first aid kit some aromatic eucalyptus-based balm that can be smeared beneath the nostrils of the rest of the crew to mask the smell. After administering seasickness pills to all, check on their health. Attend to any injuries and look for signs of shock, hypothermia, heat exhaustion, fear or panic and take remedial action:

Shock – this will be present throughout the crew to some degree. It is caused by reduced blood supply to the vital organs, and shocked survivors will look confused or scared, and will have a weak, racing pulse, cold sweats and rapid, shallow breathing. The shocked survivor should lie down with his legs and arms raised to ensure blood moves towards the vital organs. Cover him with a survival blanket to retain body heat and monitor his pulse and breathing closely. Reassure the shocked survivor that the crew abandoned safely and have everything required to survive at sea for as long as is necessary. Everyone is going to make it.

Hypothermia – if anyone shows signs of hypothermia, make sure the life raft entrance is closed to raise as far as possible the temperature in the life raft. Get the crew grouped in the centre of the life raft to share warmth, paired off back to back and each pair wrapped in a survival blanket or tarpaulin. Give the potential sufferer dry clothes if this is possible, and make sure she has gloves, boots and a hat on to prevent further heat loss. Wrap her in one of the survival blankets from the life raft survival kit and share your warmth by sitting behind her with your arms round her as she sits hugging her knees. Give the sufferer some carbohydrate rations because digesting these will create heat. If the case is severe, remove her clothing above the waist, and yours, and wrap yourselves in the same survival blanket – skin-on-skin contact is the quickest way to transfer heat.

Heat Exhaustion – this condition must be dealt with very quickly. Get the sufferer into the shade of the life raft, with the arms and legs raised above the level of their head, and dampen their clothing. Administer a salt tablet with water to replace lost fluids and minerals and instruct them to rest.

Fear – this is a normal physical response to threatening circumstances, but it must not become incapacitating or spiral into panic. Fear takes the form of cold sweating, particularly from the hands, feet and armpits, and a physical trembling caused by tremendous tension in the muscles. The eyes will dilate and dart around as concentration flips from one morbid thought to another. This inability to focus will make speech hesitant and garbled and the sufferer can become irritable as the weak, fast pulse provides an inadequate supply of blood to the brain, leaving the sufferer confused.

To reiterate, fear is natural in this circumstance. Expect it; know the symptoms and check them off as they arrive. In doing so, you will begin once again to take charge of your mental activity and think more clearly. Then take stock of your situation, remembering the knowledge and equipment you have with you in the life raft. Remember Poon Lim, and realize how much more you have going for you. Your survival chances are only as good as you believe them to be. Survival is not going to be easy, but nothing worth having comes easily.

If you see fear in others, help them to overcome their fear. By explaining away their fear, you will yourself become more confident, and that will show. Others will feed off your confidence and, before long, you will have a life raft full of people focused on survival, convinced that they will reach safety and ready to work together to achieve that goal.

Panic – this is an irrational and maladapted response to threatening circumstances, and the conscious mind becomes obsessed with catastrophic outcomes. The rational response to threat is to start thinking in survival terms and to take measures to counter the threat. 'Fight or flight' is the body's immediate reaction, and since your flight has already been made into the life raft, it is now time to fight. To prevent panic, make sure you carry out regular emergency drills onboard to make sure the crew knows where all the emergency equipment is and how to prepare it and use it.

Such drills will ensure that the conscious mind is focused on supervising the physical acts of emergency drill rather than fantasizing about horrific deaths. To counter panic, you will need a powerful new stimulus to distract the sufferer from their obsessive morbidity. This is where a slap around the face or a violent shake can be effective. Having captured their attention, explain that you are all going to make it to safety and give examples of survival at sea that show success is a matter of will, not luck. Your preparation has provided you with enough equipment to fish, collect or produce fresh water, navigate and raise the alarm. With confidence in that knowledge and equipment, and by concentrating on what you can influence rather than fretting over what you cannot, you will all survive long enough to reach safety.

EQUIPMENT

Next, conduct a complete inventory of the life raft's survival equipment and the extra equipment you have brought with you,

Abandoning ship through burning fuel

Your PFD must be uninflated. If it is self-inflating, operate the mechanism and deflate using the pressure release valve. Close your eyes, pinch your nose and jump feet first into the water. Once underwater, start swimming to windward.

including salvage. This will help later when equipment is lost or needs repairing. By reading the list, you will be able to think more objectively about the nature and composition of individual pieces of equipment rather than simply their function and appearance. Every item of equipment

Defending against shark attack in the water

In tropical climates, the turmoil of abandon ship could well attract sharks. Most will simply be curious, searching for food. If they find none, they will search elsewhere. Four types of shark are responsible for most attacks: Great White, Tiger, Hammerhead and Blue. Mako, Thresher, Grey Nurse and Ground sharks have also been known to attack if hunting in packs, but very rarely do they attack when alone.

Bleeding will attract sharks, as will urine and faeces, so bandage up as quickly as possible or hold on as long as possible. Shiny objects will also attract sharks, so remove any jewellery and place it in a pocket. Schools of fish will also attract sharks, so avoid them. If swimming, use strong, regular strokes – do not thrash in panic – and always keep the shark in view, stay alert. If a shark or group of sharks is making wide circles without sharp turns, they are simply curious. If the turns become tighter, the shark or sharks could be preparing to attack.

In this case, there are several courses of action open to you. None is guaranteed to deter sharks, but all have been known to do so. Some of these involve threatening the shark, which seems insanely bold

until you remember that the shark did not become the ocean's most successful killer by risking its own life. The shark has no natural enemies in the ocean, but the human survivor is unnatural to this habitat, and therefore an unknown quantity. For that reason alone, the shark will be circumspect. You also have the intelligence to bluff and, provided you show no obvious signs of fear, injury or distress, you stand a fairly good chance of deterring a shark attack.

A. Always watch the shark while relaxed floating – never let it out of your sight.

B. If it begins to make tighter circles, swim using strong regular strokes. If it approaches, turn and start swimming towards it, copying its own behaviour. The shark will sense a threat and turn away.

C. If this does not work, stop swimming and start slapping the water hard and regularly with the palms of your hands, shouting underwater will also add to the assault on the shark's highly-tuned senses. If the shark continues to approach, prepare for combat.

D. You will be wearing the correct personal kit, which includes soft shoes or boots.

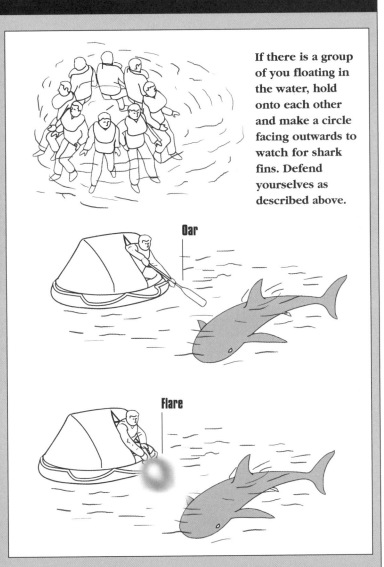

If there is a group of you floating in the water, hold onto each other and make a circle facing outwards to watch for shark fins. Defend yourselves as described above.

Oar

Flare

Keep your feet ahead of you and prepare to kick the shark's sensitive snout. If you have gloves on, you can punch its snout. Using your multitool on a lanyard, you can also attack the shark's snout, eyes and gills. If you successfully injure the shark, it should flee, taking the risk of attack with it, but its behaviour may become unpredictable. Use strong regular strokes to move away from the blood and be prepared for further attacks.

you have is multipurpose and the survivor must become accustomed to thinking in those terms.

EPIRB

Now that the life raft, equipment and crew have been checked, you should activate your EPIRB. There are two categories of EPIRB:

Category One is automatic and designed for storage in a pushpit-mounted bracket. The bracket is fitted with a Hydrostatic Release Unit (HRU), which frees the EPIRB at 5m (16ft) below sea level and the EPIRB itself has a sea water switch for activation. These float free and will need to be located using their strobe light before being tied alongside or preferably inside the life raft.

Category Two is manual and designed for storage below or in grab bags. These are better for an offshore sea survival situation because the unit can be switched on and off to save power and can be mounted inside the life raft for improved security. Most survivors would rather see their potential saviour taped to the life raft's support arch than bobbing around outside on a thin piece of line.

Both versions will operate successfully only if their aerial is vertical. The Category Two EPIRB is also fitted with a strobe light and, if mounted inside, will provoke headache and possibly nausea among the survivors. Stick duct tape over the strobe light until SAR services approach and the strobe is needed for homing in.

Bear in mind that your EPIRB's lithium battery is regulated by the IMO (International Maritime Organization) to operate for 24 -48 hours in extremely cold climates. In warmer climates, the battery can last for 100 hours or more, but you should still operate it intermittently. The EPIRB should be switched on for two hours, then off for two hours for the first 24-hour period, then on for one hour in every four thereafter. Be very careful with the battery. Depending

on the manufacturer and model, replacements may not be available. Most models' batteries are replaced during the unit's service as watertight seals and gaskets have to be refitted after doing so. There are some models that permit replacement batteries to be fitted in a survival situation, and this has obvious implications for your rescue.

It is advisable to carry a second unit, perhaps one of the smaller handheld EPIRBs or Personal Locator Beacons (PLBs), because your primary system may not work. Ensure your PLB has a built-in GPS to update your position regularly, and exercise the same caution with its battery. Remember your PLB, if fitted with the longer lasting Class One battery, may not float, and if it does the aerial may not be vertical.

Make a note of the time the EPIRB was activated in your waterproof logbook, along with details of your situation: what happened to your parent craft; where and when; what equipment and supplies you have; and how many you have onboard the life raft. As usual, positional information and meteorological data should also be recorded in the logbook.

With the EPIRB now operational, a Maritime Rescue and Coordination Centre somewhere should be working out how best to bring you to safety. To help them home in, or to attract some other form of rescue, you, as life raft skipper, will need to devise a watch system. It should involve watches of no longer than two hours – concentration starts to slip after that period, especially as the crew is likely to be fatigued.

The watchkeepers should be briefed on what to look out for and what procedures to follow if a sighting is made, including use of the handheld VHF and pyrotechnics. In rough weather, or in strong tropical sunlight, a proper lookout, through the life raft entrance, cannot be kept, but the watchkeeper should check the observation

Shark recognition

A

B

C

D

E

F

A. Blue
B. Tiger
C. Hammerhead
D. Thresher
E. Grey Nurse
F. White
G. Mako

G

port every ten minutes. If you received an acknowledgement to your Mayday call, sent before or after leaving the boat, you should have been informed of how long you could expect to wait before rescue arrived.

As your VHF has a range limited to 16–24km (10–15 miles) between yachts and ships at sea, you should expect rescue to arrive on the scene fairly swiftly. Keep your VHF on the agreed communication Channel, so your rescuer can contact you as soon as possible.

PROVISIONS AND RATIONING

Check your emergency supplies of food and water. Make a note in the logbook of what you have, and determine to use these supplies as an emergency back-up. Only if every other avenue of water collection has proved fruitless should you touch these rations. Remember, if you need to ration each crew member to less than 560ml (1 pint) per day, do not issue any food rations as they will require water to digest.

Unless suffering from medical problems, such as hypothermia or heat exhaustion, no crew member should consume rations in the first 24 hours because the body still carries plenty of food and water. This fasting will also serve to adjust the mindset of the crew into survival mode.

Urination and defecation should be discouraged because both involve passing water from the body. The withdrawal of the body's resources from the process of digestion will effectively stop the production of faeces and you will not be eating enough to produce much in that respect anyway. There are records or survivors going 39 days without passing any solids, so expect constipation. The liver will recycle your urine and extract more water, which is why urine takes on a very dark colour when water is at a premium. Don't be alarmed by this; it is completely normal.

Familiarize the crew with the equipment you have for collecting food and water, the techniques required to maximize their output, and how to store what you collect.

ROUTINE

Survivors will also need to draw up a daily rota of essential maintenance activities, some to be carried out after each watch, others once a day. This will be designed to ensure that all equipment – particularly that outside the life raft, such as the sea anchor itself and its attachment to the life raft – is regularly inspected for signs of damage, including any chafing of lines on the buoyancy chambers inside and outside the life raft. Other equipment, such as fishing gear, water collection gear, and navigational gear, should also be regularly inspected, before and after use, for any sign of wear, damage or impending breakdown.

Personal hygiene will inevitably suffer, but attempts should be made to keep the body's nodes – armpits and crotch – as free from crusted salt as possible. Injuries tend not to heal in sea survival situations because of the ever-present dampness in the life raft and the lack of vitamin provision in your diet. Wounds in these areas would be very debilitating. Many survival accounts indicate that dental health pretty much takes care of itself owing to the lack of sugar in the diet and the cleansing action of gnawing on dried fish.

Fishing gear and water collection gear should be kept free of salt. Fishing line encrusted with salt is extremely abrasive to the life raft tubes and to bare hands, especially as your hands will be covered in cuts that will not heal because of constant dampness. The water collection gear must be kept as salt-free as possible because any salt on or in the equipment will taint the water you collect.

Ensure that duties are rotated so that everyone becomes proficient in the full range of life raft duties, including navigation.

As skipper, you should be responsible for navigation and logbook entries but other crew should learn how to fulfil your duties, under your supervision, so that should anything happen to you, these duties can still be carried out.

WAITING ON SCENE

If you have an EPIRB with a built-in GPS, you do not need to worry about waiting at the wreck site for rescue because your position will be updated frequently enough for MRCC to work out your rate of drift and calculate where you should be when SAR gets there. How long it will take SAR services to relocate you depends very much on where you became distressed. If you are in the middle of the South Atlantic and well beyond helicopter range, the first contact will be made by fixed-wing aircraft or redirected shipping. If you are well away from shipping lanes, bear in mind that your rescue vessel will probably make about 480–640km (300–400 miles) per day at best towards your last reported location.

If you do not have a GPS built-in to your EPIRB, you will need to decide how long you should stay at the wreck site. This depends on how far off your intended course – known to your relatives ashore and communicated to MRCC – you will be taken by the direction of drift. Use your navigational kit to establish your position, then use your laminated routeing chart to ascertain what effect the prevailing winds

and currents will have on your drift. If they are taking you right along your course, you will not have to make a decision because SAR will search for you along that route. If, however, you are drifting perpendicularly off your course, you will be further away from where SAR is searching with every hour that passes. As life raft skipper, it will be up to you to make the call: you will have to decide when to stop waiting and start surviving. If you have not been rescued inside 72 hours, you should plan on surviving at sea for at least seven days, comforted by the knowledge that you are perfectly prepared to do so.

Above all, it is essential that the life raft's crew do not panic. Not only does panic in one crew member antagonize, unsettle and spread infectious doubt among the others, it can, if unchecked, lead to sudden bursts of potentially fatal behaviour – firing off too many flares at ships that have already passed, drinking too much water, eating too much food. The crew will need to have confidence in the soundness of their skipper's judgement, and a firm belief that they have the knowledge and equipment required to survive at sea until safety is reached. Assurances repeated calmly, firmly and with confidence will control panic. Other survivors have faced longer odds and made it back to safety, and so will you.

Panic occurs only in an unfocused mind. Every survivor should be concentrating on survival – nothing else is relevant.

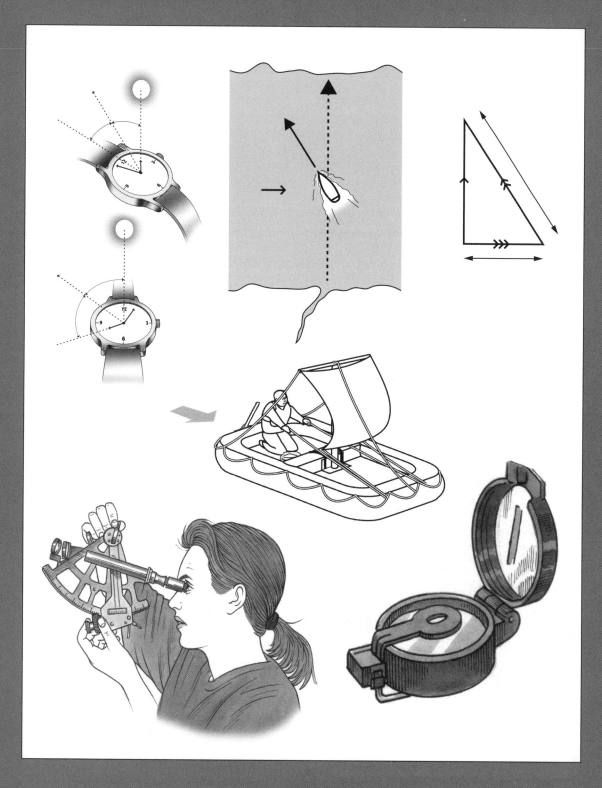

CHAPTER FOUR

Navigation

The alarm was raised 72 hours ago, but there is no sign of rescue. However, you and your crew are alive, as well as circumstances permit, focused and ready for the rigours that lie ahead. You have successfully completed the first stage of survival at sea, the next stage involves making your own way to safety.

To a great extent, the winds and the currents that prevail in your sector of the ocean will determine the direction in which your life raft travels. For this reason, you should ensure that you have included in your grab bag, or incorporated into your life raft's survival kit, laminated routeing charts (see page 35) that show vector quantities for wind and current (the commonest strengths and directions of wind and current in any given area). It would also be useful to include another chart showing the major flight paths and shipping lanes that cover the world's oceans, because contact can be made with both aircraft and ships from your life raft using your rescue kit.

It is very likely that you will have a good idea of the precise location at which the parent craft sank. Before the trauma, you will have been taking day and night sights, checking your results against a GPS perhaps, and plotting your position on a paper chart

Vectors

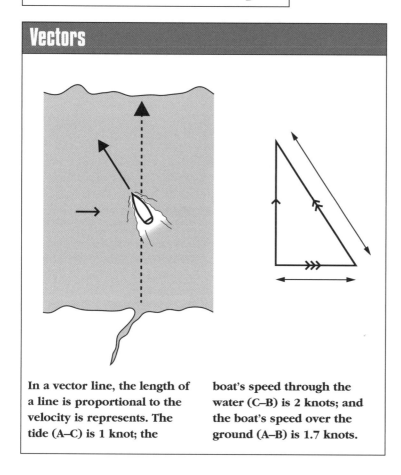

In a vector line, the length of a line is proportional to the velocity is represents. The tide (A–C) is 1 knot; the boat's speed through the water (C–B) is 2 knots; and the boat's speed over the ground (A–B) is 1.7 knots.

the four cardinal points (N, E, S and W) and four intercardinals (NE, SE, SW and NW). Within 30° north or south of the Equator, the winds – for example, the Tradewinds – are more predictable and so eight further points (NNE, ENE, ESE, SSE, SSW, WSW, WNW and NNW) are also shown.

Another method, more suitable for global routeing charts, is the vector mean of all winds in a particular location. When using a vector mean chart, remember the direction and strength indicated is only an average: if there's 45 knots of breeze from the northeast half the year and 45 knots from the southwest the other half, that's an average of zero, but it certainly won't feel that way.

Using your routeing chart, you will be able to estimate the speed and direction of your drift. Using your navigational chart, you will be able to estimate how much distance there is between you and landfall. If the speed and distance are known, then time can be calculated and a very rough ETA established. This will allow you to ration more realistically and having an ETA is a morale-booster in itself, provided it is not taken too seriously. It could vary enormously from day to day, depending on variations in wind and current strength and direction.

Depending on how much time you had to abandon the parent craft, you will have an array of navigational equipment with you. If you had time to grab your sextant and sight reduction tables (see page 30), you will be

several times a day. Just after the moment of trauma, you will have sent your Mayday message. If you are unsure of the position where the parent craft sank - perhaps you are in shock yourself and unable to think clearly - you could use the handheld GPS in the grab bag to find out where you are now. In most circumstances, you should have a pretty good idea of your location prior to the moment of trauma.

You can then check the laminated routeing charts to find the average direction and speed of the wind and current in your area. On an oceanic scale, vector quantities for wind are shown using windroses. These show the percentage frequency and the strength of winds in any given location for

Latitude and longitude

When giving positions using latitude and longitude the latitude is always given first. For example, the position of Tashkent, Kyrgyzstan is Lat 41° 20' N, Long 69° 18' E.

Latitude and longitude are measured in degrees of arc. Latitude can range from 0° at the equator to a maximum of 90° N or 90° S at the poles. Longitude can range from 0° at the prime meridian to a maximum of 180° east or west.

There are 60 minutes (60') in one degree, and 60 seconds (60") in one minute. One

minute of latitude is equal to one nautical mile (about 1.15 imperial miles). The distance represented by a minute of

longitude varies from zero at the poles to one nautical mile at the equator.

Precise positions are given in degrees, minutes and seconds (one second of latitude equals about 30m or 100ft). More approximate positions are quoted in degrees and minutes only, that is, to the nearest nautical mile. When navigating at sea, it is common practice to quote positions to the nearest tenth of a minute, using decimal notation, e.g. 56° 15.7' N, 7° 28.9' W.

able to calculate your latitude and longitude just as you did while onboard the parent craft, using the accurate watch set to GMT stowed in your grab bag or worn on your wrist. Remember to adjust for the reduced height of sight above sea level before making calculations. This will provide you with exact positional information, from which you can more accurately calculate your speed and direction of drift in any 24-hour period. While using the sextant, remember to make sure that it is firmly attached to you by its lanyard, otherwise you risk losing it and damaging your capacity for accurate navigation and thus survival. Keep the sight reduction tables in your waterproof grab bag at all times, except when referring to them, and ensure that they stay as dry as possible. Otherwise. they will become pulp in a matter of days.

Your daily position fix should be noted in your waterproof logbook using your waterproof pen and on your laminated chart

using a chinagraph pencil. If your day's run is too small to mark on your chart, mark every second or third day's run on the chart, but keep your logbook entry daily.

You should also have a handheld GPS unit in your grab bag, equipped with a lanyard and spare batteries. This unit should be considered as a handy way of checking your astronavigation if there seems to be a discrepancy, or for providing a positional fix if one is needed in a hurry – perhaps VHF contact has been made and your exact position is required quickly for SAR purposes. Remember, though, that there are any number of scenarios that could leave you with a malfunctioning or non-operative handheld GPS unit, and if you wholly reliant on GPs, you will then be left unable to navigate. The handheld GPS unit is a very useful back-up device, but should not be used as a primary navigational system.

If neither of these options is open to you, there are several techniques, none if which is highly accurate, that will give you the roughest estimate of your position. The easiest and least accurate of these is Dead Reckoning (DR). Using your recollection of the final position fix before the parent craft was lost, estimate the life raft's drift speed and direction to calculate your estimated position every 24 hours.

To estimate your speed as a result of the action of the wind, you will need an improvised log to measure how long it takes you to cover a known distance. You can use the rescue quoit to calculate this. These are generally supplied as part of your life raft survival kit with 30m (100ft) of line. You can check using your armspan if you are unsure of approximately how much line you have (your armspan from fingertip-to-fingertip is very similar to your height). Tie the bitter

end of the rescue quoit to the stern of the raft and drop the rescue quoit into the water next to the knot. Time in seconds how long it takes for the line to pull up. Then, using the time it takes to cover a known distance, you can calculate speed using the following equation:

$$\text{Speed (S)} = \text{Distance (D)} \div \text{Time (T)}$$

This will provide you with a speed in feet per second. To obtain the speed in knots, remember that

> 1 knot = 1 nautical mile per hour = 6076ft in 3600 seconds

Convert your measurement accordingly. For a distance of 100ft,

$D = 100/6076nm = 1/61nm$ (approximately) and a time of 80 seconds (as a fraction of an hour),
$T = 80 \div 3600 = 8/360$

the estimated speed

$S = (1/61) \div (8/360) = 360 \div 488 = {}^3/_4 \, kn$ approximately.

You will need to add to this figure an estimation of current speed derived from the vector quantities shown on your routeing chart – say, one knot – to arrive at an approximation of your daily distance run:

$$1{}^3/_4 \, kn \times 24hr = 42 \text{ miles}$$

Alternatively, the known distance could be the length of line between your life raft and the sea anchor which, in

Using a sextant

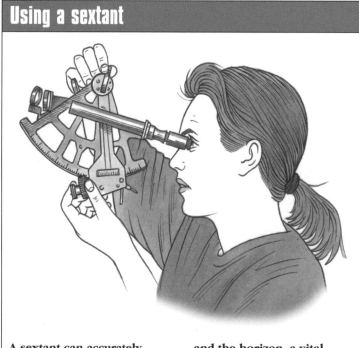

A sextant can accurately determine the angle between the sun or a star **and the horizon, a vital measurement in the practice of astro-navigation.**

Improvising a log

A

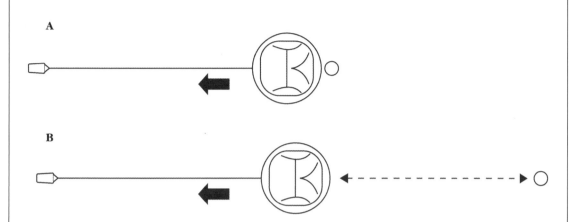

B

To estimate your distance travelled over 24 hours, you need to have some idea of your speed during that period. You can estimate speed – or improvise a log – by measuring how long it takes an object to pass through a known distance. The rescue quoit is ideal for this purpose as it is usually supplied with 30m (100ft) of line.

In light winds, when the current (harnessed by your bow-deployed sea anchor) is your major source of propulsion, secure the bitter end of the rescue quoit to the liferaft,

C

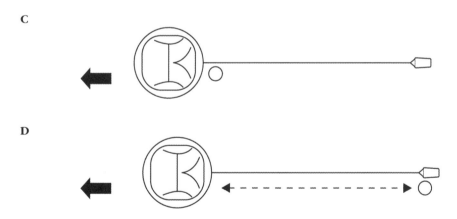

D

then drop it over the stern (A) and time how long it takes the quoit's line to deploy fully (B).

When the wind provides your propulsion (and the sea anchor is deployed over the stern for safety) you can follow the above procedure or, if you know how much sea anchor line is deployed, drop some floating refuse over the stern (C) and time how long it takes to reach the sea anchor (D).

Using the time taken to cover a known distance, an estimate of speed can be calculated using the equation: Speed = Distance ÷ Time.

Finding direction of travel

Use your handheld compass to find your life raft's direction of travel. Remember to allow for leeway – considerable leeway in a strong wind.

rough weather, will be tethered to the stern. This can be measured accurately when you take your life raft in for service or estimated by hauling in the sea anchor and measuring the line in armspans. Then drop the rescue quoit in the water and time its progress as in the previous example.

FINDING DIRECTION WITH A COMPASS

The above calculations will give you an estimate of the distance you have travelled, but you will also need to know in which direction. The routeing chart will give you an average direction of drift. However, if any breeze is blowing, it will act on your life raft and affect your drift. The life raft's survival kit will include a compass and you should also have a spare handheld compass - on a lanyard - in your grab bag navigation kit.

In light winds, when the sea anchor is tethered to the bow to harness the current, there will be little leeway owing to the wind. In this case, simply take a bearing on the sea anchor to calculate your direction of drift. In strong winds, your direction of drift will largely be dictated by leeway, overriding the effect of the current. In these conditions, the sea anchor will be tethered astern, so take a back bearing on the sea anchor or the deployed rescue quoit. Add 180° to the reading to calculate the approximate direction in which the life raft is drifting.

Check your calculations against the current direction from the routeing chart. Your actual direction of drift will be somewhere between your leeway vector and your current vector, but closer to the greater force. In other words, in a strong wind your drift will be largely determined by the breeze, and on a calm day, the current will account for your direction of drift.

FINDING DIRECTION WITHOUT A COMPASS

If you have lost or broken both compasses, you can use the sun and stars to work out your direction of drift. All you need to know is one fixed compass point; the others can be worked out from it.

During the day, use the watch set to local (or Zulu) time to find grid north in the Northern hemisphere, or grid south in the Southern hemisphere. Local time will change during the voyage, but it can be worked out using the local noon method of calculating longitude (see below).

- In the Northern hemisphere, direct your hour hand horizontally towards the sun. Grid south bisects the angle between the hour hand and 12 o'clock.
- In the Southern hemisphere, direct 12 o'clock horizontally towards the sun. Grid north bisects the angle between 12 o'clock and the hour hand.

During the night, you need to locate Polaris if you are in the Northern hemisphere and the Southern Cross in the Southern hemisphere.

Polaris – the North Star can be identified by its relation to one of the northern sky's two major constellations, Ursa Major and Cassiopeia.

Ursa Major, also known as the Big Dipper and Great Bear, is a constellation that resembles a saucepan. Find the edge of the pan furthest from the handle. Polaris lies directly above the outer edge of the saucepan, at six times the distance between the bottom (Merak) and the top (Dubhe) of the pan.

Cassiopeia is a constellation that resembles a letter W. Imagine a line linking the start and end of the W. Polaris lies on a line perpendicular to that imaginary line, above the start of the W, at twice the distance of that imaginary line.

Southern Cross – unlike Polar North, there is no star to indicate Polar South. Identify the Southern Cross (or True Cross),

Compass rose

Early compasses were marked with the main 'points' of the compass: north (N), north–northeast (NNE), northeast (NE) and so on. Most modern compasses usually have a graduated scale divided into 360 degrees.

which contains two of the brightest stars in the night sky in Mimosa and Acrux. Take care to avoid confusion with the False Cross (the stars are not so bright and the constellation less compact).

To the left of the Southern Cross' longest axis are two bright stars (Hadar nearest, Rigel Kentaurus furthest). At the point where an imaginary extrapolation of the Southern Cross' longest axis meets another imaginary line perpendicularly bisecting an imaginary line between the two bright stars, the South Pole lies approximately beneath.

ESTIMATING LATITUDE WITHOUT A SEXTANT

Having identified the location of True North (Polaris) and True South, you can now estimate your latitude. First you need to fashion a makeshift sextant using three straight objects. Three 30-cm (12-inch) lengths of dowel would be ideal, but pencils will suffice, which is why you should have three in your navigation kit. The horizontal arm should be at 90° to the vertical arm, mounted at its outer extremity. The altitude arm should be fixed at the inner extremity of the horizontal arm and sliding along the vertical arm.

Aim the horizontal arm towards the horizon and slide the altitude arm until it points at Polaris or True South. Measure the angle between the horizontal arm and the altitude arm against the compass rose on your laminated chart. This provides a rough estimate of your latitude – very rough, and errors of 5° would not be unusual. Such an error could put you 300 nautical miles north or south of your actual position.

ESTIMATING LONGITUDE

Accurate measurement of longitude was the last great barrier to navigation. It was known that the earth went round the sun once in 24 hours, and that the sun would move 15° across the heavens in one hour, and 1° in

Using a compass

four minutes. By taking a sunsight at local noon and noting GMT at the precise time of that sight, it would be possible to work out how long after noon GMT the sight was taken and therefore how far the sun had travelled since noon GMT, thus providing an accurate measurement of longitude. The problem lay in the fact that nowhere in the world was there a timepiece accurate enough to keep GMT. Timepieces were still regulated by a pendulum, and on a pitching and yawing ship, the pendulum regulation became entirely unreliable and all timepieces wildly inaccurate.

To find a solution to the problem, the British Government passed an Act of Parliament in 1714 offering £20,000 to anyone who could design a timepiece accurate to within ½° (two minutes) per day at sea. The Act also established the Board of Longitude to assess candidates. Between 1730 and 1759, John Harrison, a British watchmaker, pioneered four timepieces, H1 to H4, each a refinement of the previous one, and these finally cracked the problem. They used spring mechanisms for regulation, thereby completely removing variable gravity - and the problem of the pendulum - from the equation.

Scandalously, the Board said that his results were a fluke and offered just half the money - and that only if he handed over his designs to the Astronomer Royal. He was assured that if the resulting timepieces were found to be accurate to within 30 miles (48km), he would be paid the rest of the money. Despite the intervention of King George III, Harrison never did receive the prize money in full, but he was, eventually, officially recognized as the man who solved the longitude problem. Today, accurate timepieces are abundant, so by using a sextant to establish the exact GMT time of local noon, a precise measurement of longitude can be made.

Even without a sextant, you can make an approximate measurement of longitude using a timepiece set to GMT. Measure the exact GMT time of sunrise and sunset and divide the two to find the time of local noon. To calculate your longitude, work out how far the sun has travelled in that time.

For example, sunrise is 0802 GMT and sunset 2112 GMT. This is a difference of 13 hours, 10 minutes. Half this difference is 6 hours, 35 minutes. Therefore:

Local noon = 0802 + 6 hours, 35 minutes = 1437; and

1437 = 2 hrs 37 mins after 1200 GMT

This implies a position west of GMT meridian. The sun travels 360° in 24 hours; 15° in 1 hour; 1° in 4 minutes. A time of 2 hours, 37 minutes totals 157 minutes.

157 / 4 = 39.25°, or 39 degrees, 15 minutes West

This technique will also allow you to set your second timepiece to local time. Using these techniques, an accurate watch set to GMT, three pencils, some string and a compass rose, it is possible to make an estimate of your latitude and longitude. Using the laminated routeing charts, laminated flight path and shipping route

Using an analog watch

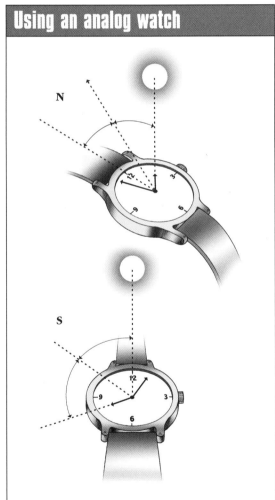

During daylight, you can use an analog watch to find Due North or Due South in the Southern and Northern Hemispheres respectively.

Major constellations

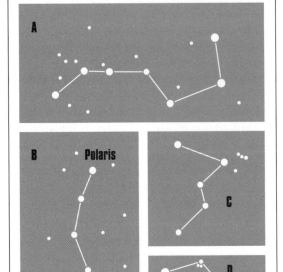

Useful constellations in the northern hemisphere: A – Ursa Major, the Plough, or the Big Dipper; B – Ursa Minor, or the Little Bear, with Polaris at the tip of its tail; C – Cassiopeia; D – Orion

exerts pressure on the earth. The amount of pressure exerted at any place on the earth depends on the density of the air, and this is affected in turn by the temperature of the air and how much water it holds. Atmospheric pressure is measured in millibars (mb) and the lines shown on weather charts are isobars - along each line the atmospheric pressure will be the same.

On the equator at midday, the sun is directly overhead and its radiation passes through the thinnest possible layer of atmosphere. Its heat energy is less diffused and therefore stronger than at any other point on earth. This radiation heats the Equatorial air and, because hot air is less dense than the colder air north and south of the Equator, the hot air rises creating an area of low pressure at the Equator. As the heated

Finding Polaris

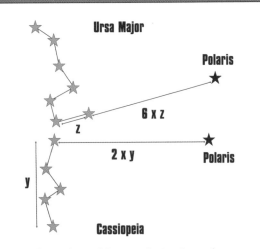

At night, Polaris (the North Star) can be located using its relationship to two of the northern sky's major constellations, Ursa Major and Cassiopeia.

For Ursa Major, multiply the distance between Merak and Dubhe (z) by six; for Cassiopeia, multiply (y) by two.

charts, you can also make estimates of your speed and direction of drift. Together, these will enable you to work out potential points of rescue, potential landfalls and an ETA - all essential information for the survivor.

WINDS

The gases that make up the atmosphere have mass and the effect of gravity on that combined mass means that the atmosphere air rises into the less dense atmosphere further from the earth, it cools and begins to descend back to the surface of the earth, forming a convection cycle. Some of the heated air travels onwards to the Polar regions while the rest descends between around 30° North or South.

Meanwhile the colder air at 30° North or South of the Equator is at relatively higher pressure, for two reasons:

cold air is denser, and therefore exerts more pressure on the earth's surface;

the warm air that rose from the Equator has cooled, becoming denser, and thus descends into this region, increasing the pressure.

The difference in pressure is known as a pressure gradient and air will move from high pressure to low pressure along that gradient to equalize atmospheric pressure.

Average atmospheric pressure is 1013mb, but it ranges somewhere between 950 and 1050mb over the earth's surface. The difference between the average pressure and maximum low pressure is greater than that between average and maximum high pressure. This means that the wind tends to move faster towards low pressure than towards high pressure, and this is why low pressure tends to bring more violent weather.

The earth's rotation means that the wind does not move directly from high pressure to low pressure. The earth rotates, while space does not and the area between these two – the earth's atmosphere – absorbs the resulting friction. Put simply, wind is deflected to the right of the pressure

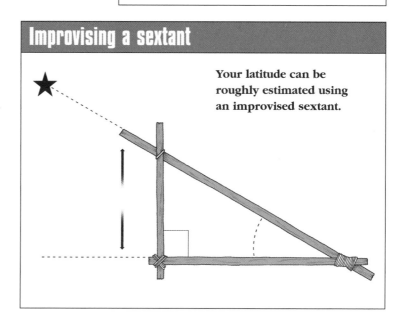

Improvising a sextant

Your latitude can be roughly estimated using an improvised sextant.

gradient in the northern hemisphere and to the left of it in the southern hemisphere. This is known as the Coriolis Effect. For this reason, wind moving away from an area of high pressure, or towards an area of low pressure, is instead deflected around its centre in a spiral. This creates weather systems, where the warm, rising air and the cool, sinking air interact.

CURRENTS

The second major factor affecting navigation is current. Nowhere in the world's oceans is completely still. Investigations of the oceans' greatest depths have shown that life exists where light has never penetrated. This proves the presence of oxygen in the water and, since life needs a renewable supply of oxygen, this means that even the deepest water is in motion.

The cause of this motion is the wind. Prevailing winds sweep across the surface of the world's oceans, driving surface water through air-water friction into drift currents. These do not exactly follow the prevailing winds that cause them, again because of the

Global currents

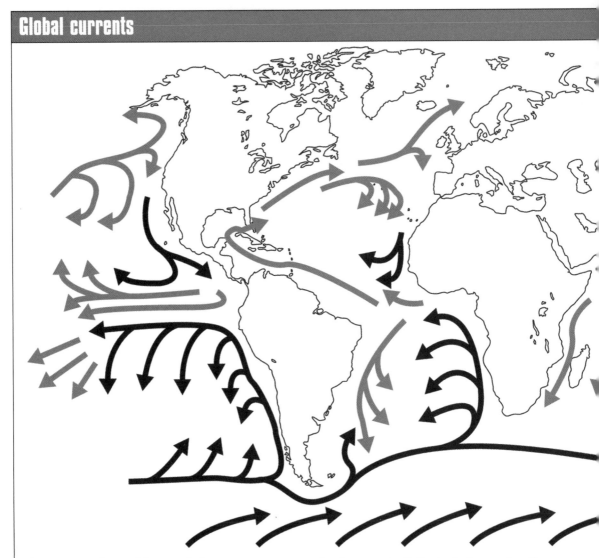

The currents that swirl around the oceans are collectively influenced by the prevailing wind, the Coriolis Effect, and continental coastlines. In extreme southern latitudes, where there are no landmasses to deflect wind or water, the current is driven by the strong westerly winds of the 'Roaring Forties' and 'Furious Fifties'. Along the Equator, the influence of the Coriolis

Coriolis Effect. This makes currents in the northern hemisphere deflect to the right of the wind direction, and in the southern hemisphere, deflect to the left of the wind. The result of this is that, in the northern hemisphere, currents tend to circulate clockwise, while in the southern hemisphere they rotate anticlockwise. The effect is least pronounced at the Equator, where the drift is predominantly westwards and caused by the flows west from West Africa to the Caribbean, feeding the Gulf Stream flowing northeast from the Caribbean towards Europe, and the Azores current flows south to link up with the North Equatorial current again, creating a clockwise circulation of water. In the South Atlantic, the Brazil Current flows west along the Equator before being deflected southwest by the Brazilian coast. Then it meets the Antarctic Drift at Cape Horn and flows east towards Cape Town where the Benguela Current deflects north, then east, along the coast of southwestern Africa before joining up with the Brazil Current, creating anticlockwise circulation.

SAILING LIFE RAFTS

Life rafts are designed solely for survival at sea. Most are either square or hexagonal, because these are the most stable shapes on the water and present the smallest likelihood of capsize regardless of the life raft's orientation to the waves. Most are also equipped with ballast bags – sacks attached to the underside of the life raft that fill with water and whose aim also is to prevent capsize. On some older life raft models, such as that carried by the Robertsons on their 13-metre (43-foot) schooner *Lucette*, the ballast bags can be tripped (tied flat to the bottom of the life raft). This offers improved progress through the water, but the safety against capsize that the bags are designed to give is lost. Also, as the Robertsons discovered, the constant flexing of the life raft's structure means that any loaded lines in contact with the buoyancy chambers will chafe against the chamber and eventually wear a hole in it. Modern designs are required by the IMO's SOLAS regulations to be fitted with self-deploying ballast bags.

The unfortunate corollary of these safety features is that the average life raft simply cannot sail. The square or hexagonal shape is stable on the water, but unstable

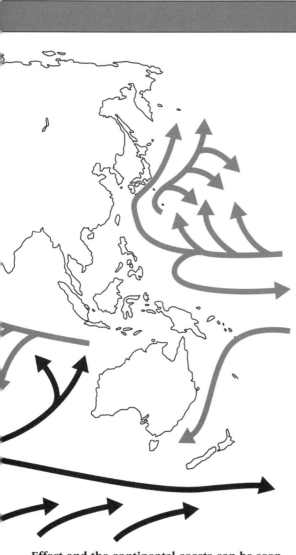

Effect and the continental coasts can be seen, creating a clockwise rotation for currents in the northern and an anticlockwise rotation in the southern hemisphere.

earth's rotation, but increases towards the Poles. The currents are also deflected by the coastal contours on the continents.

For example, in the North Atlantic, the North Equatorial current near the Equator directionally, which makes sailing in any direction other than that dictated by the current very difficult. Even if a mast were erected and a system of foils (including a leeboard and a rudder) improvised, the ballast bags would provide so much drag in the water that the net gain in speed would be negligible. The differential forces of the wind in the sail and the drag from the ballast bags would also place great stress on the mast and rigging. This in turn would stress the structure of the life raft – its welds, seams, strong points and ballast bags – raising the possibility that the life raft would tear apart beneath you. Add to this the increased risk of capsize presented by the sail and sailing a square or hexagonal life raft is not a viable option in most circumstances.

Many military life rafts are rectangular in shape and do not feature ballast bags. These can be sailed with considerably more success than the standard shapes but are also less safe and stable as a direct result of their design. Nor, because of their essentially covert nature, are they brightly coloured. They do not feature automatically inflating canopies or strobe lights fitted to the exterior, nor any of the other safety features required on civilian life rafts. If you were to buy one from military surplus, it would be secondhand by definition, and getting it serviced would be problematic. Hence, a life raft designed for civilian use is recommended.

However, the value of a spare craft, an inflatable dinghy or rigid tender, is well documented and best illustrated by the Robertsons' experience over 38 days adrift in the Pacific. Although their wooden schooner *Lucette* sank just one minute after being attacked by a killer whale, they successfully launched their life raft and their GRP dinghy. As they abandoned ship, the dinghy itself, named *Ednamair*, became swamped but had enough buoyancy to remain afloat. Extra buoyancy in the form of fenders or closed

cell foam should be securely attached under the thwarts, or a rubbing strip of buoyant material added around the exterior gunwales to make sure that your dinghy does not sink. An inflatable tender is naturally buoyant, but clearly less robust and durable than a rigid one.

The Robertsons' dinghy served a number of purposes. Initially it was used for storing useful items salvaged from the hull – remember, there were six of them crowded onto a six-man life raft. Then it entered service as a tug: by erecting a mast from the oars that were stored under her thwarts and using a salvaged sail, they were able to use *Ednamair* to double their rate of progress. She also acted as a butcher's shop, where the fish and turtles they caught would be gutted, dressed and dried for storage on the rigging. This served to keep the life raft a good deal cleaner than it otherwise would have been and also allowed for disposal of offal at a greater distance from the life raft, deterring the unwanted attention of sharks.

Ednamair ultimately proved their saviour too. After 17 days, it became clear that they could not physically manage to keep the life raft usefully inflated (their manual bellows had given up shortly after they abandoned ship and they had been inflating by mouth since then). They conducted a merciless inventory of their survival equipment and disposed of bulky items of minimal use, then transferred the remaining stores into *Ednamair* and set about salvaging everything of use from the life raft – in other words, the canopy, the one remaining useful buoyancy chamber. Finally, all six moved into *Ednamair* and soon learned the art of perfect trim, spurred on by the fact that there were just 15cm (6in) of freeboard between them and the Pacific.

ERECTING A MAST

Use the dinghy's oars because the life raft's paddles are generally 0.9–1.2 metres

(3–4 feet) and therefore less than ideal for this purpose. With some of the salvaged line, you can quickly erect a main mast using one oar and secure the second to the masthead as a yardarm from which sail can be made.

Inflatable dinghy

Before starting any physical work, construct the mast mentally, working out not just which materials you will need, but also, if there is anything you lack, what can be used in its stead. Prepare everything you need in advance.

Start by preparing your sail. If you have managed to salvage a sail, cut a section from it as wide as the oar is long and 1.5 times as long as the sail is wide. If you can, punch holes in its four corners and reinforce them with sail repair tape from the sailmaking kit or duct tape from the utility kit. If you cannot, tie lines tightly around the corners.

If you did not manage to salvage a sail from the parent craft, explore other options. A tarpaulin would be an ideal replacement. The survival blanket could be used, and this has the added bonus of raising visibility because of its reflective qualities. However, it will not be so strong as sailcloth and will probably tear easily. If there is any spare clothing in the life raft, that could be sewn together using the sewing kit or the sailmaking kit. Some of the plastic sheeting could be used, but make sure it is surplus to your water collection requirements – water is your first, most essential priority.

Next, lash one of the oars to the other. The yardarm oar should be cross-lashed around its centre to the inboard end of the main mast oar so that it lies perpendicular to the mainmast oar on the leading edge of the mainmast. Attach the sail, furled with gaskets, to the yardarm and add extra lines at each end of the yardarm to act as stays and also for trimming it. You can now erect the mast.

Remember that you will need to protect the dinghy floor, which is probably single-

Improvising a mast

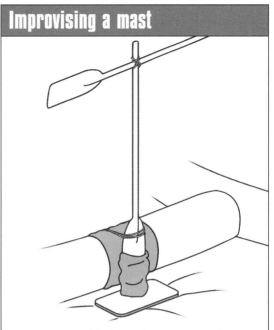

Wrapping the blade of the oar in tough material and using a chopping board as a mast base will prevent damage to the life raft floor.

skinned, from the sharp edges of the oar's blade. This can be done by wrapping the blade in thick material, such as sailcloth or a foul weather jacket, before strapping the oar to the centre of the middle thwart. Remember to wrap some soft cloth round the thwart where the oar will be lashed to prevent the lashings chafing through the inflatable thwart's skin. If there is still too much stress on the dinghy's floor, you could place something solid and smooth-edged beneath the wrapped blade – a chopping board would be ideal if you have a spare; otherwise a shoe would be nearly as effective. The mainmast is now in place.

Attach the lines secured at each end of the yardarm to the grab line around the dinghy and at the stern. When under sail, you will need to watch the points where the grab

Improvising rigging

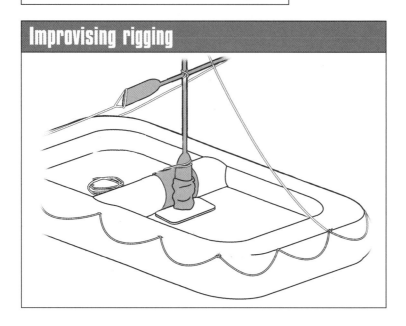

will need to strengthen the mainmast's lashing to the centre thwart and check it regularly. Also lash the tow line to one of the grab lines at the stern of the dinghy to add more directional stability to the dinghy, but remember to protect against any chafing on the dinghy's buoyancy chambers with soft cloth. This should make sure that the dinghy's stern does not swing out, risking capsize.

Attach the other end of the tow line to a bridle on the bow of the life raft. Attaching a heavy sinking weight halfway along the tow line will serve to dampen the shockloads imposed on the secure points at

line is attached to the dinghy because the drive of the sail may tear the grab line free. If you believe the strain to be too great, you could attach second stays to each end of the yardarm to spread the load and add another from the top of the mainmast to the stern of the dinghy. Finally, add another stay from the mainmast head to the bow of the dinghy, and make sure that this stay will run below the sail when it is in use. Your rig and sail are now ready for use.

The towing line should be attached to a bridle secured to two of the grab lines at the stern of the dinghy. Do this only as long as the grab lines are strong enough to stand the strain. If you doubt whether they are, you can attach the tow line to the mainmast, but you

Improvising a leeboard and rudder

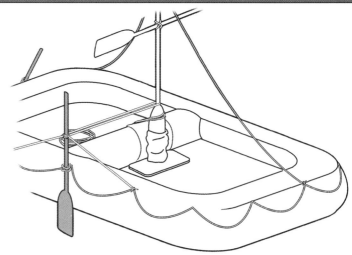

The performance of your dinghy can be improved by adding a leeboard and rudder. Remember to guard against chafe wherever there is contact with the raft's buoyancy chambers.

Lashing the yardarm to the mast

Diagonal lashing is the most effective way of securing your mast. Two diagonal lashings should be followed by vertical lashings each end of the horizontal.

Secure the yardarm to the top of the mast as shown. Check this lashing regularly for signs of wear or potential failure.

either end of the tow line. If you have nothing heavy and expendable on the life raft, you could fill a fender with seawater and use that. Whatever you use, make sure it is firmly attached and that it will not chafe through your tow line. Protect the tow line with a soft cloth.

Release the gaskets furling the sail and pass the sheets (the lines from each of the lower corners of the sail) through the grab lines either side of the bow and lead them aft. These lines will be used to trim the sail, but remember you should never tie both of these lines off. If a sudden gust should catch the sail, the stays could tear out the grab line securing points or, if they hold firm, the dinghy could capsize. So always have at least one of the lines in your hand ready to release if you feel the rig is overpowered. By releasing one line, the wind will spill out of the sail and depower the rig instantly. Remember to harness yourself to the dinghy so that, in the event of capsize, you will not lose touch with the dinghy, even if you are knocked unconscious.

The presence of sailing crew in the towing dinghy will add some stability to the craft, acting as a counter to the weight and power of the rig above the dinghy. Without that counterweight, the dinghy will slew around ahead of the life raft, fighting the resistance of the life raft and the sea anchor, if deployed, briefly before capsizing. Also, in the event that the towing line breaks or pulls free of the life raft, the crew in the dinghy will be able to strike sail and paddle back to the life raft. A further benefit is that, in a dinghy and without the canopy to obscure the field of vision, a much more effective watch can be kept.

If the weather is such that the sailing crew is unable to remain in the dinghy without risking exposure, devise a tripping line for the sail.

If you are in an area of reliable, gentle winds that do not whip up steep waves, you can 'trip' (open the end of) the sea anchor to cut down its drag or bring in it in completely to reduce your drag and increase your speed. This will also give you the chance to conduct

Sailing an inflatable dinghy

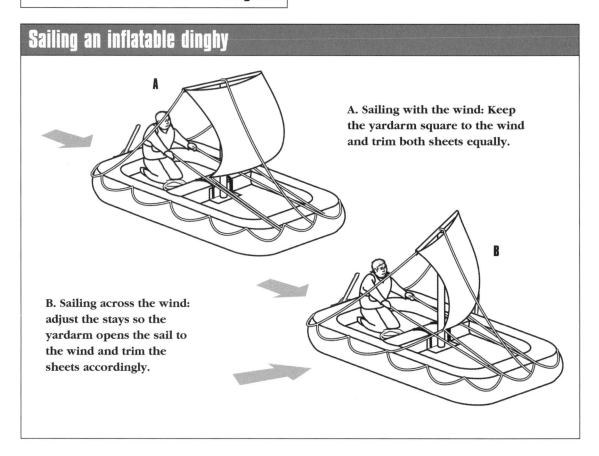

A. Sailing with the wind: Keep the yardarm square to the wind and trim both sheets equally.

B. Sailing across the wind: adjust the stays so the yardarm opens the sail to the wind and trim the sheets accordingly.

a thorough check of your sea anchor and carry out any maintenance. If you are in an area of the ocean where cold and warm currents interact, or where strong winds cause large waves, the subsurface waters, rich in nutrients, promote the growth of plankton. A sea anchor is the perfect device for trapping this vitamin-rich resource.

As part of your daily maintenance rota, always check the attachments of the rigging to the grab lines – these are the weakest points of the rig and the most difficult to repair. The oars and sail are designed for strength, but the dinghy is not designed to handle these loads. Also check for chafing at the point where the towline passes over the stern, and add a protective soft cloth if there are any signs of wear.

Rigid dinghy

If you have a rigid dinghy, the process of constructing and erecting your rig is very similar but you should rig the dinghy to sail stern first. Regardless of how efficient your rig is, you will not be able to sail faster than the wave train (15–20 knots) and if your dinghy is rigged to sail in its usual orientation with the bow leading, waves will break over the stern and swamp it. The bow is the most seaworthy section of the dinghy so that should face the waves as they sweep under you. Your dinghy may not be fitted with grab lines, so you will have to improvise strong points, perhaps by boring holes in the gunwales and fitting U-shackles, or by using the thwarts if these are strong enough.

Your sailing crew or watchkeeper should

always keep a weather eye and strike sail if there is a risk of overpowering the rig or the towline. The small distance gains you make by holding sail longer than is wise will be greatly exceeded by the downtime caused by having to effect repairs. You will be expending valuable energy and losing valuable fluids in carrying out the work and using your limited supplies of equipment at an unnecessary speed.

SAILING ANGLES

The rig as described is very basic and designed to work best when travelling directly before the wind – in short, dead downwind. If the wind is in the east and you want to travel west with the current, you will make excellent progress. If the wind is in the west, however, you must lower all sail and attach the dinghy by its bow to the stern of the life raft. Then deploy the sea anchor from the bow of the life raft to utilize the favourable current and minimize the distance lost because of unfavourable winds.

If you are heading west with the current and the wind is in the north or south, it is still possible to make good progress, but you will need to improvise underwater foils to prevent your dinghy being blown downwind. If we imagine the wind direction to be gravity, it is possible, with difficulty, to balance an object on a single point of support, but it is much easier and more secure to place the object on two fixed points. These fixed points will be a leeboard and a rudder. A leeboard acts like a centreboard on a sailing dinghy and stops it from being skimmed downwind across the water by the wind. The rudder, the second point of support, adds directional stability to the dinghy. It also gives enhanced control over the direction of travel, but as you are towing a life raft, this is fairly superfluous.

The life raft paddles will be used for the foils. One should be lashed to the grab lines on the leeward side of the dinghy level with the thwart. Place a soft cloth between the dinghy and the paddle to prevent chafing and add stays fore, aft and athwartships to the mainmast to keep the leeboard in position. The rudder will be mounted on the dinghy's stern and lashed to the grab lines, again using soft cloth to prevent any chafing.

By adjusting the yardarm stays, turn the yardarm so it is at $45°$ to the direction of the wind, still filling the sail. Adjust the sheets (attached to the sail's lower corners) likewise. You are now trimmed for reaching. The wind is exerting a transverse strain on the mainmast, pushing it to leeward, so you should add an extra stay from the masthead to the windward grab rail to counter this strain. The life raft itself has ballast bags to act as leeboards, but it also has considerable windage (area above the waterline that catches the wind), so you will need to adjust your rudder to find the optimum angle for towing.

SAILING WITHOUT A DINGHY

If you have no dinghy, it is possible to optimize the life raft for sailing. Inflate the buoyancy chambers to their practical maximum – but don't overinflate – and the life raft will ride higher in the water, presenting greater windage. If the wind is not too strong (not whipping up waves, in other words), you could also open the life raft canopy and attach the sea anchor to the bow so that the life raft entrance faces the wind and the canopy itself acts as a sail. This will provide a cooling breeze for the occupants and may also help to dry out some of the soaked equipment inside the life raft. If the wind picks up and waves start to splash over the buoyancy chambers at the entrance, move the sea anchor back to the stern of the life raft, turning the entrance back to leeward.

Any extra windage you can offer, or drag you can reduce, will increase your speed. If you are on watch, sit on the tubes at the entrance, making sure you are suitably dressed to avoid exposure, wearing your PFD and harnessed to the life raft. The wind on your body will drive the life raft along very slightly faster. Get the rest of the crew to lie around the edges of the life raft floor, where the floor meets the buoyancy chambers. This will reduce the drag caused by the bulging life raft floor and again add an extra tenth of a knot to your speed.

You could also investigate kite-surfing equipment as an alternative means of harnessing the wind. Use the smallest kite to avoid being hauled out of the life raft and make sure that flying the kite does not involve too much exertion on your part. If the kite is coloured brightly, this will also raise your visibility.

SEA ANCHOR

The life-saving value of this piece of equipment in very rough weather has been proven by several maritime disasters. The sea anchor, or drogue, slows the life raft when towed through water just as a parachute slows a dragster when towed through air. In doing so, it ensures that the life raft does not surf down the faces of waves and capsize in the trough at the bottom, but is instead dragged back safely over the crest of as the wave passes harmlessly beneath the life raft.

To ensure correct function, the tether should be half the wavelength, so if the life raft is on top of a wave, the sea anchor should be at the bottom of the trough behind the life raft. Remember that wavelength and oceanic swell are different. Oceanic swells can have a wavelength of anything from 60 metres (200 feet) up to 800 metres (½ mile) and will never be steep enough to jeopardize your life raft. Waves generated by strong winds will typically have a wavelength of 15–45 metres (50–150 feet) in open ocean. If you do not have a sea anchor, these waves can flip your life raft or break over it, crushing it and the crew under hundreds of tons of water.

The sea anchor itself and all its associated lines and attachments should be regularly and carefully examined for signs of wear. In rough weather, as the life raft begins to accelerate down the face of waves, the sea anchor will brake that acceleration and jerk the life raft back to safety. This imposes considerable shock loads on the sea anchor system. When you consider the weight of the life raft uninflated, then add not just the weight of water captured in the ballast bags (up to 45kg/120lb per bag) but also the weight of the occupants and the equipment inside the life raft, you begin to get some idea of the strain placed on the system.

Should the original and replacement sea anchors become lost, improvising a repair is not difficult. However, it will not be so effective and will be more prone to loss. A collapsible canvas bucket, a foul weather jacket, a sailbag or a piece of sailcloth could easily be used as sea anchors, but because sea anchors spin as they travel through the water, these will need regular unravelling unless a spinner can be improvised. This spinning could weaken and then snap the sea anchor line unless some method of accounting for, or stopping, the spin can be devised. If using a foul weather jacket, one of the pockets could be weighted to reduce the tendency to spin.

An alternative to the sea anchor, often used by sailors, is to stream lines aft. Take lengths of line and attach something heavy, but expendable, to their ends, then secure the bitter end to the stern of the life raft and allow the line to stream behind. This method does not provide anything like so much drag as the sea anchor, but it will act as a decelerant. Another option is to tie the lengths of line together; one long line will provide more resistance than several shorter lines. However, with this method, losing one line means losing all the lines attached after it. If you have one very long piece of line, tie

Towing a life raft with a rigid dinghy

The dinghy, rigged to sail, is proceeding stern-first for greater seaworthiness. Both ends of the towline are attached using bridles and there is a damping weight attached to the middle of the towline. After completing a maintenance check, the dinghy crew should keep watch for potential rescue, fishing or water collection opportunities.

each end to the aft quarters of the life raft and stream the looped line with an expendable weight attached to its apex.

You can increase the progress made by adjusting your life raft's trim. Unlike the sailing scenario, when using the current, the more drag you can present, the better. Deflate the buoyancy chambers a little so that the life raft is still firm and retains its shape but rides lower in the water, presenting greater drag to the current. The crew should sit in the middle of the life raft's floor, bulging it to increase the drag still further. As with the sailing situation, the increase in speed will be imperceptible, but it could add as much as 16–24km (10–15 miles) a day to your 24-hour distance. More important still is the psychological effect. The crew will be working towards the same goal, which helps to breeds team spirit and boost morale.

VIGILANCE AND MAINTENANCE

Help you and your crew to concentrate on survival by not allowing yourselves the time to wander. The survivor should be focusing on survival, nothing else. An excellent and useful method of occupying your mind and improving your survival chances, other than watchkeeping, is to conduct regular visual and physical checks on your equipment. Check all the secure points, such as the sea anchor attachment and tow line attachment: are they in the same condition as the last time you inspected them? If they have deteriorated, what can you do to stop that and make good the attachment? Is there a back-up system to prevent the loss of vital equipment attached to these points? How would you improvise a replacement if the attachment were to break? Share any ideas you have, because you – or they – may have missed something glaringly obvious.

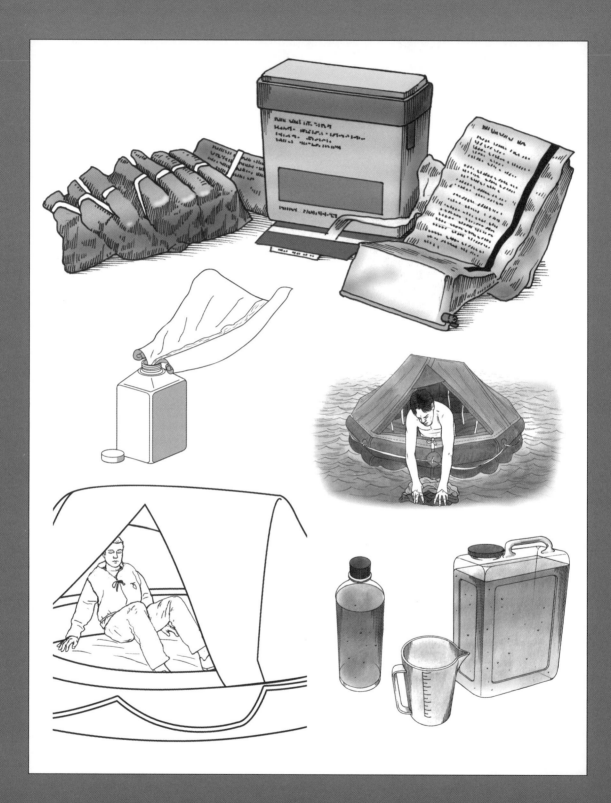

CHAPTER FIVE

Water supply

If you have to survive at sea for longer than a week, your relationship with fresh water is very simple: life means water, and water means life. Your stores of fresh water should be absolutely secure, their consumption closely rationed, and no opportunity to add to them should be spurned.

The ocean covered the entire surface of the earth 3500 million years ago. Today, since the emergence of landmasses as a result of tectonic and volcanic activity, the oceans now cover just over 70 percent of the earth. It is the presence of this abundance of water that gives the earth its unique position – in our solar system at least – as the only planet to sustain organic life. When astronauts first ventured to the moon, the earth's barren satellite, and looked back at earth as the rest of the universe might see it, they dubbed it the Blue Planet, precisely because of its extensive liquid mantle.

But as Coleridge's Ancient Mariner remarked, when becalmed '[a]s idle as a painted ship, Upon a painted ocean,' the irony of fresh water shortage at sea is that there is 'Water, water everywhere, Nor any drop to drink.' Sea water is about four per cent salt – far too high for human consumption under normal circumstances.

Indeed, if you were to drink 568 ml (1 pint) of sea water, your body would need to use twice as much - 1.2 litres (2 pints) - of its fluid to cleanse the body of the salt imbibed. The drinking of sea water is a slightly contentious issue, as we will discover later, but the massive weight of evidence indicates that sea water dehydrates the body and leads to kidney failure. As a properly equipped and prepared survivor at sea, you should not consider sea water as an alternative to fresh water, nor should you need to resort to drinking it. Fresh water is essential for human function.

WATER MEANS LIFE

The average man consists of 70 per cent water and the average woman 60 per cent. In a healthy man weighing 65kg (145lb), there are 40 litres (70 pints) of water. Of this 26 litres (46 pints) is intracellular and 12 litres (21 pints) extracellular - 2.5 litres (4 pints) in blood plasma and 9.5 litres (16 pints) in interstitial, or tissue, fluid. To remain healthy, he needs to drink 2-3 litres (3½-5¼ pints) per day, all of which will be lost during the course of the day through excretion, moisture in exhaled breath, perspiration, and invisible water loss as water evaporates through the skin, even when sweat glands are inactive.

Even at rest, out of the sun in a temperate climate, the body will lose 1 litre (1¾ pints) of water per day. Moderate activity in a temperate climate raises that loss to 3 litres (5¼ pints) per day. In tropical climates, even avoiding activity during the hottest part of the day, water loss will be 5 litres (8¾ pints). If this fluid is not replaced, normal human function will suffer. In temperate regions, inactive and out of the sun, the human body can retain some fitness for 5-7 days without any water, and sustain life for 10-12 days. With 500ml (¾ pint) of water per day, some fitness is retained for 10-14 days and life sustained for 20 -24 days.

If the average male is 60 per cent water, a loss of 1-5 per cent of that water leaves the survivor feeling thirsty, irritable and nauseous, perhaps reporting a headache and fatigue, but unable to think clearly. The loss of water thickens the blood, reducing blood pressure and denying the brain the oxygen it needs to function normally, producing these symptoms and an increased heart rate as the body tries to compensate for the drop in pressure. Losing 6-10 per cent of this fluid will increase the intensity of the headache, deepen the sense of thirst as the mouth dries, and speech will become slurred. The survivor will feel faint and dizzy, perhaps with impaired vision, and experience difficulty with motor coordination. Losing 11-3 per cent of the body's fluid leaves the survivor delirious and drifting in and out of consciousness, possibly deaf and with greatly reduced vision. As the tongue swells and the throat dries, he will lose control of the swallowing reflex and his motor coordination will be severely impaired, making any movement difficult. These symptoms are caused by the brain overheating and swelling, and, by this time, death is imminent.

For all these reasons, survival at sea is not possible without fresh water. There are three sources of fresh water available to you while adrift on the ocean: bottled supplies, desalinated sea water and captured freshwater.

Bottled supplies

Previously, it has been specified that the abandon ship locker should contain, in addition to your waterproof grab bag and the life raft, two 35-45-litre (8-10-gallon) containers, tied together at their handles and three-quarters full with fresh water - between 55 and 68 litres (12 and15 gallons) in total. Four people adrift in a life raft in a tropical climate, drinking four pints per day - towards the lower end of the healthy daily

Bottled water

Remember to leave an air gap in each bottle of water so they will float if dropped overboard during abandon ship. A measuring jug or cup means equal rations.

range in a temperate climate – will consume that amount in about a week. The five Robertsons and one friend were adrift for over five weeks after losing *Lucette*. When Steve Callahan's *Napoleon Solo* sank in the Atlantic, he was adrift for nearly 11 weeks. When Maurice and Maralyn Bailey lost *Auralyn* in the Pacific, they were adrift for nearly 17 weeks. These are exceptional tales of survival but, for obvious reasons, there are no tales from those who failed to survive.

Only when every other source of fresh water is exhausted should you consider opening those two containers. If you do, ration yourselves to the bare minimum essential for human function. The normal daily range is 2.25–3.5 litres (4–6 pints), but, as mentioned above, just 560ml (1 pint) per day can sustain life for up to three weeks. The Robertsons managed to survive for up to a week on as little as 280 ml (½ pint) per day without any serious deterioration in mental or physical function. Your life raft is not a

health farm, and you and your crew are not there to get, or even stay, healthy. You are there to survive, to keep yourselves alive until you reach safety. To do so will require a tremendous amount of self-discipline and you must come to terms with this as soon as possible. It will make your existence in the life raft much simpler.

This is why preparation is so important. Remember to refresh the water in these large containers whenever you reach port, and check the containers themselves for damage. Taste the water before discarding it. Has it been contaminated by salt? If so, you will need a new container, or at least a new screw-top. Is there any discoloration of the container? It may need treating with a fungicide. Maintain these containers well because, in a life raft, their contents will end up maintaining your life.

Desalinated sea water

This process involves the conversion of sea water, of which there is no shortage, into fresh water, of which there is. There are several methods of desalination. Some are fast and easy, some are slow and laborious, and in terms of taste, the results vary from mineral quality to fairly unpleasant, but all produce fresh water. There are three methods of desalinating water – chemical, reverse osmosis and distillation.

CHEMICAL DESALTER KIT

Chemical desalination relies on the reaction between a silver-based chemical and the salt (sodium chloride) in sea water. These kits are lightweight and each one contains enough chemical to make eight pints of water, at nearly 560 ml (1 pint) per hour. The water left in the bag once the reaction is complete is not especially palatable, but it is 100 percent potable and the kit is totally effective, provided the equipment is not damaged. Single-use solutions to water shortage, like the chemical desalter, should

Desalter kit

These kits use a chemical reaction to remove the salt from sea water. The production rate is about 560 ml (1 pint) per hour and, although the results are not especially pleasant, the water produced is completely potable. Use only when supplies are dangerously low.

be used only when fresh water supplies are running dangerously low and there's no sign of any rain. Once the kit has been used, that's it – it cannot be used again.

REVERSE OSMOSIS PUMP

The reverse osmosis pump works by forcing sea water through a filtration membrane at high pressure, thus removing the salt from sea water. Using the Survivor-06 model as an example, 24 hours of pumping at 40 strokes a minute will produce 27.25 litres (6 gallons) of potable water at almost 1 litre (1¾ pints) per hour with brine as a waste product. The drawback is that the high pressure upon which the system relies is generated by the survivor using a handpump, and this can be exhausting. To limit the loss of fluid and salt from the body in using the pump, it should be used only at night and in shifts.

At 1kg (2¼lb), the 06 pump is a light piece of kit, considerably lighter than the 27.25 litres (6 gallons) of water you would need to replace it for just 24 hours. It is not cheap, but it produces fresh water on demand and for that reason it deserves a place in every grab bag.

There is also a Survivor-35 model. Although considerably more expensive and heavier at 3kg (7lb), it features a longer handle to make pumping easier. The 35 produces 4.5 litres (8 pints) after one hour's pumping at 30 strokes per minute. Some maintenance is required for both models (the pump is sold with biocide that you can apply yourself at the required intervals), and you should get it serviced at least every three years. A well-maintained reverse osmosis pump is the only way you can guarantee a limitless supply of fresh water in mid-ocean.

SOLAR DISTILLATION

Rainwater collection is impossible without clouds, but clear skies and calm seas make solar distillation a viable alternative for producing fresh water. As a sea survivor you must learn to explore and exploit every possible source of fresh water. The principle is very simple: in warm, sunny conditions, the water in sea water evaporates, leaving behind a concentrated salt solution. The water that evaporates is fresh water and the aim is to collect this. There are solar stills on the market, but they are easy enough to improvise.

Saturate a dark piece of cloth in sea water and place it in the bottom of a large watertight container. In the middle of the large container, place a smaller, watertight container – this is your collection vessel. Place clear plastic sheeting over the large container and weight it in the centre so that the weight hangs just above the collection vessel. Then use duct tape (always useful for repairs) to create an airtight seal between the sheet and the large container. Place the improvised still in the sun and the fresh water will condense on the sheet and roll down, gradually dripping into the collection vessel.

If conditions are flat-calm and you have no dark cloth, you can place sea water itself in the bottom of the container but the slightest motion could mean saltwater slopping into your collection vessel and contaminating your hard-earned fresh water. Also, dark colours absorb heat quicker and saturating a dark cloth means that there is a

greater surface area from which the water can evaporate, meaning faster evaporation and a better rate of production.

This is a slow and fragile method of making fresh water and has proved to be a considerable source of disappointment to survivors at sea. After hours tending the equipment frequently under a blazing sun, the first sip of your hard-earned water could reveal salt contamination, and all your time and effort has been wasted. You should be prepared for the occasional disappointment, but it is not a complicated system, so you should be able to find out where the problem is and improvise a solution.

Captured Freshwater

Fresh water will be available to you in one or more different forms, depending on your location. Rainfall occurs over every ocean in

Reverse osmosis pump

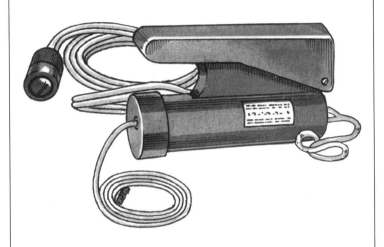

After your life raft, PFD, clothing, and EPIRB, the reverse osmosis pump is the most important part of your survival kit. It produces fresh water from sea water on demand provided it is well maintained.

Keeping cool in tropical climes

It is vital the survivor avoids fluid loss through sweating. If resting in the shade during the heat of the day does not prevent sweating, dampen your clothing in sea water and your body heat will be drawn away as the water evaporates.

the world to a greater or lesser extent and this offers an excellent opportunity to rehydrate the body's interior and clean its exterior. In colder climates, water can be recovered from ice, but it must be melted first to avoid lowering the body's core temperature to a dangerous level and so risking hypothermia.

RAINWATER

Clouds are formed of hundreds, or even thousands, of tons of condensed fresh water vapour. The sun's radiation on the surface of the sea causes fresh water to evaporate from the sea water and this rises until it reaches an altitude that is cold enough, and where the air is humid enough, for the water vapour to condense on tiny airborne particles, such as salt crystals or sand. High cloud, that is, 5485–13715 metres (18,000–45,000feet) is formed largely of ice crystals. Mid cloud, 2440–5485 metres (8000–18,000feet), and low 0–2440 metres (8000feet) cloud are both formed from water droplets.

These droplets are disturbed by upcurrents and other airflows, such as those that occur ahead of a warm front in a low pressure system. As they move, they collide with other water droplets, becoming larger. Once their weight is too great for the cloud to support, the droplets fall as rain.

CLOUD TYPES

There are 13 classifications of cloud, but only nine are regularly experienced. Each of them carries with it a varying probability of rain, and indicates what weather can be expected over the next 24 hours.

High Cloud:

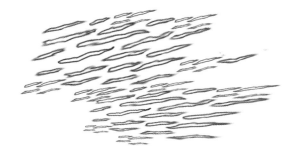

Cirrus (Ci)

In texture, it appears as a delicate and thin white cloud, silky and fibrous because of the ice crystals of which it is composed. The sun passes through it easily, leaving daylight at sea level unaffected. In form it is the most variable of all the cloud types, appearing as straight streaks or curves of cloud – usually parallel – or tufts with streaks whipped off them. The streaking is as result of the cloud being blasted by the jet stream at high altitude.

At sunrise and sunset, its height means that cirrus will be the first to glow and the last to dim respectively, and it always contributes to spectacular sunsets. At night, cirrus will not obstruct stars, but it will diffuse their light slightly.

Cirrus generally indicates changing weather. If accompanied by lower cumulus clouds and followed by cirrostratus, you are near a rain-bearing, low pressure system. The relation between cirrus and cumulus will tell you what you can expect. In the Northern Hemisphere, face the wind so that the cumulus is moving straight over your head. If the cirrus is approaching from your left, the weather will improve, becoming warmer and drier. If the cirrus approaches from the right, prepare your collection equipment and expect rain because a warm front is approaching. The reverse applies in the Southern Hemisphere.

Cirrocumulus (Cc)

This is also high cloud but lower than cirrus and less disturbed by the jet stream. It will appear as a near-regular pattern of tufted cloudlets or thicker streaks. Often described as a mackerel sky, it appears dappled, or rippled like the sand on a beach. These will not diminish sunlight during the day, but could obstruct the dimmer stars at night.

Cirrocumulus is associated with dry weather generally, but if the cloud thickens, taking on a grey appearance from below as the sun's light is blocked, and starts to lower, expect rain.

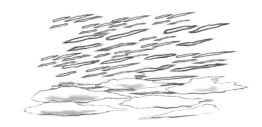

Cirrostratus (Cs)

This appears during the day as a white, milky smudge across the sky, a thin white veil of cloud. If mixed with cirrus, it will form vague parallel bands across the sky. It is the ice crystals in cirrostratus that give the sun and the moon their 'halo' effect, surrounding them with a glowing disc, but cirrostratus is not thick enough to obscure either.

Cirrostratus always indicates a change in weather. Watch for cirrus clouds lowering and becoming cirrostratus, giving the characteristic appearance of 'grey mare's tail' in the sky. If this cloud continues to thicken and lower, the ice crystals will melt into water droplets and form altostratus cloud, and you can expect rain within 24 hours.

Mid cloud:

Altocumulus (Ac):
This is formed of many small, flattened, globular cloudlets that can be thick enough to block some sunlight and appear grey on their underside. Altocumulus is usually arranged like a slightly disorganized cirrocumulus (it is also sometimes known as a mackerel sky) and has a loose order to its formation, sometimes appearing as bands of cloud. Generally blue sky is visible between them, but sometimes they merge.

Sometimes the bands appear like huge rolling ocean swells sweeping across the sky, leaving bands of blue sky in the troughs. These cannot be confused with cirrocumulus because these bands are much thicker and will be grey beneath. When caught by the sun early or later in the day, altocumulus can refract many spectral colours vividly and creates a very 'painterly' sky, but if this cloud lowers and thickens,

expect short, thundery showers that won't last. Be prepared to deploy your collection equipment at short notice.

Sometimes it will appear to be 'turreted' – taller and with a castellated appearance to the cloud tops, like small-scale cumulus clouds, and scattered by altitude. This usually forecasts thunderstorms.

Altostratus (As)
This is similar to cirrostratus, veiled and fibrous, but thicker. It does not obscure stars, but it does make them appear as if they are being viewed through ground glass, diffusing their light and giving rise to the expression 'watery sky'. If thicker, it can reduce the sun and moon to a vague blur or hide them completely.

If this cloud lowers, thickens and darkens, or if low level grey 'scud' (nimbostratus or stratus fractus) forms below it, expect continuous rain, or snow in colder climates, in a few hours' time.

Low cloud:

Stratocumulus (Sc)
These are layers or long patches of soft, globular white cloud, often appearing grey

beneath. They tend to form more or less regular lines or waves across the sky, usually in one direction but occasionally in two. Blue sky is usually visible between the waves, but often these waves join to form an overcast sky, softer and more regular in formation than stratus. Occasionally this appears as parallel rolls of cloud with blue sky visible between them; this is known as roll cumulus. At night, they tend to give way to clear skies.

Stratus (S)

Stratus is low cloud, about 150–610 metres (500–2000 feet) at its base. It is similar to fog in appearance, a more or less continuous layer of cloud. When broken up by strong winds beneath the base of nimbus or cumulus, it is known as stratus fractus, or 'scud' (so-called because of its rapid speeds at low level in the strong winds of a depression). It can be thin enough to appear as a haze, but is usually much thicker.

Nimbostratus (Ns)

This is classic rain cloud. It is a low, uniform, dark grey layer that blocks daylight, but seems to be lit from within. This gives the impression of a thin layer of cloud, but nimbostratus could be the underside of a cumulonimbus reaching up thousands of feet, or may extend up to the level of altostratus above. It is the visible underside of a very thick composite cloud and usually seen at the core of a low pressure system.

Its base is generally 150–610 metres (500–2000 feet), but it can reach sea level or rise up to 1220 metres (4000 feet). If the cloud is deep enough, it will appear darker, much more so than stratus, and will give continuous, steady rain or snow, depending on the climate. It often appears smudged or blurred as rain obscures the cloud base, and 'scud' is often seen scooting beneath.

Cumulus (Cu)

These are flat-based, brilliant white and sharply defined cotton wool clouds with domed tops and protuberances that cast shadows on the cloud itself. With the sun behind them, they appear dark with luminous edges. They vary in size enormously, from the small tufts of cotton wool that litter the Tradewind skies to the vast cumulonimbus thunderclouds, and this variation is caused by strong updraughts.

These updraughts are associated with turbulence within and below the cloud. Often cumulus merges with altocumulus, then forms cumulonimbus thunderclouds.

Cumulonimbus (Cb)

These are the biggest clouds. They are mountainous, flat-bottomed cumulus clouds that rise up to the level of cirrus clouds. From beneath, they resemble nimbostratus but, whereas nimbostratus rainfall is continuous, cumulonimbus rainfall is showery. Where the top of the cloud meets the jet streams at that height, the water droplets freeze into ice crystals and are whipped into the characteristic brilliant white 'anvil heads' associated with thunder. These heads will be visible over the horizon long before the body of the cloud appears, so if you see it, make sure your collection equipment is ready to go.

The rain or snow showers may be mixed with hail and thunderstorms of varying severity, so your chances of collecting a great deal of water are good. However, their showery nature may frustrate your collection efforts as showers dance on the ocean around you.

LOW PRESSURE SYSTEMS

In the Northern Hemisphere, the surest sign of rainfall is cumulus approaching at low level and cirrus at high level. Behind the cumulus, you will see a haze of cirrostratus and below it nimbostratus, its base obscured by rainfall. This marks the warm front and, as it approaches, visibility will deteriorate, the wind will strengthen and back (move anticlockwise), and rainfall will increase. As it passes, the rainfall will become showery, perhaps fading to drizzle, the temperature will rise, visibility will be poor and the wind will veer (its direction will move clockwise).

As the showers from the stratus and stratocumulus start to stall, you might see between gaps in the cloud base huge towers of cumulonimbus marking the cold front. There will be heavy rain, squalls, possibly hail or thunder, as the cold front passes and the rain will lighten abruptly with occasional showers from cumulus clouds. The wind will become gusty but generally veer further, visibility will improve and the temperature will drop as the system moves away.

COLLECTING RAINWATER

Most life rafts are now fitted with a gutter system to channel rainwater from the canopy into a collection bag, but there are drawbacks to this system. As a general rule, the canopy will be covered in salt spray, whipped off the waves by the wind. As the rain begins to fall, this salt will be washed off the canopy and into the collection bag, contaminating the fresh water. This is not a serious problem if the rain keeps falling steadily. The first bag can be used simply for wetting the lips and washing injuries and sea water sores. The second bag, collected from a cleaned canopy, will be potable. However, rainfall is often showery, a brief burst and then suddenly over. Even a brief shower could provide you with 560 ml (1 pint) pint of water if your collection system is clean and effective.

After sea survival periods of several weeks, the coating of the canopy, usually orange or yellow, is severely degraded by the sun's ultraviolet radiation and the degraded material contaminates the water. This water is fresh, but it will taste foul and brackish because of the contamination and could induce vomiting if taken orally. This water, up to 560ml (1 pint), can be taken rectally using the enema kit. As the canopy degrades further, it loses its waterproofing and water runs through rather than down it, preventing effective collection. For these reasons, you should have a water collection sheet and storage boxes stored inside the life raft (off the life raft floor and away from any sea water), kept ready for instant deployment when it starts raining. The survival blanket could be used for this purpose and your grab bag should contain any number of alternative collection surfaces – plastic sheeting, rubbish sacks, a tarpaulin, a section of a salvaged sail, foul weather jackets and trousers, and life jackets. Make sure no water escapes your catchment system by improvising guttering at the sides of the sheet and a completely watertight method of draining the collected water into resealable plastic containers.

One or more of these plastic containers – preferably the larger ones – can also be installed on top of the inflatable arch and held in place using bungee or shock cord retainers to increase your catchment. If you managed to salvage a dinghy and the rain looks set to last long enough to haul it back to the life raft, more containers can be placed in the dinghy. Alternatively, you could create a cover for the aft section of the dinghy (the forward section will be sheltered by the sail and the mast will prevent you from using the full surface of the dinghy). Put a hole at its centre so that rainwater drains into a plastic box beneath it. Collecting rainwater is all about maximizing your salt-free catchment area.

Despite your best efforts, it is very likely that anything and everything in your life raft will eventually end up with a coating of salt. The wind blows spray off the surface of the sea and where sea water doesn't manage to reach, the wind certainly will. As the water

Solar still

The solar still works by using heat energy from the sun to evaporate fresh water from sea water. It is critical that the plastic sheeting is taped round the outer edge of the larger vessel to form an airtight seal, and that the still remains level so that the weight always hangs over the collection vessel.

evaporates in the heat of the day, tiny salt crystals are left coating any surface in contact with the air. Unless your equipment is stored in resealable plastic boxes, your best efforts to keep your water collection equipment free of salt will be frustrated by airborne salt. If you are using a survival blanket as a collection device, it is sensible to store it in a resealable plastic box if you can spare the storage space. But if your collection device is a section of sail or a tarpaulin, this will not be an option. In that case, make sure that when your watchkeeper reports rain approaching, you rinse the collection device in the sea. This will dissolve the salt crystals much faster than would be possible using rainfall and leave you with a surface that can quickly be washed by the rain to let you begin collecting fresh water.

Rainwater collection is without doubt the fastest way of boosting your supply of fresh water. If you are in an area of regular rainfall, along the Equator or in the temperate zones at 30-50° North or South, you will quickly perfect your collection equipment and become well-drilled in its deployment and use. Remember also that the most effective collection device is your stomach, but your mouth does not present a large catchment area. Devise for yourself a funnel of some description using the range of impermeable options onboard your life raft to increase your mouth's catchment area. Once your collection equipment is deployed, drink as much rainwater as possible and also rinse your clothes and your body free of salt.

There are a variety of devices in your grab bag in which water can be stored. The resealable plastic boxes, screw-top bottles and plastic zipper bags are ideal because they can be securely closed. They are also either transparent or translucent, which means that you do not need to open the container, and risk losing some of its contents, to find out how much water it contains. The condoms in the utility kit will, once cleaned, provide you with a great deal of fresh water storage – several pints each. Once filled, however, they are very fragile, so their storage will need careful consideration– seaboots are one option.

Remember to look at your equipment as a survivor should, in terms of form rather than function, and composition rather than purpose. This way, you will find many other storage options. If it can be spared without endangering its contents, your waterproof grab bag, once emptied and cleaned, offers watertight storage for many gallons of fresh water. The fenders you salvaged from the parent craft will make excellent, extremely robust fresh water containers (provided they do not leak) and so long as you do not fill them right up, they will still be buoyant. If the pressure release valves are simply designed, the chambers of the life raft itself can be used to store fresh water. The inflatable floor or the lower chamber should be used; adding weight there will improve the life raft's stability, a very desirable side effect in rough weather.

To retrieve the water, you will need to pass the tubing through one or more of the pressure release valves, which means the chamber will deflate while you are filling or draining it with water.

Provided you do not store too great a weight of water in either chamber or attempt to retrieve water from both the floor and the lower chamber at the same time, the life raft will retain enough buoyancy to remain afloat. Do not use the canopy arch tube – weight this far up will have the reverse effect on stability.

CONDENSATION

In temperate climates, or in climates where there is a great diurnal range of temperature, dew will collect in the morning. There is always a certain amount of moisture suspended in the air, and this will condense on surfaces that are cooler than the ambient temperature. For instance, it is easier and quicker to increase the temperature of air rather than the earth. When the sun rises, it warms the air but the ground warms slowly and is cooler than the air. Airborne moisture therefore condenses on the ground as dew.

The same principle applies at sea. Every survivor loses water as airborne moisture with every breath exhaled. This water is fresh, and during the night, this moisture condenses on the inside of the canopy, which is cooler because the air temperature is higher inside than outside the canopy. This water can be collected using a clean cloth or a sponge but the collection device must be dedicated solely to this purpose. It cannot be used to sponge out sea water or to wipe salt from buoyancy chambers or it will contaminate any fresh water that has been collected.

You will also find dew on the raft's exterior, gathered in the canopy guttering around the buoyancy chambers. Sponge this up with a cloth and remember that to check for salinity, because of the presence of salt crystals on the canopy, before considering it drinkable.

Condensation can also be collected by other objects. Your radar reflector, if deployed, will warm slower than the surrounding air and airborne moisture will condense on its surfaces. It will be dripping with dew as the sun rises and the dawn watchkeeper should be briefed to collect as much of this as possible.

If the weather at night is calm enough to ensure that no sea water splashes onto your collection sheet, the night watchkeeper should deploy it on the life raft canopy because moisture in the air will condense on the sheet. You will not collect much water, but every drop of fresh water you can collect improves your chance of survival.

ICE

In colder climates, water can be obtained from ice and snow. Collecting snow will be relatively easy because it can be scooped off the canopy of the life raft directly using

Snow and ice

collecting vessels. Take care not to scoop snow too closely to the surface of the life raft canopy; otherwise, you will risk contaminating the melted snow with salt encrusted on the canopy. Remember that snow is considerably less dense than water and a large amount of snow, even tightly compacted, will produce a significantly smaller volume of water.

In blizzard conditions, the snow will form a crust of ice on top of your life raft and this will need to be removed regularly to avoid stressing the life raft structure and jeopardizing its stability with too much extra weight aloft. Fortunately, the canopy is flexible, so this can be pushed or punched off from inside the life raft without risking exposure by having to venture outside. This ice should not be collected, for it will be contaminated with salt whipped off the surface of the sea by the wind.

Never ingest snow directly. If the ambient temperature inside the life raft is too low to melt the snow, you can place pieces of compacted snow in your mouth and wait for them to melt before swallowing. This is not ideal as the cold will burn your lips and tongue, and even lower your core temperature. Provided you drink slowly, leaving enough time between bites of snow for your mouth, throat and stomach to return to a comfortable temperature, your core temperature should not suffer. To ensure there is no fall in core temperature, eat something, preferably carbohydrate, at the same time so that your digestion starts and your metabolism is stimulated. Both biological processes will raise core temperature as a by-product of their activity. Remember that in very cold climates, you will need a fresh water ration of at least 470ml (about ¾ pint) per person per day for eating carbohydrate to be permissible, and at least double that if you have access only to dried protein rations.

If you are in an area of icebergs, you could find yourself in considerable danger at any time. Not only is it obviously extremely cold, but your life raft could be crushed easily between two colliding floes or torn by growlers. Also, near icebergs and glaciers, your life raft could be crushed by a sudden iceslide as huge sections of ice weighing hundreds of tons shear from the main body of ice. This is likelier to occur on the sides of the iceberg that are in the sun.

However, survival is a desperate business and if you are severely dehydrated, this may be your only viable source of water. Some of the ice around you will be fresh and can be melted for consumption. Ice loses its salinity after about a year. New ice appears grey and milky in colour, hard with the crystallized salt, whereas older ice has a bluish tinge, softer corners and can be cleaved easily from the iceberg or floe and melted to produce fresh water. Once you have collected enough ice, paddle quickly away from the iceberg or the face of the glacier until you are at least as far away as the ice face is tall.

In these climates, water itself will freeze if removed from the comparative warmth of the sea. If you fill a container with sea water at nightfall and leave it secured to the outside of the life raft and out of the ocean, the sea water will freeze overnight. The water will freeze at the edges first and in the centre last, and all the salt will be concentrated in the centre of the container. If the sun rises shining, the dawn watchkeeper should make sure each side of the container is exposed to direct sunlight for ten minutes or so, enough to melt the ice at the sides, top and bottom of the container. If there is no sunshine, bring the container inside the life raft and wait for the ambient heat to thaw out the ice at the edges. When you can see melted water gathering at the bottom of the container, open the container and drain the melted water. Taste the water to check that it is free of salt before drinking.

RATIONING WATER

The human body under normal circumstances in a temperate climate needs 2-3 litres (3½-5¼ pints) of water per day to ensure normal function. In a sea survival situation, this is not an option as your supply of fresh water will inevitably be limited, probably severely. Even if your life raft or grab bag includes a watermaker, you must make provision for the fact that it may malfunction - a seal may blow or the membrane might degrade and the spares kit may have been lost when you abandoned ship. You must build up a stockpile of water to ensure that you and your crew have the best possible chance of survival.

To protect your reserves of water, ration the amount of water you and your crew drink each day. This is why the measuring jug

Conserving energy

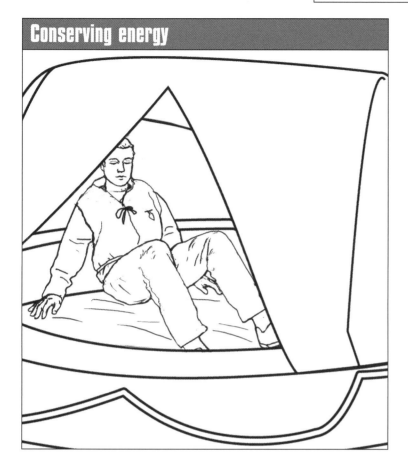

water. Use the rubber tubing in the utility kit, some petroleum jelly for lubrication and the funnel to administer 560ml (1 pint) of water rectally.

From 24–72 hours, the ration should be 470ml (about ¾ pint) per person per day. Beyond 72 hours, the ration should be reduced to 280ml (½ pint) per person per day from the reserve supplies. Supplement with water collected from the other sources described above. Cracked lips, dry mouths and physical weakness are symptoms that should be expected, but if there are any signs of mental dysfunction – confusion, poor coordination, delirium – consider increasing the ration temporarily.

In tropical climates, it is likely that you will need to increase the ration to as much as 940ml (about 1½ pints) per day as you and your crew will be losing more a lot more water through sweating.

or cup is included – to ensure that everyone gets the same ration. Instruct your crew to swill their ration about their mouths and gargle with it. If any of your crew is suffering from heat exhaustion, burns or has lost a lot of blood, they will need water to restore the body's electrolytic balance, help the burns to heal and allow the body to produce more plasma respectively. Otherwise, no water should be issued during the first 24 hours in the life raft.

Those suffering from seasickness will be dehydrated but to provide them with a ration of water would be wasteful – they will simply vomit it up again. An enema should be administered to ensure that their body rehydrates effectively without wasting any

As a general rule it is a good idea for you, as life raft skipper, to make daily checks on the health of each of the life raft crew for signs of dehydration or malnutrition that go beyond those exhibited by yourself and everyone else in the life raft. If one is in worse shape than the others, increase their ration for a couple of days, cut down on their duties and keep a close eye on their vital signs – pulse and respiration – for indications of further deterioration. Holding a brief conversation with a potential casualty will give you some idea if there is any sign of mental deterioration.

Drive to survive

If the will to survive is strong enough, anything is possible. The example of Mexican Pablo Valencia is highlighted in a US Air Force survival manual. He was stranded without food or water in the Arizona Desert. For eight days and seven nights, he walked 240km (150 miles), crawling the last 13km (8 miles) naked, in daytime temperatures of 50°C (120˚F). A loss of 11–13 per cent of body weight in fluids is considered fatal, but when Valencia was found, he had lost 25 percent of his body weight through dehydration. His body was blackened by dehydration and burns, and lacerations to his body did not bleed because his blood was so thick. He was also deaf and virtually blind and unable to speak. After three days of intravenous rehydration, his senses returned and he made a full recovery. In survival terms, he had got everything wrong, but he lived because he wanted to live. He refused to accept that he would die. This is another illustration of the power of the drive to survive. If your instinct to survive is strong enough, you are capable of the most incredible – impossible – feats of endurance.

CONSERVING WATER

As important as collecting water is making sure you lose as little as possible. Your body has already stopped the process of defecation, which is a major source of water loss, and urine is being recycled by the kidneys. Still, there are many steps to take to minimize your water loss. In tropical climates, where the risk of dehydration is greatest, sweating should be regarded as being as serious as bleeding. Make sure you remain completely inactive during the warmest part of the day. Either side of noon, make sure you dampen your clothing in sea water – soak, then wring it – so the evaporation draws heat away from your body. Don't overdo it; if you are spending much of the day sitting in a pool of sea water, you will aggravate and spread existing sea-water sores. You need to balance the importance of not sweating with the importance of looking after your sores.

You will need to remain shaded inside the life raft. If you do not have a canopy, you must improvise one as soon as possible if you hope to survive for more than a week. Shaded inside the life raft, you should rest and try to sleep with your mouth and eyes closed. You lose a considerable amount of water through your mouth in exhaled breath, and by breathing through your nose you can limit this loss considerably. This applies equally to survivors in cold climates: the steam your breath creates is fresh water being lost. Wear something over your nose and mouth to capture that water as it is exhaled; this should also allow you to reinhale at least some of it.

While shade is critical, you will also need airflow around the life raft's interior to help the sea water evaporate from your clothes and to prevent heating still air with your own body heat. If you are crossing a shipping lane or passing under a flight path, reduce watches to 30 minutes each, and make sure that sunhats, sunglasses, collars, sleeved shirts and full-length trousers are worn. If you are nowhere near potential sources of rescue, abandon external watches in favour of internal watches, resting in the shade and taking a glance outside every 10 minutes.

If there is enough space inside the life raft and the floor is relatively dry, lie down so that as much of your body as possible is in contact with the life raft floor. This will feel cooling, though the experience may be made unbearable by the constant battering that the underside of the floor receives from inquisitive fish. In this case, sit on something forgiving - a sleeping bag, section of sail or fender - with your arms away from your sides and your legs spread. This will allow heat to escape from the nodes of the body, the armpits and crotch, the warmest areas on the body's surface.

If your water ration is sufficient to allow you to eat - 0.94-1.8 litres (1½-1¾ pints) per person per day, depending on whether you are eating carbohydrate or protein rations - make sure you rest immediately after eating as the digestive process will generate heat and any activity will add to this.

DRINKING SEA WATER

The medical line on drinking sea water is that it is counterproductive in survival terms. Sea water is up to four per cent salt - four times the concentration of salt in the healthy human body. The body needs salt for electrolytic balance, but there is too much salt in sea water. The kidneys extract the excess and expel it from the body in urine but this requires water.

If there is insufficient water in the body to expel that salt in urine, then the kidneys will begin to suffer. Continued consumption for any extended period will lead to kidney failure, coma and death. This has been well documented in the past. However in 1951-52, France's Dr Alain Bombard conducted an experiment that claimed sea water was not as poisonous as believed. In an inflatable raft conspicuously named *L'Heritique*, Bombard crossed the Atlantic from Las Palmas in the Canary Islands to Barbados in 66 days.

He contended that survivors died at sea not because of thirst and starvation but because of fear and idleness. To prove this theory, he set out from Las Palmas - without

supplies, he claims - and survived on the fish he caught, juice he squeezed from those fish, plankton, rainwater and sea water. He never suggested that sea water is good for the human body - far from it - but he did say that a maximum of 0.9 litres (1½ pint) per day could be imbibed for a maximum of five days without any long-term damage to the renal system. The purpose of this was not to replace fresh water in the body, but to replenish the levels of salt lost through sweat and to survive until rainfall could be collected to flush the system, or to stretch out inadequate supplies of fresh water.

His claims are disputed, in particular by, by the German Dr. Hannes Lindemann. Lindemann was inspired by Bombard's adventures but extremely sceptical, both as a doctor and a sailor, about his claims. To test them, Lindemann crossed the Atlantic alone in 1955, in a 7.6-metre (25-foot) dugout canoe, and took 65 days to reach Haiti from the Canary Islands. Nine months later, he crossed the Atlantic again, from the Canaries to St Martin, after 72 days in a 5-metre (17-foot) folding kayak. Lindemann conducted experiments of his own and concluded that sea water was not in fact potable. Nor, he claimed, could he extract any useful amount of juice from fish flesh. He also claimed, in his book *Alone at Sea*, that witnesses at the Real Club Nautico in Las Palmas report that Bombard, before leaving, loaded his raft 'to the brim' with 114 litres (25 gallons) of fresh water and enough food for three months at sea. Also, Lindemann claims that Bombard twice collected supplies from ships he encountered in the Atlantic.

There seems to be little middle ground between these two arguments, but it is clear that drinking sea water is an option only if you have exhausted your supply of fresh water. To reiterate, if the option is death by dehydration, then you could try sea water to buy you a few days while you wait for rain.

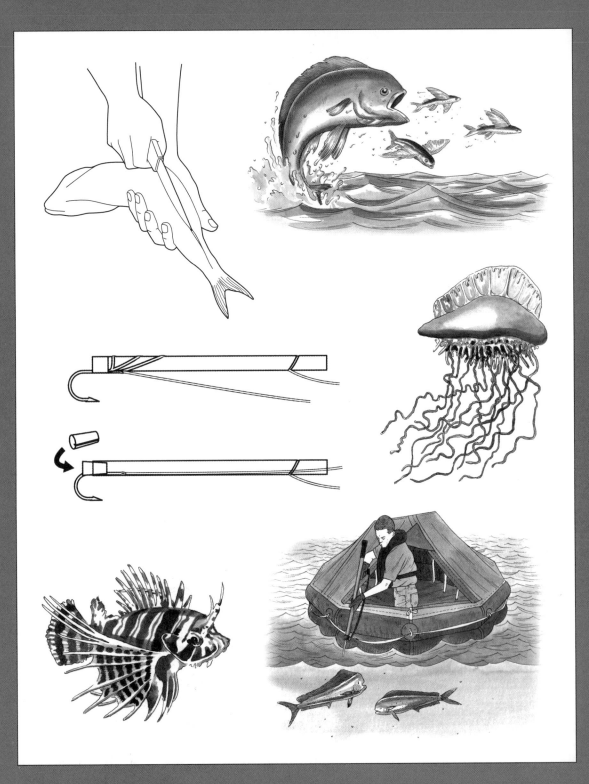

CHAPTER SIX

Food supply

Once your fresh water supply is established, you can turn your attention to sources of nutrition. There are a certain number of nutritional requirements to meet if you are to ensure that your body continues functioning usefully, and the ocean can provide them all.

It is well documented that the human body can function normally without food for up to 30 days, and support an increasingly weakened form of life for 60 days or more before death. If sufficient fresh water is taken daily, hunger pangs will disappear within a week, but survivors will be moody and irritable. This will affect survival chances because the life raft crew will be turning on each other, undermining morale rather than focusing on survival. Lack of food also means the survivor is physically weakened, physically less durable and mentally more distracted from his survival tasks.

You will lose weight – remember that you are trying to survive, not to stay healthy. The limited amount of fresh water available to you will mean that you will be eating the minimum amount of food, and quite possibly nothing at all on some days. Your carbohydrate rations should be jealously guarded, and these will take on huge value.

In practical terms, they supply an almost instant burst of energy; in psychological terms, they are a luxurious reminder of civilization and safety – your ultimate goal. You should touch them only when energy and morale throughout the crew are reaching debilitatingly low levels or if one of the life raft crew is suffering from hypothermia.

Lighting fires onboard inflatable life rafts is not recommended, so you will have to develop an immediate fondness for cold, raw and, typically, slimy foods. Nor is there any room for sentimentality when it comes to catching and killing fish to whom you may have become attached, particularly if you are a solo survivor. Steve Callahan, adrift and alone for 76 days in a life raft, used to refer to the school of dorado fish (known as mahi-mahi in the Pacific) surrounding his life raft as his 'doggies', but he never intentionally missed a chance to catch, kill and eat one.

Although he began to recognize individual fish by identifying their markings, and to appreciate their company, he never lost sight of the fact that survival is about life and death. Evolution has decreed that the most successful survive, and he needed to maintain his strength. His survival depended on their death. It is a simple equation – often brutal, but that is nature's way, red in tooth and claw.

NUTRITION

Under normal circumstances, the human body requires nutrition from a range of sources to remain healthy. Broadly, there are six categories: water, as discussed in the previous chapter; carbohydrate; protein; fats; vitamins; and mineral salts.

Carbohydrate

Carbohydrates are formed of carbon, hydrogen and oxygen. The hydrogen and oxygen are present in the same proportion as water and as a consequence, they require

Carbohydrate

Carbohydrate provides for short- to medium-term energy needs. The potential survivor at sea should ensure a good supply of boiled sweets, chocolate, glucose tablets, cereal bars and biscuits in their survival kit.

much less of your valuable extracellular water supply during digestion. Carbohydrates are digested in the alimentary canal in the form of monosaccharides, such as glucose and fructose. Carbohydrates also exist in the form of disaccharides (sugars, such as sucrose and lactose) and polysaccharides (such as starch and cellulose). Most of these will be broken down in the alimentary canal and absorbed as monosaccharides.

Their primary function is the supply of short- and medium-term energy and heat. If there is a lack of carbohydrate in the body, proteins will be broken down to supply that energy and heat. These proteins are drawn from the muscles and organs, resulting in muscle wastage and impaired organ performance, neither of which is desirable, particularly in a sea survival situation. If carbohydrate intake exceeds the body's requirements, the excess is stored as fat in the adipose tissue beneath the skin. This provides the body with insulation against heat loss and these reserves of fat can be drawn upon when energy is required.

The primary sources of carbohydrate in daily life are pasta, rice, bread, biscuits, confectionery, fruit, vegetables and cereals. Many of these sources will not be available to you in mid-ocean, so when preparing your sea survival plan, you should make sure you have an adequate supply of durable carbohydrates, such as biscuits, chocolate, glucose tablets and boiled sweets. Carbohydrate is also found in some seaweed.

Proteins

Proteins are composed of amino acids, linked chemically in a way unique to the particular protein. Amino acids are subdivided into two categories: essential – those that cannot be synthesized in the body; and non-essential – those that can.

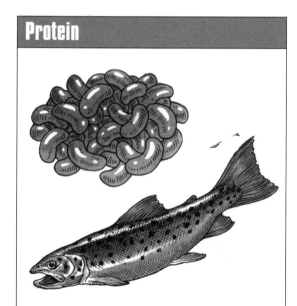

Protein

Protein is required for cell and tissue repair, digestion and healthy blood. At sea, fish will provide your main source of protein.

A complete (or first-class) protein is one that contains all nine essential amino acids. Incomplete (or second-class) proteins do not contain all the essential amino acids. All foods containing protein are broken down during digestion and the proteins absorbed through the lining of the intestine.

Proteins, or more particularly amino acids, are composed of carbon, hydrogen, oxygen, nitrogen, and minerals such as zinc, iron, copper, iodine and sulphur. They are vital for the growth and repair of cells and tissue, the synthesis of enzymes used in digestion, and the healthy balance or proteins and antibodies present in blood plasma. They can also be converted into an energy source, but the conversion process requires water. Protein is also the only supply of nitrogen to the body and without that element, cell renewal, tissue repair, immunity from infection and blood health decline. If protein intake exceeds requirement, the nitrogen is detached and excreted while the rest is stored as fat.

Complete proteins are found in meat, eggs, milk, milk products (except butter), soya beans and fish, incomplete proteins are supplied by pulses and cereals, such as beans and lentils, and in most seaweed. Provided you can fish, you should not want for protein, but remember that digesting protein will require more of your extracellular water supply than carbohydrates and that this water must be replaced. Eat fish and eggs (from female fish and turtles) only if you have a plentiful supply of fresh water.

Fats

Like carbohydrates, fats are also composed of carbon, hydrogen and oxygen, but in a different proportion to that found in water. They subdivide into saturated and unsaturated fats. Saturated, or animal, fats are found in all animal sources of protein, but are particularly high in dairy products, red meat and oily fish, which also supply

Fats

Fat is required in the chemical reaction that converts carbohydrate into energy and also transports vitamins. At sea, oily fish and fat from large fish and turtles are sources.

cholesterol. Unsaturated, or vegetable, fats are primarily found in vegetable oils and derivative products like margarine, and these also supply several polyunsaturated fatty acids important for blood clotting.

Fats are used in the chemical production of energy and heat. They also help vital organs, such as the kidneys and the eyes function normally, and are used to transport and store the fat-soluble vitamins A, D, E and K. In excess, it is stored as fat. When fat enters the duodenum, at the top of the small intestine, the stomach takes longer to empty and this delays hunger. Animal fat can be found around the bottom of the organ cavity in fish and around the organ cavity in turtles.

Vitamins

Vitamins, or vital amines, are essential in very small quantities for normal metabolic function and health. They are subdivided into fat-soluble and water-soluble.

Fat-soluble vitamins are:

Vitamin A (retinol) – found in dairy products, egg yolks, fish liver oil, fish fat and some seaweed, but can also be synthesized from carotene, which is found in fruit, green vegetables and carrots. Vitamin A is essential for normal vision, fighting infection and bone development.

Vitamin D – found in eggs, dairy products, fish liver oils and fish fat, but can be synthesized by the sunlight on cholesterol in the skin. It helps bones and teeth develop normally and maintains their health.

Vitamin E – found in nuts, egg yolk, cereals, dairy products and some seaweed, Vitamin E prevents scotomas (blind spots on the retina) and anaemia.

Vitamin K – found in fruit, leafy green vegetables, fish liver and some seaweed, Vitamin K helps blood to clot.

Vitamins

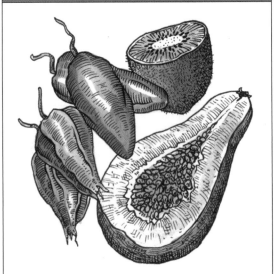

Vitamins are vital for metabolic function and health. Sources at sea include seaweed, fish and plankton in addition to multivitamins.

Water-soluble vitamins are:

Vitamin B complex – there are eight B vitamins and most are found in yeast, eggs, liver, nuts, fish and most seaweed. Five are important for normal function.

1. Thiamine (B_1) is essential for the conversion of carbohydrate into energy. Deficiency causes beriberi, a disease that wastes muscles, damages nerve function, reduces immunity and ultimately kills.

2. Riboflavine (B_2) is associated with healthy eyes and skin.

3. Niacin helps to reduce cholesterol production and in the break down of fat, releasing energy.

4. Pyridoxine (B_6) is essential to the immune system.

5. Cyanocobalamin (B_{12}) ensures healthy bone marrow and normal nerve function.

Vitamin C – found in fresh fruit, particularly grapefruit, lemons, most seaweed and plankton. It prevents scurvy (which causes swollen gums, anaemia, internal bleeding, tissue disrepair), and any deficiency will manifest itself as scurvy after two to three months.

Minerals
The essential minerals are calcium, phosphorous, sodium, potassium, iron, and iodine, and these are required in very small amounts for all body processes.

Calcium – found in dairy products, some seaweed and fish (usually by eating the bones of smaller fish), it promotes healthy growth of bones and teeth, blood clotting and muscle function.

Phosphorous – found in oatmeal, cheese, liver, kidney and sea fish, it works with calcium to promote healthy bones and teeth and is also involved in energy storage.

Sodium – present in meat, eggs, salt, fish and seaweed, it is involved in muscle function and tissue repair, but is critical for electrolytic balance (healthy body fluids).

Potassium – widely available, especially in fruit, vegetables, seaweed and shellfish, it serves a similar function to sodium.

Iron – found in liver, kidney, eggs, wholemeal bread, green vegetables, prawns, shrimp and seaweed, it is essential for blood oxygenation and the conversion of carbohydrate into energy.

Iodine – found in sea fish and seaweed, it is involved in metabolic function. Low levels inhibit the conversion of carbohydrates, proteins and fats into energy. Just 6.4 square centimetres (1 square inch) of seaweed contains the recommended daily allowance of iodine.

In a sea survival situation, however, many of the conventional sources of nutrition will not be available. This is not to say that you will starve. In terms of food supply, the area covered by your life raft is 200 times more bountiful than that same area on land. Many of the carbohydrates, vitamins and minerals required daily are freely available, although many are incorporated in protein-rich foods. To eat them you will need fresh water, illustrating once again just how critical fresh water is to your survival.

FISHING
Fish will provide the main staple of your diet and you will quickly learn the finer points of the art of fishing. It will be a completely different experience from sitting on a riverbank because the fish will come to you. Lie on the inflatable floor of the life raft without any protective layer between you and the floor, and you will soon appreciate this. The fish will nudge, buffet and even charge any bulge in the life raft floor. As you lose weight, this will become increasingly uncomfortable, even painful. The life raft itself, indeed any floating debris, attracts fish because marine life – gooseneck barnacles and algae – grow beneath it and also because it provides shade, an unusual phenomenon

Dorado and flying fish

Dorado, also known as dolphinfish and mahi-mahi, feed on flying fish. They are very powerful so provided you don't hook into one bigger than your fishing equipment can handle, you should be able to eat and dry plenty of meat from a single catch. Check the stomach for flying fish – these will be partially digested and therefore require less of your body's fluid to digest completely. They may even fly into your life raft.

on the ocean surface and therefore worthy of inquiry. The crustacea attract smaller fish, such as triggerfish, and these in turn attract bigger fish, such as dorado.

Dorado are powerful fish, strong-bodied and very fast. They need to be to catch their main prey, flying fish. These remarkable fish have huge pectoral fins that act as wings. With a burst of power from their tails, the flying fish leaves the water and glides across the surface of the water, occasionally up to 6 metres (20 feet) above sea level, at speeds of up to 20 knots, sometimes for distances of 395 metres (1300 feet), although more

typically 30–60 metres (100–200 feet). Their heads are shaped like an inverted triangle – eyes facing down so that they have a good view of any potential predators beneath them. However, this means that they have poor forward vision and could well end up in your life raft, in the towing dinghy or even slapping you about the face. If you are sailing at night, you can improve the chances of catching a flying fish by playing a light on the sail – bright lights attract all fish at night, although flying fish are the only ones that will deliver themselves right to you.

In deep ocean, just about every fish that you can catch is edible and, stomach and intestines excepted, every part of it can be eaten. Useful fluid can be extracted from the eyeballs and between the vertebrae, but it is protein-rich and will make demands on your extracellular water supply. If your catch has flabby skin or flesh that remains indented when pressed; sunken, dull eyes; an unpleasant, strong odour; and pale, shiny gills, it is diseased and should not be eaten. Nor should it be used for bait because you risk contaminating your next catch. If you are in an area of polluted water, the fish you catch are likely to be polluted too. In this case, the flesh should be safe, but do not eat any of the offal. Healthy fish look like healthy fish with bright scales and eyes and red gills, and they have a fresh, slightly salty, but never distinctly 'fishy' odour.

If you are in any doubt regarding the health of any fish you have caught, try a taste test. Eat a very small amount of the flesh. If it tastes unusual, harsh, bitter or salty, spit it out at once and discard the fish, checking the area for sharks first. Even if your sample tastes all right, there is still a risk that the flesh is dangerous – some fish toxins are both tasteless and odourless. Wait for an hour while you cut the fish into strips for drying, to see if there is any reaction. Most poisons work quickly, so if nothing has happened within an hour, you can be almost certain the fish is edible. The first signs of toxins are numbness to the lips and tongue, toes and fingers, itchiness and sensory confusion. This will be followed by vomiting, dizziness, the loss of the ability to speak, paralysis, and even death. However, if only a very small amount has been eaten, the developing symptoms are unlikely to conclude fatally. But do make sure you have sampled only a very small amount: these toxins are very powerful, and just 25g (1oz) of the liver of the pufferfish can kill a man in 30 minutes or even less.

Poisonous fish

If you are near coastline or reefs, avoid fish that do not conform to stereotype. A fish with a beaked mouth is a reef dweller and, as such, could be carrying ciguatera poison from the blue-green reef-living algae on which it feeds. In mid-ocean, however, the fish will be edible. The triggerfish, for example, can probably be found feeding on the marine life growing on the underside of your life raft. If caught in mid-ocean, its flesh will be free of toxins and can be eaten, but its tough skin and bony structure make it a hard-earned and unrewarding meal.

As well as beaked fish, avoid fish with box-like shapes, fish that inflate when threatened, those with hard, armour-like scales and those with stunted or missing ventral (belly) fins.

Venomous fish

Again, these are largely coast-dwelling fish and are instantly recognizable as dangerous. They are typically either flamboyant, with flowing fins and dorsal spines, or ugly, with dorsal spines. The most venomous of all is the stonefish. It is stone-coloured, hence the name, and therefore difficult to spot when lying in shallow coastal waters. It is squat, warty and slimy in appearance and the venom in its dorsal spines can kill a man in six hours. If the dose received is not fatal, the survivor can expect to be in excruciating, crippling pain for 12 hours.

If you are stung by a venomous spine, remove the spine using tweezers. Then flush the wound with sea water and allow the wound to bleed by keeping the hand or foot low and pinching the area. This will clear some of the toxin before it enters the blood stream. Then cover the wound with a clean dressing and treat the victim as you would treat someone suffering from shock. If heat loss is a risk, cover the victim and raise their extremities – except the affected one – to concentrate the blood in the vital organs.

Poisonous fish

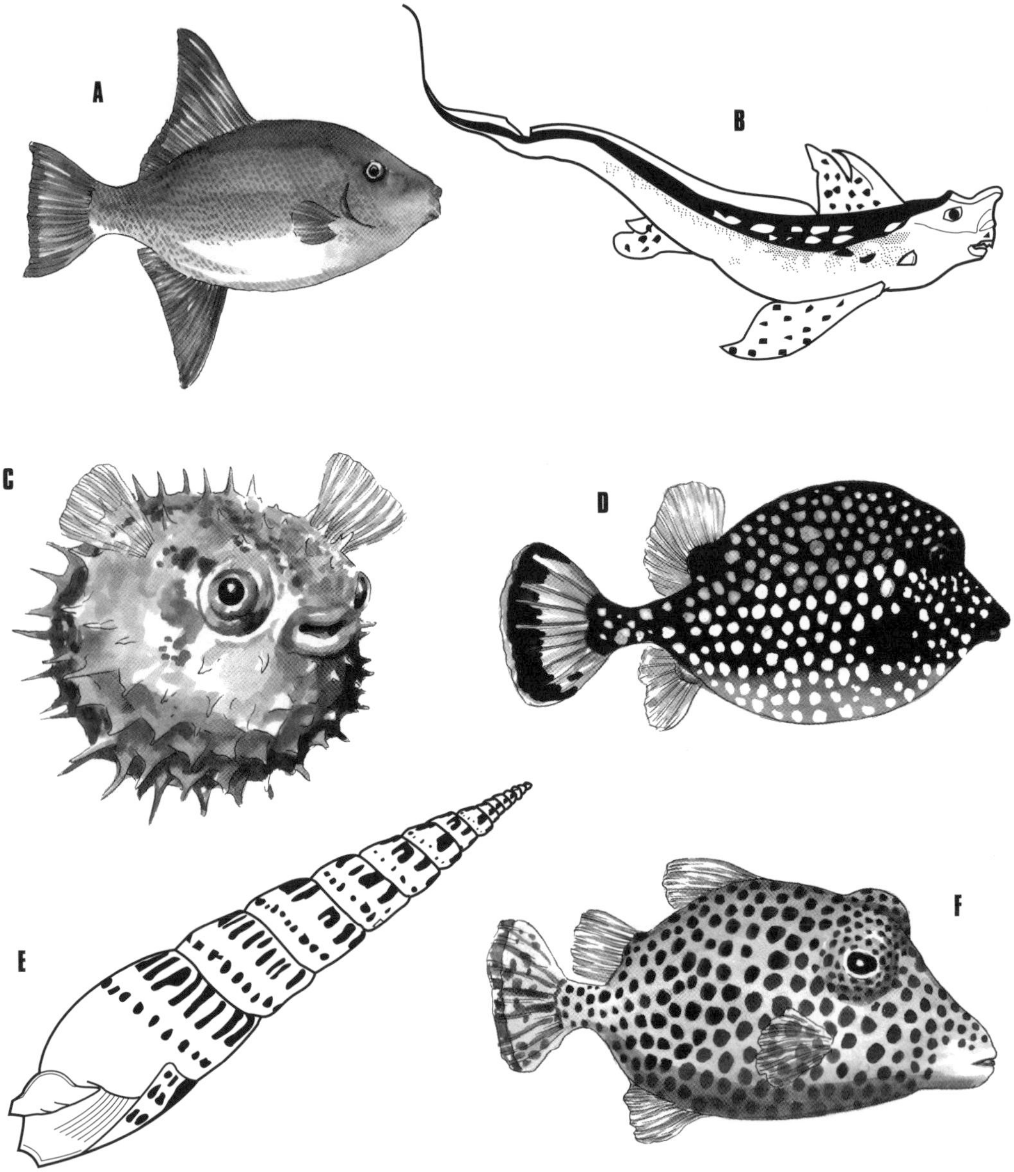

A. Trigger fish
B. Rockfish
C. Porcupine fish

D. Cowfish
E. Terebra shell
F. Boxfish

Venomous fish

A

B
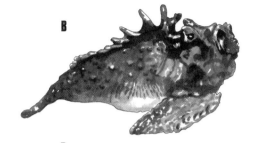

C
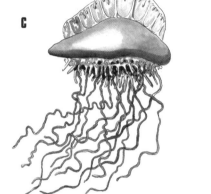

D

E

F
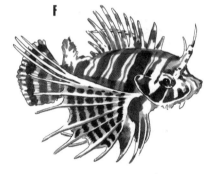

G

H
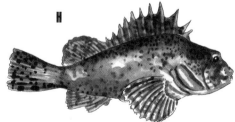

A. Weever fish
B. Stonefish
C. Portuguese man-of-war
D. Siganus

E. Surgeon fish
F. Lionfish
G. Zebra fish
H. Scorpion fish

Dangerous fish

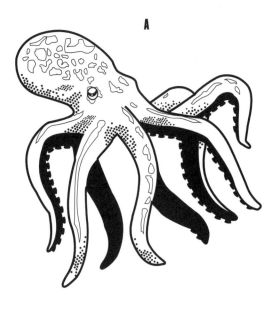

A

A. Octopus
B. Swordfish
C. Barracuda

Attacks by octopus and swordfish are not widely reported but the barracuda, particularly the Australian sub-species, have been known to attack man or steal catches. If caught, larger ones 1.2–1.8 metres (4-6 feet) should be cut free but smaller ones can be landed. Watch out for the razor sharp teeth.

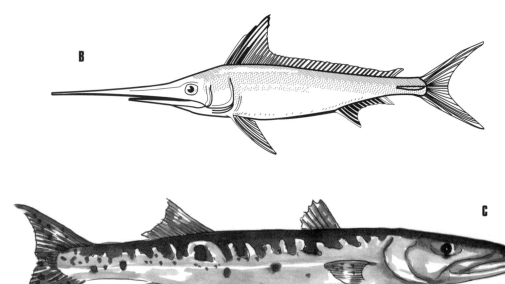

B

C

Monitor the victim's heart rate and respiration. It is possible he will stop breathing as the toxin takes hold, so be prepared to administer artificial respiration.

If several spines punctured the skin, you should bleed the wound for longer and then apply a tourniquet above the wound. Heat some water in a container using a handheld flare if you have no other method of heating water, taking care not to damage the container or the life raft, then bathe the affected area in the hot water for 20 minutes. Remove the tourniquet, then treat as for shock. The potency of the toxin will be reduced by this heat treatment.

Another venomous fish you are more likely to encounter is the Portuguese man-of-war jellyfish. These are actually a colony of thousands of organisms comprised of four different types of jelly fish, each specialized in either floating, catching food, digesting or reproducing. They sail the oceans using their opaque kidney-shaped flotation sacks as sails and trailing tentacles up to 18 metres (60 feet) long in their wake. Any fish coming into contact with these tentacles are paralyzed by the sting, then killed and eaten. For humans, the sting can cause severe pain, a rapid drop in blood pressure and faintness, all usually associated with shock. Death has been known to result, but most simply bear red weals across their skin for several days.

Dangerous fish

Like sharks, barracuda have been known to attack man. These are long, torpedo-shaped fish, some 0.9-1.8 metres (3-6 feet) in length, with dark blue-black backs and silvered bellies. They usually inhabit tropical shoal waters, and are bolder when swimming in schools. The Australian barracuda is reported to be more aggressive than its Caribbean or Pacific cousins. Near coasts, they may also carry ciguatera poison, so do not eat barracuda that have been caught near coasts or reefs.

Another potential danger is the sea snake, occasionally found in mid-ocean. It has a scaled body, but is distinguishable from the land variety by a flattened fin-like tail. They do not usually attack, but can become aggressive in the mating season. Their fangs are short, so serious attacks are rare. However, the sea snake has a venom ten times as poisonous as its land-bound cousin. Treat as you would for venomous spines.

HOW TO FISH

Hooks, spear tips and harpoons can all inflict serious damage to your life raft and consequently your survival chances. If you salvaged a rigid dinghy from the parent craft, always fish from that. It is less stable than the life raft, but you will be much more sensitive to trim and able unconsciously to balance the dinghy when landing fish. You can kill, gut, dress and dry the fish in the dinghy and avoid covering the life raft floor with fish blood and offal. If you salvaged an inflatable dinghy or have only the life raft, you will need to keep uppermost in your mind that you risk puncturing a buoyancy chamber while landing fish.

Before you start to fish, prepare everything you will need to kill and land the fish safely. If you fish from a rigid dinghy, all you will need are gloves, long sleeves of tough material to protect your arms – your foul weather jacket would be ideal – clothing to guard against exposure, a sharp knife and a huge amount of patience. If fishing from an inflatable dinghy or from the life raft, make sure the buoyancy chambers over which you are fishing are protected by thick material, such as a tarpaulin, a salvaged sail or a foul weather jacket. You will need to keep a sharp, sheathed knife within arm's reach and a chopping board to protect the inflatable floor while killing, gutting and dressing the fish. Also make sure you have some resealable plastic boxes to store the offal as bait and a plastic bag for any waste

Lures

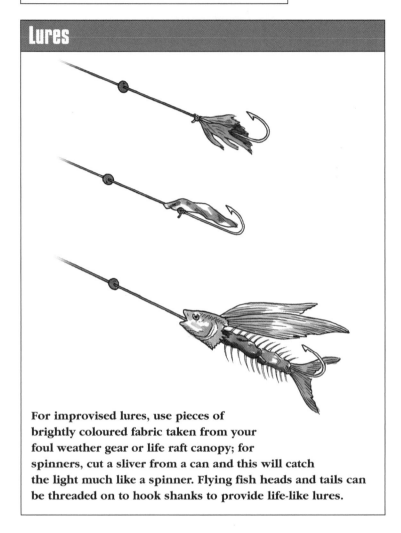

For improvised lures, use pieces of brightly coloured fabric taken from your foul weather gear or life raft canopy; for spinners, cut a sliver from a can and this will catch the light much like a spinner. Flying fish heads and tails can be threaded on to hook shanks to provide life-like lures.

back to break the neck, taking care not to stick yourself with the hook. If the fish is too large, or has sharp teeth, you can kill it by sliding a knife into the gills and breaking the spine with the tip, but always take care not to puncture the life raft while doing so. If the thumb and middle finger are pressed onto the fish's eyes, some fish become temporarily paralysed, making them easier to kill. If the fish is fighting hard and you are not comfortable using the knife close to the life raft, stun the fish with a sharp blow on top of the head, then land it and kill it. If you catch a fish that you suspect has venomous dorsal spines, do not land it until you have cut off the spines. If you are unable to do so, attempt to cut the hook out and let the fish go.

If fish are proving shy, you can attract them during the day by creating areas of shade. Your life raft should encourage fish to approach,

materials like scales and blood. You can dispose of these after ensuring there are no sharks in the area by throwing them as far across the wind as possible. If you throw them up or downwind, you risk catching up with them or snaring them with your sea anchor.

Your catch should be killed before landing it, but try not to spill any blood outside the fishing craft because sharks will close in quickly. With a smaller catch, this can usually be accomplished by placing your fingers in its mouth and pulling the head

but if it does not, create other areas. If you managed to salvage a sail, float it on the surface of the water just outside the life raft entrance, and fish will be drawn to its shade. If you have no sail, you can use a foul weather jacket, a survival blanket, a garbage bag, indeed anything that will float. Another way of luring fish to you is to is to take a handful of bait, fish entrails or stored fish that has gone bad, and agitate it in the water just outside the life raft entrance, but always check first to make sure there are no sharks in the area. Sharks have an extraordinary

Constructing a gaff hook

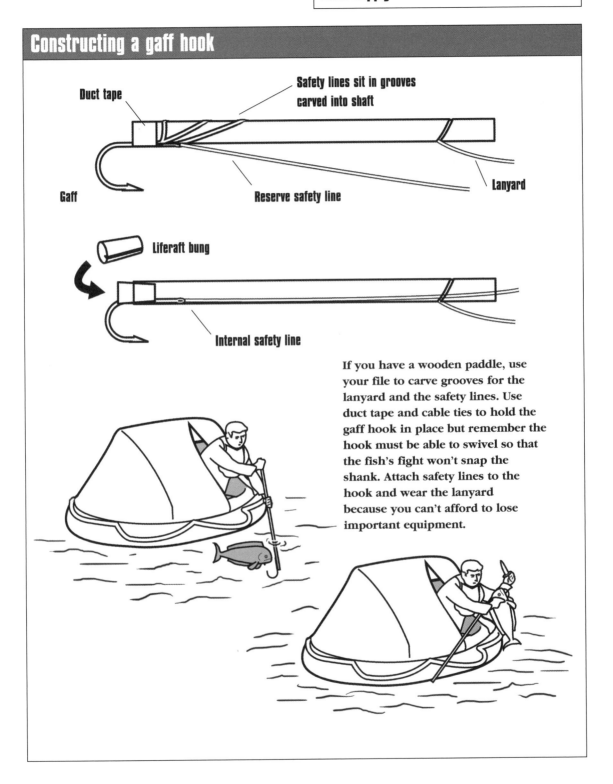

Duct tape

Safety lines sit in grooves carved into shaft

Lanyard

Gaff

Reserve safety line

Liferaft bung

Internal safety line

If you have a wooden paddle, use your file to carve grooves for the lanyard and the safety lines. Use duct tape and cable ties to hold the gaff hook in place but remember the hook must be able to swivel so that the fish's fight won't snap the shank. Attach safety lines to the hook and wear the lanyard because you can't afford to lose important equipment.

sense of smell and the entrails will attract any sharks in the area, so keep watch for fins at all times. If you see any, stop fishing.

At night, playing the flashlight beam on the surface of the water will also attract fish. This is a popular trick used by commercial deep sea fishermen and they tend to use stroboscopic lights to maximize the effect.

LINE FISHING

The life raft survival kit includes a fishing kit, and you should use this first. It will probably be inadequate for most of your line fishing requirements. As you lose line, hooks and fish, you will develop an appreciation of how easily these losses can occur and how critical they could become. You will also learn a great deal about tying knots; which lures and baits work best; what you are likely to catch; and exactly how far you can fight fish without risking your equipment.

Remember when line fishing that salt crystals will collect on the line. If you get a bite and the line loads while it is wrapped around the hand, these crystals can cause deep lacerations to the hands. Clean the gear regularly using the life raft sponge and always use the reel, or fish with gloves if you have no reel. Sea water and reduced vitamin intake will mean the skin does not heal so well as it usually does, and such lacerations will not heal but instead ulcerate and become septic.

On no account should you attach the line to either the life raft or yourself. If you are fishing with a strong line tied to your life raft and a shark or a large fish takes the bait, you are risking capsize at the very least, and possibly a shark attack. If the line is attached to you, you could be hauled overboard. If you catch something that is putting up that degree of resistance, it is much better to cut it free and put down to experience the loss of the hook, lure, bait and line. Remember, you (not the shark) has had a lucky escape. Always look for sharks before you start

fishing. If there are any swimming about, do not fish. Wait until they leave before casting. Otherwise, they will take your catch and your gear at the very least, and could become frenzied enough to attack your life raft.

When using your grab bag fishing kit, use the stronger line if you have a choice. If the fish you catch are much lighter than the line's breaking strain, you can change down, but always start with the strongest. Also start with the bigger hooks. If you get no bites and reel in to find your bait has been eaten off the hook, choose a smaller one, but for the same reasons of economy, start with the larger. Also start with the wire leaders to prevent your hook and bait being bitten off by larger fish biting through the line. Before and after using your fishing gear, check it thoroughly. Make sure the line is free of salt and not cracked or fractured and that the hooks are securely attached and sharpened.

If you run out of lures or spinners, you can improvise replacements using ribbons of coloured material from your foul weather gear, or a small section of the life raft canopy. Spinners can be replaced by cutting up pieces of tin can or using small sections of the survival blanket. In terms of bait, fish offal and spoiled fish are ideal: if a flying fish should stray into your life raft, eat the flesh, then thread hooks through the head and tail to make a lifelike lure. These lures should be towed across the surface of the water to maximize their attraction to fish.

Line itself is more difficult to replace, but you can extract and tie together strands taken from spare lengths of line, from sails or tarpaulins or any other fabric. It won't be so strong as nylon fishing line and you will need to scale down your intended catch to avoid losing hooks. If you run out of hooks, there are many options open to you provided you look at your equipment in terms of its components rather than its function. Any metal is useful; cans, safety pins, nails and springs can all be bent or cut into useful hooks, and wood can be carved into a hook shape. You could also use a gorge hook. This is a straight section of metal or wood with barbed or jagged ends that is secured around its middle and buried in bait. When the bait is taken, the strain on the line deploys the gorge laterally, catching in the fish's throat.

SPEAR GUN

One of the recommended components of your grab bag is a spear gun with spare power bands, shafts and tips. This is an enormously effective way of spearing fish – fast and accurate. Provided that you do not aim for excessively large fish and that you check the gun thoroughly before and after use, your equipment should provide you with the fish you require throughout the survival period. You will need to lean outside the life raft and aim directly downwards to avoid missing your target and to account for the refraction of light through the water.

Spear fishing

Always aim vertically downwards to avoid missing your target owing to light refracting in the water. Patience is the key: pick a fish of a manageable size to avoid damaging your equipment, and hit the strike zone with your first shot. Take care when landing the fish to avoid holing the buoyancy chambers with the spear tip. Stun the fish if it is fighting.

Exercise enormous patience before firing to make sure you get the fish you want and hit it in the strike zone - just behind the head. Narrow misses will tend to deter fish from nearing the life raft.

The greatest care must be taken when bringing your catch to the life raft. If it is still thrashing, there is a risk of the tip of the harpoon tearing the life raft, so kill or stun the fish before landing it. Always remember to attach the spear gun's lanyard to yourself. Unlike line fishing, you will be able to make sure the fish you select is not too large for your equipment, so using the lanyard is essential to make sure vital fishing equipment is not lost.

SPEARS

Spears can be improvised in a number of ways, using oars or paddles for shafts and knives, metal barbs or even fish bones strapped securely to the end. Particularly when using knives, you must make sure they are very securely attached; you cannot afford to lose them.

Use line, duct tape, cable ties and hose clips to fasten the improvised tip to the shaft and always attach a safety line to the knife itself. This means that if the knife works loose during use, it will not swim away lodged in the escaping fish. If you are down to your last knife and have nothing else to use as a cutting edge, you can use the hacksaw, knife or file to turn the end of the paddle itself into a barbed spear tip.

Again, to avoid missing your prey, aim directly downwards while leaning outside the life raft and wait until you can spear the fish you want in its strike zone. Once used to the refraction, you should consider using an arc strike. This involves swooping the spear tip in an arc through the air and into the water, hitting the fish horizontally in the strike zone, just behind the pectoral fin, and lifting it clear of the water in one movement. This will ensure that the fish cannot writhe off the spear and be lost, that your equipment is stressed for the absolute minimum amount of time, and that there is little risk of damaging the life raft.

Make sure that the fish you strike at is not so large that you will struggle to lift it clear of the water or risk breaking the spear itself, and wait until you can hit the strike zone. Again, keep a very good lookout for sharks. If they show up, bring your gear in immediately and do not start again until you are sure that they have left the area. Remember to attach the spear's lanyard.

GAFF FISHING

If there are plenty of bold fish about, this is perhaps the most productive method of fishing. Use the largest hook you have - at least 4 cm (1½ inches) from shank to barb and probably larger - and make sure it is attached to the end of the paddle in such a way that it can rotate to account for the fish fighting once hooked. Otherwise enormous strain will be placed on the hook's shank and its tethers, and the hook could be lost. You should add a safety line to the gaff hook, in addition to wearing the shaft's lanyard, to ensure that it is not lost. Once again, you must exercise great patience and selection before striking to avoid damaging your equipment and deterring fish from approaching the life raft.

HAND FISHING

Even if you have no fishing equipment, you can still go fishing. Agitating bait in the water outside the life raft entrance will attract fish - and sharks too, remember. Once you are certain that the fish is neither poisonous nor venomous, you can grab it. The scales will provide you with a good grip and aim to grasp the fish around its tail.

DRESSING FISH

In tropical climates, your catch will spoil in about 30 minutes if it is not prepared properly. When the catch is killed and

Spear fishing

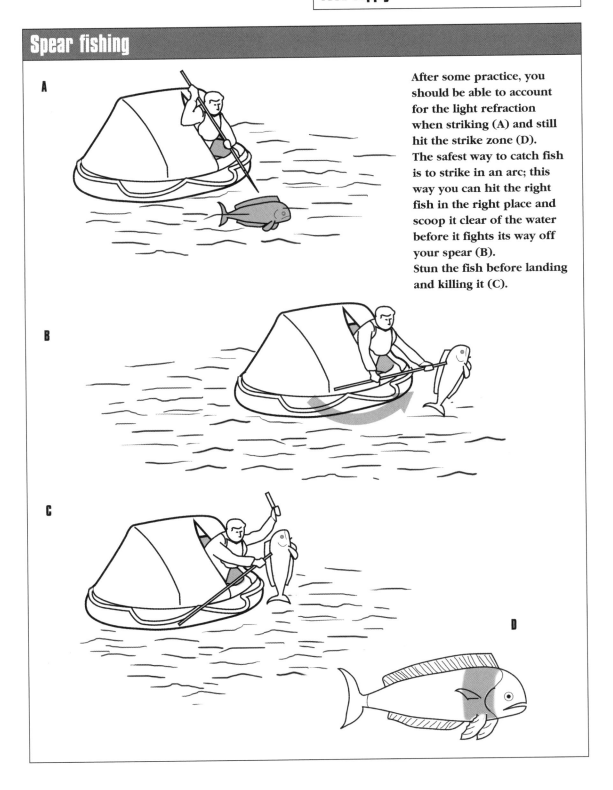

After some practice, you should be able to account for the light refraction when striking (A) and still hit the strike zone (D).
The safest way to catch fish is to strike in an arc; this way you can hit the right fish in the right place and scoop it clear of the water before it fights its way off your spear (B).
Stun the fish before landing and killing it (C).

landed, remove the head by cutting around the gills and through the spine, and cut off the tail (there is some meat on the fish's head and fluid in the eyes, so do not discard). Bleed the fish dry; it will keep much better if the flesh is free of blood. Remove its skin and cut the fish from the anus to the head to gain access to the organ cavity and remove all the organs. Keep the liver and heart, and always check the stomach contents – you could find several more fish, and these are likely to be partially digested, which means that they will require less of your extracellular water supply to complete digestion. Keep the rest of the offal for bait.

Once the organs are removed, cut the fish into sections 30 cm (12 inches) long, then start carving off strips about 2.5cm (1 inch) thick and wide. In bright sunlight, the fish will dry quickly, but if the weather is a little overcast, cut narrower strips, about 1cm (½ inch) thick, so that they will dry more quickly. Once these strips are ready, hang, tie or thread the strips on the rigging of the dinghy to dry. If you have no dinghy, remove the salt from the areas of the life raft canopy and buoyancy chambers facing the sun, or use some salt-free sheeting, and lay them out. Once the strips are dry, store the fish in a resealable plastic box.

In wet conditions, the fish will not dry and what you can't eat will spoil. You should be collecting water if it is raining, and you will not be able to fish in rough weather, so this is unlikely to be an issue.

With the strips of fish now out to dry, you can scavenge meat from the head, extract the eyes and remove the gelatinous nuggets from between the vertebrae. Eat only a small amount of liver, which is extremely high in vitamin A; an excess of this vitamin will need to be expelled from the body as urine, therefore contributing to your dehydration.

Store the bait in a resealable plastic bait box. Before you dispose of the bones, check that there are none that could be used as spear tips and ensure that there are no sharks in the area.

If the fish was not properly dried before storing, it will spoil. Spoiled fish smells strongly – the odour is unpleasant – and will discolour between the layers of muscle. Don't eat it – you risk food poisoning. The resulting vomiting will cost you dearly in terms of fluids and minerals.

SHARKS

Never attempt to attract sharks to your life raft or dinghy – you could provoke an attack. If there are several sharks circling your life raft, nudging and brushing their bodies against the buoyancy chambers, there is a chance that their rough skins will damage your life raft. As they make passes by your life raft entrance, attack them with a paddle, aiming for the snout, eyes and gills, to deter them from attacking. If they are not deterred by your attack and begin to turn tighter circles, hold a flare or attach it to the end of a paddle, then ignite it and jab the shark with it as it passes. This will be particularly effective at night, but it is very much a last resort as flares are not replaceable and can damage your life raft.

However, if a lone shark approaches and it is less than 1 metre (3 feet) long, you can attempt to catch it. You should always wear gloves while fishing, and in this case they will protect your hands from the sandpaper-like skin of the shark. Grab the shark's tail just forward of the tail fin and immediately stun it with a blow to the head from a heavy object, to avoid being caught by its razor-sharp teeth in a struggle and to avoid any damage to your life raft. Once it is motionless, kill the shark by stabbing it in the eye, then land the shark and remove the head to ensure that it is dead and fully bled. Should you catch a shark while line fishing and be able to wrestle it to the life raft, grab it around the tail and kill it in the same way.

Landing a fish

A fighting fish, particularly one still on the spear, can cause devastating damage to your life raft. Once clear of the water, hold it by the gill and stun it with a blow to the head, then land it and kill it. The head contains some meat and the eyes are filled with salt-free fluid. The tail can be discarded, the intestines used for bait, the rest can be eaten.

Dressing large fish

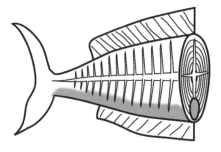

With the head and tail removed and the organ cavity emptied, cut the fish into 30 cm (12-inch) sections and carve the flesh off in strips 2.5 cm (1 inch) wide, and 1 cm (½ inch) or 2.5 cm (1 inch) deep, depending on drying conditions.

TURTLES

The Robertsons and the Baileys both caught and ate turtles. Turtles are attracted to the marine life below the life raft, and there is also some evidence to suggest that their approaches may be concerned with mating. Once they are near the life raft, grab one of the rear flippers and hang on tight – there will be a struggle. Make sure you have gloves and are wearing thick-sleeved clothing because you will be scratched and nipped by the turtle's flippers and beak. Grab the second rear flipper and turn the turtle upside down before hauling it in.

Use a knife on the turtle's carotid artery, either side of the front of the neck, to kill it and bleed it dry. This is not a process that should be attempted outside the dinghy because the blood will attract fish and sharks and possibly provoke a frenzied attack. Make sure the reptile is thoroughly bled, otherwise the meat will spoil quicker.

To dress a turtle, take a knife to the underside of the shell and cut around its edge using a sawing action. This will be a difficult task with anything other than a keenly honed knife, but it will be easier with younger, smaller turtles, whose shell will be thinner.

Once you cut around the edges from the front to the rear edge of the shell, closely undercut the section of shell, starting from the head end because muscle will be attached to it, then lift it clear. If you have no knife, you could attempt to cut the shell with a section of tin can, but remember to wear gloves, otherwise you will cut your hands badly. If you are unable to breach the shell, remove the flippers and pull the meat out through the flipper apertures.

Most of the turtle's muscle is used for propulsion and will be located around the flippers. The forward flippers are the stronger pair and therefore provide more

Gutting and dressing small fish

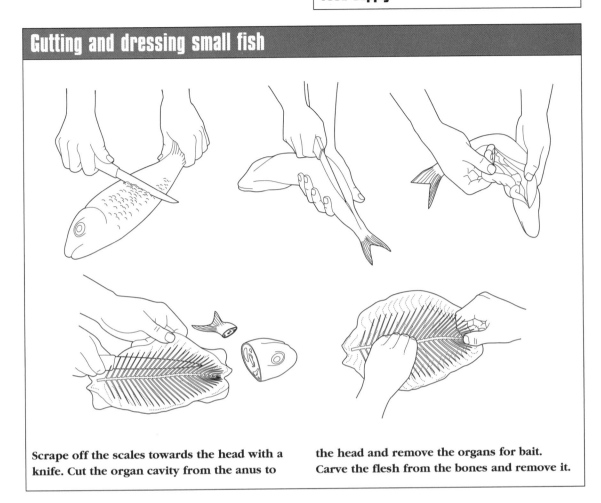

Scrape off the scales towards the head with a knife. Cut the organ cavity from the anus to **the head and remove the organs for bait. Carve the flesh from the bones and remove it.**

meat. The muscle for the rear flippers is centred over the pelvic bone.

The female can be distinguished from the male by the tail: if the tail extends beyond the shell, the turtle is male. In the female, you may find a clutch of eggs, deep yellow in colour and soft-shelled, just forward of the pelvic bone.

Once again, the flesh should be cut into thin strips, and what you cannot eat immediately should be dried in the same way as the fish flesh. The heart can be eaten, but the rest of the organs should be used for bait only. Around the edge of the organ cavity, you will find deposits of fat. These should be stored because they will release oil after a period of storage and this oil has several uses. It can be used to calm rough water around the life raft if it is deposited overboard, but it can also be applied to the skin to provide a degree of protection for salt water sores and cracked skin. The fat itself can be chewed but, as with all food, you must have a good supply of water if you are to eat anything.

The bones of the turtle contain edible, nutritious marrow. The smaller flipper bones can be gnawed for nutrition. For larger bones, remove the knuckle and dig out the marrow. A wire leader could be used to achieve this.

BIRDS

Seabirds are more common in the Southern Hemisphere than in the Northern. All seabirds are edible, but tempting them to land is difficult. Poon Lim ingeniously and successfully used a small 'nest' of seaweed to tempt a bird to land, but bait (organ bait or rotten fish) is probably the most effective method. This can be placed in the dinghy or on the canopy of the life raft. Once the bird has landed, there are several methods of catching it. Like Poon Lim, you could attempt to grab it with your gloved hand, but if you are not successful, the bird is unlikely to attempt another landing. Placing the bait inside a snare made of fishing line has proved to be successful. Once the bird's feet enter the snare, pull it sharply to snare its feet.

Another method is to bury your smallest fish-hook, attached to a line, in the bait. When the bird takes the bait, pull the line to lodge the hook. If you have no hook, try a jagged piece of tin can buried in bait with a hole punched in it to attach the line. This can be placed on the canopy or, if the bird is unwilling to land, towed behind the life raft, tempting it to dive. You could also try throwing the bait into the air to see if you can catch it on the wing. If

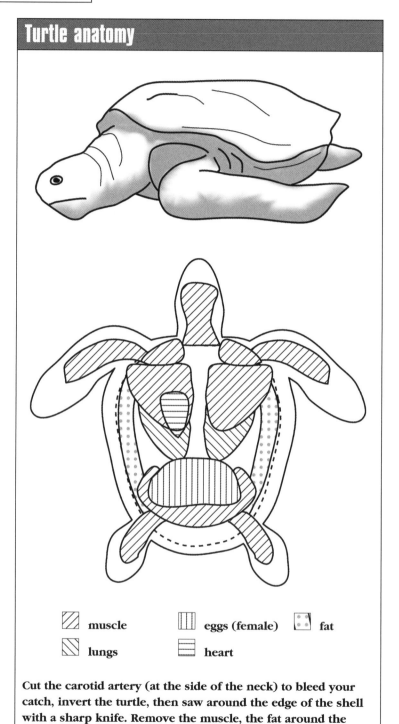

Turtle anatomy

muscle   eggs (female)   fat

lungs   heart

Cut the carotid artery (at the side of the neck) to bleed your catch, invert the turtle, then saw around the edge of the shell with a sharp knife. Remove the muscle, the fat around the organ cavity and the eggs, if you have caught a female.

the bird is large enough to make a decent target, you could consider using a spear gun, but be extremely careful not to puncture the canopy chamber. A paddle could be used to knock the bird from the air or to stun it once it has landed, or throw a net to trap the bird. If you have no net, a jacket with weighted pockets could be used.

Having caught the bird, break its neck by pulling the head backwards sharply. Remove the head and feet, keeping them for bait, and skin the bird. The meat should be eaten raw, the fat underneath the skin can be stored and the oil later extracted, and the bones can be gnawed and the marrow extracted. Feathers can be used as lures for fishing.

SEAWEED

Seaweed, a form of algae, is an excellent source of nutrition. Various species contain incomplete protein, slow-release carbohydrate, iodine, calcium, iron, vitamins A, B complex, C, E and K. However, the amount of protein they contain means that they should not be eaten without a good supply of fresh water. Some of the breeds can be eaten raw, but the varieties found offshore are often too tough to eat straight away. Try, but otherwise it should be wiped free of sea water, sun-dried and crumbled before being eaten.

Seaweed can be found floating in the ocean. Sargasso weed is common in the northwest Atlantic and other species torn from coastal rocks can also be found drifting. It can be caught using casting nets, gaffs, paddles, grapple hooks, and you may find some snared on your sea anchor when you bring it in for maintenance or when sailing.

CRUSTACEA

When you catch seaweed, search it for small shrimp, fish and crabs, which often hitch rides on the drifting weed. These can be eaten straight away. Barnacles will be attached to the underside of the life raft, but they will be difficult to reach. The danger of damaging the life raft while removing them should be seriously considered before using anything sharp. There will also be barnacles attached to the sea anchor line and these can be removed when servicing the sea anchor or sailing.

PLANKTON

Plankton is so rich in nutrients that whales – the world's largest creatures – live off it almost exclusively. It is an excellent source of vitamin C, carbohydrate, protein and fat, and is effortless to catch. It is found predominantly at the confluence or cold and warm currents and where continental submarine profiles cause different layers of water to mix. Wherever whales are found, plankton is plentiful.

During the day, plankton is too deep to catch but at night it will be abundant at the surface and easily caught. Your sea anchor is a perfect plankton trap and you can also use any woven fabric towed behind the life raft overnight to trap plankton. It smells extremely unpleasant, but it is an excellent source of many nutrients and as such a boon for the survivor.

CHAPTER SEVEN

Attracting rescue

Passing ships and aircraft offer a chance of rescue, but not a guarantee. While survival remains your overriding priority, rescue represents its successful conclusion and every chance to bring your mission to an end should be taken – but always remain realistic.

When sailing across oceans, the sailor will become accustomed to barren horizons stripped of any trace of humanity or civilization. Seabirds, dolphins and whales bring exciting reminders that life extends beyond the shore, but their presence is usually fleeting and the sailor is soon alone again. Imagine, then, the excitement of seeing a ship. Sailors on yachts stare transfixed as a large craft rises over one horizon and dips behind another, and may even attempt to make contact as it arcs by, using a radio check as a pretext.

If sighting a ship is exciting for sailors on seaworthy yachts, it is a hundred times more so for survivors in a life raft. Life at sea is primitive, uncomfortable and potentially brief; ships represent opulence and, most importantly, safety - an end to your survival ordeal. On sighting a ship, the euphoric anticipation of rescue will soon turn to confusion as the ship makes no change in its

Keeping a lookout

Make sure you are dressed appropriately for the conditions, not forgetting your PFD and harness, and that you have the signalling equipment you need close at hand. Use your eyes, ears and nose to detect signs of shipping, aircraft or land. You should also conduct a visual maintenance check on the life raft and its equipment.

heading, frustration as you realize you have not been seen, and to disbelief an finally, despair as it steams over the horizon, trailing your hopes, still unseen, in its wake.

This harrowing experience is well known to survivors in life rafts. Modern navigational equipment and the resulting reduced emphasis on watchkeeping makes it almost more likely that you will be run down rather than rescued by passing ships. The survivor soon learns to appreciate that, while she is looking at a ship - several thousand tons of painted steel - she is floating in a small hexagon of rubber and air. At distances over 3 km (2 miles), even a good watchkeeper would struggle to spot such a small object.

You should certainly attempt to make your presence known to the ship's bridge, but you should also be prepared for the probability that you will not be seen. Don't let frustration lead to desperation and cause you to fire off too many flares in the hope of being seen. Once a ship has passed, it has passed - even the best watchkeepers won't be looking astern.

Experience has shown time and again that cargo ships, tankers and cruise ships will be highly unlikely to notice a life raft. Most sea survivors have been rescued by fishermen. The Baileys and the Robertsons were saved by deep-sea fishermen, from Korea and Japan respectively, while Poon

Lim and Steve Callahan were rescued by coastal fishermen. The reason for this is that most ships are simply charged with getting from port A to port B safely and economically. Routeing charts will have been examined and a passage punched into the GPS, weather information will arrive via satellite communication, and a DSC VHF watch is obligatory. But otherwise, the ship's crew will be expecting an uneventful passage.

Fishermen on the other hand are highly vigilant. Despite the use of modern innovations, such as side-scanning sonar equipment, locating fish still relies heavily on educated guesswork. After years of experience, trawler skippers will begin to rely on their intuition and this will be influenced by the conditions around them: the weather; clouds, sea state, time of day, water temperature, presence of seabirds and other signs of marine life. All of these indicators are outside the bridge, scattered as far as the horizon. For this reason your life raft stands a much greater chance of being spotted. It is still just a chance, however. As survivors, your lives are in your own hands and you cannot rely on others for rescue.

WATCHKEEPING

As life raft skipper, you will have devised a watch system soon after abandoning ship. Watches should not last longer than two hours because concentration levels drop

Hand signals

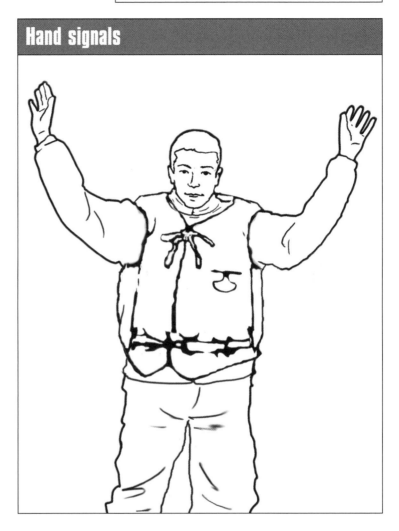

after that period and vital rescue opportunities may be lost.

The watchkeeper should be appropriately dressed for the conditions outside to avoid exposure. As he will be sitting on the buoyancy chamber at the life raft entrance, he should be wearing both PFD and harness to avoid falling overboard, or to prevent drowning if he does go overboard. Scan the horizon through 360° regularly, looking for ships, their lights at night, or smoke from the funnels, which could indicate a ship's approach before it is visible. Keep the binoculars close to hand to

Global Maritime Distress and Safety System (GMDSS)

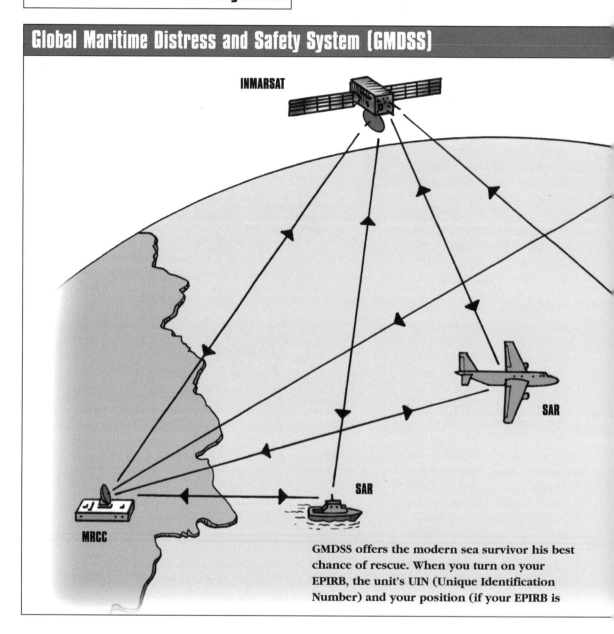

INMARSAT

SAR

SAR

MRCC

GMDSS offers the modern sea survivor his best chance of rescue. When you turn on your EPIRB, the unit's UIN (Unique Identification Number) and your position (if your EPIRB is

verify a possible ship sighting, but remember when using them to use the lanyard, otherwise you risk losing them over the side.

While on watch during the day, you should also conduct a visual maintenance check on the outside of the life raft. Check the chambers and the grab ropes, any fishing lines that are deployed, that the sea anchor is still deployed and has not been lost, and look for any seaweed or floating debris. If there is a school of fish nearby, notify the skipper to arrange a fishing detail. Likewise, if you see a bank of cumulonimbus cloud approaching from windward or a low grey scud of

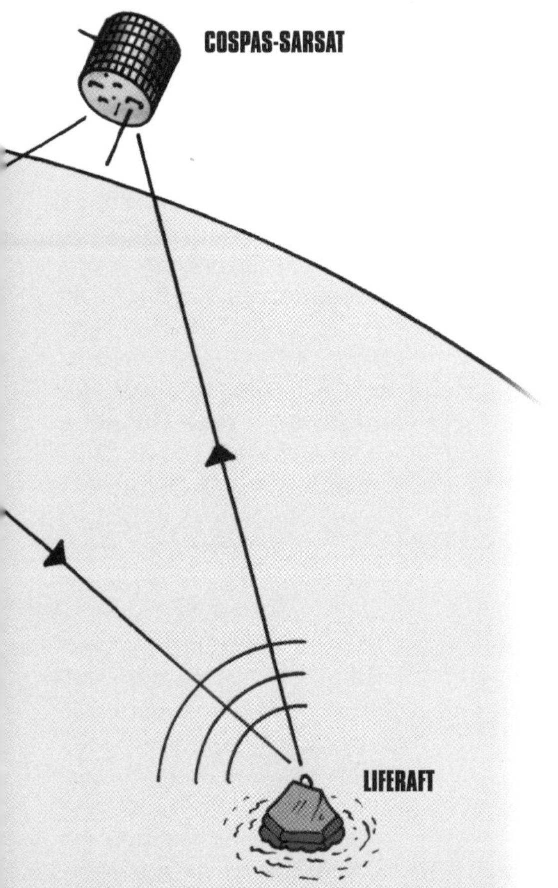

COSPAS-SARSAT

LIFERAFT

fitted with a GPS transmitter) will be transmitted via one of two satellite networks to a shore-based MRCC (Marine Rescue and Coordination Centre) within 5 minutes.

If conditions do not allow the watchkeeper to maintain a 360° watch outside - it is too rough or too hot to sit outside - the watchkeeper should use the observation port in the life raft canopy to monitor the situation outside in rough weather, or look out 360° every 10 minutes in hot weather.

To prevent any unnecessary waste of signalling equipment and damage to morale from unrealistic expectations, the life raft skipper should make his crew aware that, while every chance should be taken, they should never expect to be spotted. Instigate a plan of action on sighting a vessel and brief the watchkeepers on what procedures to follow and how to signal effectively. The entire crew should know where signalling equipment is stored, how and when to use it and, more importantly, when to stop using it. The entire crew will also need to know the EPIRB operation schedule in use at any given time and be given clear instructions about when it should be switched on and, more importantly, when it should be switched off to conserve battery life.

EPIRB

If poor watchkeeping is the downside of technology at sea, then the EPIRB (Emergency Position Indicating Radio Beacon) is unquestionably the upside. The EPIRB works using the GMDSS (Global Maritime Distress and Safety System), and GMDSS represents the biggest step forward in technologically assisted rescue at sea since radio was invented. Guglielmo Marconi, an Italian engineer, invented radio communication in 1895. Fewer than five years later, on 3 March 1899, a freighter rammed the East Goodwin Lightship anchored 16 km (10 miles) off Deal in Kent on the southeast coast of England. Radio was used to send a message to a shore station at nearby South Foreland and help was dispatched immediately.

nimbostratus, inform the skipper and deploy water collection equipment. At night, you may feel rain approaching, sense a drop in temperature or a change in the wind, and notice that it is getting darker very quickly, with the horizons and the stars becoming obscured.

EPIRB

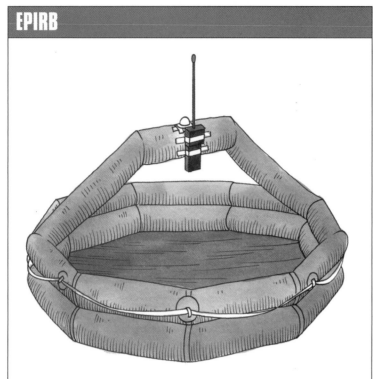

The EPIRB should be mounted inside the life raft, taped onto the canopy arch tube, with the aerial deployed vertically. Tape over the strobe light for the comfort of those within the life raft until it is needed to help rescue to home in.

Little changed in terms of raising the alarm until the 1960s, when it became clear that satellites could play a huge role in sending distress signals. In 1976, the International Maritime Satellite Organization was launched (INMARSAT) to provide emergency satellite communications for distressed vessels. As technology advanced and became more efficient, GMDSS was adopted by the IMO's member states and by 1992, the system was ready to be phased in. All ships built after February 1995 were required to be fitted with GMDSS-compliant equipment and all vessels over 300 tons (295 tonnes), plus certain classes of passenger and fishing vessels, had to be GMDSS-compliant by 1999. Almost 100 years to the day after radio saved its first lives at sea, mariners could rely on a system which would ensure that, no matter where they found themselves in distress, their plight would be known.

The EPIRB with built-in GPS is undoubtedly your single most important piece of signalling equipment. It has a range of 370 km (200 miles) to reach the satellite networks monitoring the 406MHz (COSPAS-SARSAT) or the 1.6GHz (INMARSAT) frequencies. If the EPIRB in your grab bag is well maintained, has a working battery and is fitted with a GPS receiver and transmitter, you can be almost certain that, when it is correctly operated and deployed, your UIN (Unique Identification Number) and location will be flashing on a screen in a MRCC somewhere in the world within five minutes, probably three.

The device is battery operated, however. Once the battery is flat, you have no way of helping SAR to home in on your exact location. Like everything else in a life raft, battery use should be rationed and always make sure that there is some power left. Battery life will be extended considerably if you operate your EPIRB at regular intervals – by turning it on and off. This has the added effect of letting MRCC know that yours is not a signal received from an EPIRB that has been knocked overboard by a wave, but rather indicates sea survivors alive and waiting to be rescued.

Battery life is regulated by the IMO to be at least 24 hours at a temperature of -20°C (-4°F), and you should always assume that this is how long it will last – the worst case scenario. Your battery should last up to twice as long at 0°C(32°F), and four or five times longer at temperate or tropical temperatures – but don't rely on this longevity. During the first 24 hours, the EPIRB should be switched on for two hours, then off for two hours. Thereafter, it should be used for one hour in every four. In cold climates, this schedule means that your EPIRB should work for 72 hours but, since you will need some reserve battery life, you should adjust the schedule. Switch on the EPIRB for two hours in every four for the first 12 hours, then one hour in every four for the next 36 hours. You will have been transmitting your position and indicating that you are still alive for 48 hours in total, having used 15 hours of battery life.

After that, you will need to become even more conservative in its use. Drop it to 30 minutes in every four hours, or perhaps just 10 minutes, but keep the schedule regular so that SAR can work out your transmission schedule and time their arrival to coincide with transmission. If there are no signs of rescue after

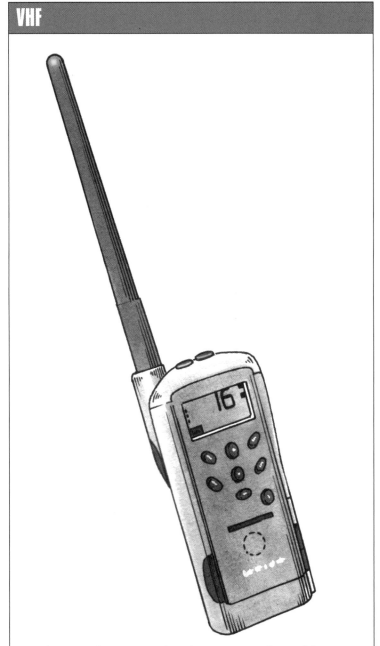

VHF

VHF (Very High Frequency) radio is commonly used for routine and emergency maritime communications. DSC (Digital Selective Calling) VHF also features a Distress button that, when operated, automatically alerts all DSC receivers in range of your MMSI (Mobile Maritime Service Identity).

Using your VHF

VHF waves travel in straight lines, so you need to see the recipient's aerial at least. DSC signals, transmitted digitally, are received complete even at the limits of operating range, unlike analog signals, used for voice contact. So even of your DSC distress alert has been received, it is possible that voice contact will not be possible.

72 hours, no aircraft flying low in your area, you will need to drop the schedule again, say to 30 minutes at a set GMT time each day.

The EPIRB represents your best chance of rescue. For that reason, a second handheld PLB (Personal Locator Beacon), again with built in GPS, is a hugely important addition to your grab bag. This technology is still quite expensive, but if you decide not to purchase it, you will find yourself with plenty of time in the life raft to wonder if the money you saved was better spent.

DSC VHF

Digital Selective Calling (DSC) is another innovation brought in by GMDSS. In non-emergency situations it can be used, as its name suggests, to contact an individual recipient - or recipients - by using their unique MMSI number, thus avoiding a broadcast to all receivers in the area. It does not use the satellite constellations, but instead standard VHF broadcasting. Rather than transmitting via an analog signal however, over which voice calls are usually broadcast, it sends a pulse of digital information containing your vessel's MMSI, a call type (routine in everyday use), and your position on Channel 70. The selected receiver bleeps until answered, and voice contact can then be made using an agreed working channel.

In emergency use, a button on the unit is depressed, instantly sending out your MMSI, a Mayday call type, the time, and your position (if the unit is interfaced with your GPS unit) on Channel 70. All receivers in the area – other yachts, ships, even a coastal station if within range – will bleep until your call is acknowledged. Voice contact will be made on Channel 16 (156.8MHz), the internationally recognized distress channel, or Channel 13, now designated the bridge-to-bridge communications channel.

There are handheld DSC VHF units. They will have an MMSI but, as the unit is likely to be used on various different craft – the life raft in this case – the number will be misleading in terms of the vessel's identity. Transferable MMSI numbers are being introduced so that SAR services do not spend their time looking for the wrong craft. However, unless these handheld units are connected to a GPS unit, the position must be entered manually using buttons that are far too small for fingers numbed by cold. Soon manufacturers should be able to provide these handheld DSC VHF units with a built-in GPS receiver to make the position programming superfluous and the positional information accurate. Without positional information, the VHF broadcasts a Distress Alert to all receivers in the area, but voice communication must be used to give position.

These DSC units can be used if a ship or other vessel is sighted. If you can see the craft, you can be confident that your Distress

Using smoke canisters

During daylight, rescue can be attracted using smoke canisters. These are more effective in light winds and for helping aerial SAR services to home in on your position.

Alert will be received and that voice contact can be established. The craft's DSC VHF will bleep with your Distress Alert, and voice communication can be established on Channel 16 and your position given – either latitude and longitude or a position relative to the craft if you are unable to give an exact position. This should bring an end to the crushing experience of watching the sterns of potential rescuers sailing over the horizon, but it does rely on an alert signals officer on watch onboard the passing ship. If your Distress Alert is not acknowledged while the craft is still in VHF range, it is unlikely that voice contact can be made.

If shipping is seen, alert the life raft skipper at once. Then switch on your GPS and DSC VHF. Ensure the DSC VHF is switched to full power and send a Distress Alert by pressing the red distress button. Follow up your Alert straightaway with a Mayday call and identify yourself as the life raft, giving your distance and position relative to the ship. For example:

- Mayday Mayday Mayday
- This is life raft off your port quarter, life raft off your port quarter, life raft off your port quarter
- Mayday
- This is life raft off your port quarter
- My position is two miles, repeat two miles, off your port quarter (give latitude and longitude if you have accurate readings from your GPS)
- I am adrift and in distress
- I have four persons onboard
- I require immediate assistance
- Over

Await a response on Channel 16.

If you have a non-DSC VHF, send the same Mayday message, but send it on Channel 13, the channel now used for bridge-to-bridge communication by shipping. Ships are obliged to maintain a watch on Channel 16 until 2005, but how rigorously this duty is observed before that date is open to question. Other craft will be listening using dual-watch on Channel 16 until 2005, by which time every ocean-going craft will be expected to be GMDSS-compliant. If you have any kind of handheld VHF, check whether it is genuinely waterproof and not just splashproof. If the latter case, the unit should be kept in a waterproof pouch at all times. These pouches also work for handheld GPS units.

The survivor should also bear in mind that VHF range is restricted to line of sight at sea level; 4.8–8 km (3–5 miles) from life raft to yacht; and 8–16 km (5–10 miles) from life raft to ship. But your VHF signal can be received by overflying aircraft at a range of 320 km (200 miles). Most aircraft will be monitoring VHF Channel 16 and can relay your distress call.

You should have replacement batteries for your handheld VHF, but an alternative to these is a portable solar panel. This is mounted on the canopy facing the sun and produces 6V or 12V power for your VHF or GPS units using a cigarette lighter power cord. Make sure that your VHF and GPS batteries are rechargeable and that the units can be powered by one of these voltages.

PYROTECHNICS

Pyrotechnics play an important role in rescues, and this makes them a grab bag essential. But as a signalling device, they are some way less than perfect. The smaller, less expensive and more easily stored ones last only a few seconds and are of limited use in attracting rescue. Larger ones may last for five, even 10 minutes, but they are expensive and bulky and even these have drawbacks. To light stoves or smoke cigarettes in a life raft would be ridiculous, yet one of our primary signalling devices can easily burn a hole in a buoyancy chamber, even if used correctly. However, if VHF is not an option for contacting passing craft, and SAR services are not overflying the area looking for you,

Signalling with a mirror

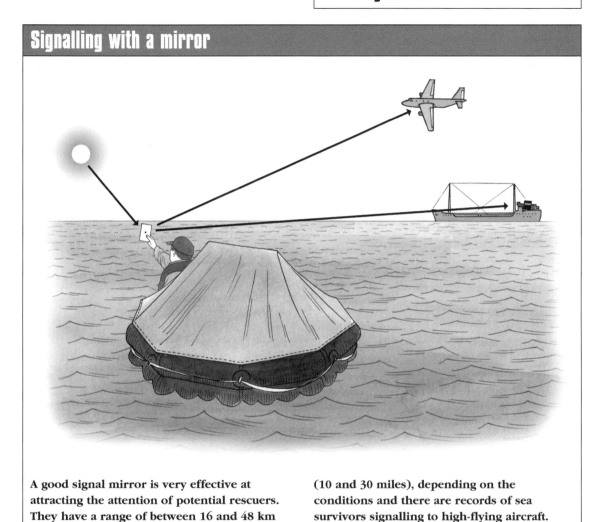

A good signal mirror is very effective at attracting the attention of potential rescuers. They have a range of between 16 and 48 km (10 and 30 miles), depending on the conditions and there are records of sea survivors signalling to high-flying aircraft.

pyrotechnics offer perhaps the best chance you have of being noticed.

Smoke canisters are intended to aid relocation in daylight, but if there is any wind, the smoke will quickly be dispersed. Even from the air, they provide a veiled signal. In light winds, they are more noticeable, but SOLAS approved canisters last for only three minutes. This is why you should load up on flares. Smaller flares requiring a launcher are suitable only for inshore use; they do not last long enough nor burn bright enough for use offshore.

You must ensure that your flares are within their expiry date. Inspect them regularly to make sure they have not been degraded by water. You may also want to vacuum-pack them in plastic to ensure they are kept dry. They are generally kept in a plastic canister with a screw-top lid, and the canister itself is kept in the waterproof grab bag. If your flares are out of date, buy new ones. Don't discard the old ones; provided they have been looked after, they will probably work. It has been said that flares are like blessings - you can't have too many.

As part of your survival training, it would be a good idea to fire some of your out-of-date flares to make sure your crew is familiar with their operation. They are fairly straightforward to use, but the more training you can give your crew, the more confident they will be in using survival equipment. Unless you are in open space well inland and away from any potential fire risks, you will need to notify the local Coastguard and Harbour Authority that you will be training with flares. Better still, enrol your crew on a sea safety course, where they will learn to fire flares, use PFDs, and launch, right and board life rafts.

ATTRACTING RESCUE

Having established VHF contact with another craft, or spotted an SAR vessel or aircraft in your area, flares will be required to help indicate your location. If winds are light, use parachute flares. These will stay airborne for longer, giving your rescuer a better chance of spotting the flare. Stand with your back to the wind and fire downwind slightly, at 10-15° to the vertical – they will turn back into the wind and deploy at a height of 240-300 metres (800-1000 feet). If the cloud is low, fire the flare downwind at 45° to ensure that the flare stays below the cloud base, at 150-210 metres (500-700 feet). If the winds are stronger, a rocket flare will be more useful because it presents less windage. As with all rocket flares, do not fire them at SAR aircraft. Rocket flares are visible for 24-48 km (15-30 miles), depending on the level of the cloud base and on whether anyone is looking your way.

After launching your rocket or parachute flare, deploy a smoke canister (for daylight use only, and preferably in calm or light winds) and activate a red handheld flare. The airborne flare will give potential rescuers

only a rough indication of where to look, and the handheld red flare will help to pinpoint your life raft within that area. These are visible for 8 km (5 miles) in good visibility, but remember to wait until you can see your potential rescuer. If a fixed wing SAR flight has flown past, wait for it to approach again before firing your handheld flare. Exercise extreme caution when using handheld flares. To avoid damaging your life raft, always deploy them from the leeward side and hold them at the base, at arm's length and at an angle of 45°.

An alternative to the pyrotechnic smoke canister is the dye marker. This is a plastic sachet of soluble dye that colours the water, raising visibility from the air during daylight. In calm waters, these remain visible for up to three hours, but they disperse considerably quicker in rough weather. When airborne SAR are searching your area, the streaming marker is a useful rough weather alternative to the dye marker and the smoke canister. This is a floating strip of brightly coloured plastic that is attached to and deployed from the life raft. It has the advantage of posing no risk to your life raft, lasting indefinitely, being reusable and unaffected by strong winds.

ATTRACTING ATTENTION

If you have no VHF, DSC or otherwise, flares can help you to attract rescue. They are considerably more effective on overcast nights, a little less effective on bright cloudless nights, and of little practical use during the day unless the vessel is passing close to you. Remember, it is pointless to fire flares at a ship that is beam-on or heading away from you. You must have a view of the bridge to have any hope that the watch officer will be able to see you. Otherwise, you are simply wasting your flares.

If you have activated your EPIRB, fire one or two flares, a rocket and a handheld red, because it is possible the MRCC has received your EPIRB signal and redirected shipping in

Attracting attention

During daylight, your silver-coloured survival blanket can be waved to catch the sunlight and help SAR services to home in on your position. Alternatively, it could be attached to a paddle and waved higher for increased visibility.

the area to search for you. In that case, a more thorough lookout should be in operation and your flares stand a much greater chance of being noticed.

Heliograph

In bright conditions, the signal mirror, or heliograph, is the best method of attracting attention. It has no working parts so, loss or breakage aside, it will always work. The larger

the mirror, the better because it will reflect more of the sun's energy and therefore produce a stronger flash. Glass mirrors provide the best reflection, although there are some excellent plastic ones available that are a near-match in performance. The steel ones tend to distort and thick ones are very heavy, and all steel will corrode to some extent, reducing the reflective surface. The reflection from a good quality mirror,

10 x 12.5 cm (4 x 5inches), will be easily visible for 16 km (10 miles) at least, 4 8km (30 miles) in good conditions. Survivors have signalled high flying aircraft with mirrors.

Authentic heliographs have a reflective aiming spot mounted in a hole in the centre of the mirror. These make aiming easier, but it is not difficult to aim your reflection. Hold the mirror just below eye level with one hand and hold the other hand in front of you, in the general direction of the target you wish to signal.

Move the mirror until the sun's reflection hits your hand, then move your hand so it is aimed directly at the target and move the mirror so that the reflection follows your hand. Move your aiming hand away and wiggle the mirror very slowly and slightly so that the reflection moves up and down and side to side by very small degrees. This is another survival art that can be practised and perfected by you and your crew before a survival situation develops.

Whatever mirror you end up taking, make sure it has a secure lanyard attachment to prevent loss. If you lose your mirror, remember there is another in the life raft survival kit. If you lose that too, you can improvise, although the results will be far less impressive. There are mirrors on your sextant (but do not dismantle it), or use the lid of a tin can, a section or survival blanket wrapped tightly around something flat, the blade of a highly polished knife, and even a credit card hologram.

Whistle/Foghorn

These will be of no use whatever for attracting aircraft, but if SAR vessels are on location searching for you, they will be listening as closely as possible (but note that various power plants and generators will be operating). A good whistle blast can be heard for up to 3 km (2 miles), not quite so far in foggy conditions, but it will make a sound considerably greater than you could manage with shouting or any other technique and it requires very little effort to operate. It is light and small, so you should carry one, in addition to the one attached to your PFD, in your pocket kit.

Flashlight

In a mid-ocean survival situation, it is probable that the batteries powering the strobe light on your PFD and life raft will have expired. Strobe lights are of limited use over larger distances because their light, intense and blinding at close range, is diffused over a wide area. A carefully aimed flashlight is considerably more effective, particularly the survival models that allow you to focus the beam. You should use the international distress signal SOS in Morse code – flash three short beams, three long beams and three short beams.

When using a flashlight, you will need to listen with great care to discern the direction from which potential rescue is approaching and then play the beam very slowly over that area. Generally, the vessel's lights will make them visible to you long before you are visible to them, so turn on your flashlight only when you can see at least the loom of their lights.

In fog, your beam is diffused quickly by the moisture in the air, but the flashlight will create a glowing beam or loom. If rescue is approaching by sea, but you are unsure of the direction, play the beam through 360°, aiming it at 45° like a searchlight. If rescue is approaching from the air, play the beam along the surface of the sea to maximize you visibility and to avoid blinding the pilot with the glare of direct light.

Another way you can improve your visibility from the air is to play your flashlight beam on your sails, if you are sailing. You could also use the flashlight inside the life raft to create a glowing canopy, or attach a survival blanket to the life raft canopy and play your beam on that.

Chemical light sticks

You should have one of these as part of your pocket kit. Once operated, there is no way of turning them off and they are one-use only. The normal intensity light sticks last on average 10 hours and are useful for creating a working light, but they are not useful for attracting attention or rescue. The high intensity light lasts 30 minutes and the very high intensity light last five minutes. Both of these are visible from a distance of 1.6 km (1 mile), the latter more easily when swung about the head on the end of a lanyard. These are useful for MOB situations and can be used instead of a flashlight to attract SAR close by in the area.

INCREASING VISIBILITY

There are several ways to increase your visibility for SAR services, other than those methods already described. Most involve creating something eye-catching to break up the featurelessness of the horizon or the ocean. Most manmade structures involve corners and straight edges. These are very rare in nature, so if you can create those shapes, they will stand out against nature's soft, irregular shapes.

To make your life raft more visible to seaborne SAR services, use your paddle as a flagstaff and attach brightly coloured or regularly shaped material to it using duct tape, hose clips, plastic cable ties or spare line. You will have among your life raft possessions a tarpaulin, a survival blanket, a foul weather jacket, a section of sail or a brightly coloured sleeping bag. Attaching these to your paddle and waving them regularly in the air will make your presence known to anyone who looks your way. Regardless of whether your life raft is visible or not when SAR glances your way – you may be lost in the trough of an ocean swell – this flag will be visible against the uniform ocean backdrop.

For airborne SAR services, you could consider floating a salvaged sail on the surface of the water, using fenders to keep it buoyant if it does not float by itself. You could do the same with a survival blanket and place another on the canopy of the life raft. These will catch the sun and stand out against the ocean's expanse. If there are several life rafts floating tethered together, bring them as close as possible without contact being made to give SAR a larger target to find. If you have any oil, either from turtles or fish, pour this around the life raft to smooth the waters – this will stand out at a distance.

On a calm sea, bouncing hard against the buoyancy chambers from the interior will send out concentric waves from your life raft. These will be small individually but highly visible against the ocean swell as a series of circular waves centred on your life raft. In rough weather, this is not a useful strategy; your waves will be overpowered by the wind-driven waves.

PREPARING FOR RESCUE

Once SAR has made visual contact and has been heading directly for you for at least 20 seconds, prepare the life raft for rescue. Make sure everything inside the life raft is firmly tethered so that nothing tangles with survivors as they exit. Put on and inflate your PFD to avoid drowning should anything go wrong during rescue. Take down sails and masts and bring in all lines, such as fishing lines and sea anchor. Cut free the towing dinghy (but only when you are absolutely sure that you are about to be rescued).

Partially deflate the life raft chambers and partially flood the interior. Both of these measures will improve the stability of the life raft, making the rescue procedure easier. The final measure is to listen carefully to instructions given by the SAR personnel – they are the experts. Do not move unless you are told to do so, remain calm and take one last look around you. Your ordeal is over.

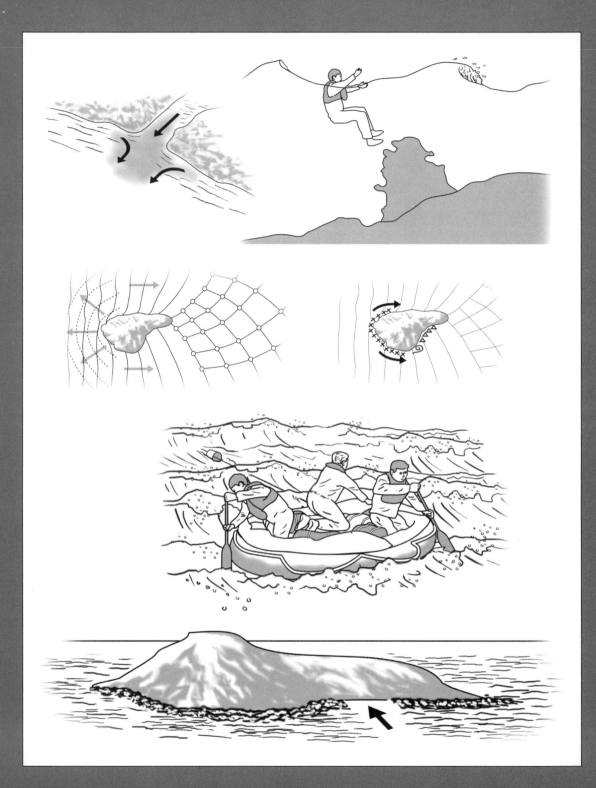

CHAPTER EIGHT

Making landfall

Sooner or later, you will find land, and land means safety. But coasts are killers, and to avoid failing at this final stage of the ordeal, you need to know when, where and how to land.

With the range of signalling devices you have at your disposal, the strong likelihood is that you will be able to raise the alarm. The EPIRB is most likely to aid your swift recovery than any other piece of equipment. Either SAR services will be dispatched or a vessel passing through your area will be re-routed to collect you.

Close to land, but before reaching it, your chances of rescue will increase. Intercontinental shipping routes converge on major and minor coastal ports, and continental traffic uses the coast. Deep sea trawlers operate in oceanic areas where warm currents meet cold and plankton – the bottom link of the oceanic food chain – thrives. These areas are typically near the edge of the continental shelf and, once the trawlers have their catch, they too will converge on ports. Unless you are in Polar regions, you should notice a great increase in the amount of seaborne and airborne traffic as you approach land, and you should always be ready to attract its attention and hasten your rescue.

Naturally, if you are presented with the choice, you will opt to be rescued as soon as possible, but you should be doubly committed as you near the coast because landing your life raft on an unfamiliar shore is not easy. More mariners meet their fate dashed on the border of land and sea than in the open wilderness of the ocean. Any sailor will tell you that the worst situation they can possibly envisage is finding themselves without steerage in a gale and being driven onto a rock-strewn or reef-lined lee shore – and this is a fair comparison with your situation. You may be delighted to see land once again after so long in the wet, featureless expanse of the ocean, but your joy – indeed you and your crew – could be short-lived.

NAVIGATING TOWARDS LAND

With sextant, GPS and charts, you will be able to work out your exact position daily. You will know how the wind and currents are affecting your progress and, as you near land, you will be able to work out where you are likely to land and what awaits you when you do. Even without these navigational tools, you will be able to locate your approximate position using the navigational methods already described (see Chapter Four). However, these methods will be too approximate to ascertain either what your likely landing will be or, unless you are heading for a continental landmass, that you will make landfall at all. You should make every effort to attract the attention of any passing vessel or aircraft, because the chance of guaranteeing a landing on an island 16 km (10 miles) long when your navigation is accurate only to 480 km (300 miles) is not great.

There are many indicators of land, and these will be of varying use depending on

your equipment. If you can erect a mast and fly a sail on a salvaged dinghy, you can tow your life raft in directions other than that dictated solely by the wind and currents. If you have rigged a rudder and leeboard, you can technically sail to windward, but the ballast bags on the life raft mean that it is unlikely you will be able to do better than to 'beam reach', or sail directly across the wind. Without a dinghy, your landfall will be largely decided for you.

PRIMARY INDICATORS OF LAND

Your watchkeepers should be briefed to keep an eye out for the following indicators of land:

Driftwood, vegetation and garbage

Keep an eye out for floating objects. Most beaches are strewn with all sorts of flotsam and jetsam. Just as the waves deposit seaborne detritus on the windward side, so can they set landborne detritus adrift from the leeward side. If you notice types of seaweed that you have not encountered before, or tree branches with foliage still attached, coconuts or palm fronds, an island probably lies windward. The fresher the vegetation looks, the closer land will be. Keep a particularly keen eye open for vegetation after a storm has passed, because wind will have stripped the island's leeward side of a fair proportion of its foliage.

Another indicator is garbage. While most sailors will be downcast at the sight of man's clutter littering the oceans, you should take it as a sign that there is land to windward, although it is possible that this litter has been dumped illegally by a passing ship. Plastic tends to form the majority of our floating garbage – bottles, bags, and sheets – but just one or two floating items do not indicate land nearby. If you can see 10 or 20 items around your life raft, that is a positive sign that land lies to windward. If possible, grab one of the plastic bags because this will carry some indication of where it came from: the language on cartons and other packaging, a phone number, even an address. If you have no precise navigational tools, this will enable you to work out where you are and where the wind and currents might land you.

Disturbed wave patterns

During your survival period, you will become accustomed to the oceanic swell and possibly even rely on it for steering, so regular is its direction. Any deviation from this steady pattern of rolling swells will be noticeable very quickly because your ride

will become considerably less comfortable. As swell passes an island, it 'refracts', or bends around it, producing a characteristic pattern of wave interaction in the lee of the island. At the nodes where wave crests combine, a larger wave peak will be seen, and a deeper trough where troughs combine, and two swell patterns will be discernable on the water's surface. The angle that bisects the approach of these two patterns indicates approximately the direction in which the island lies.

Also noticeable will be the absence of any swell from its previous direction as this will be blocked by the island.

Wave interference

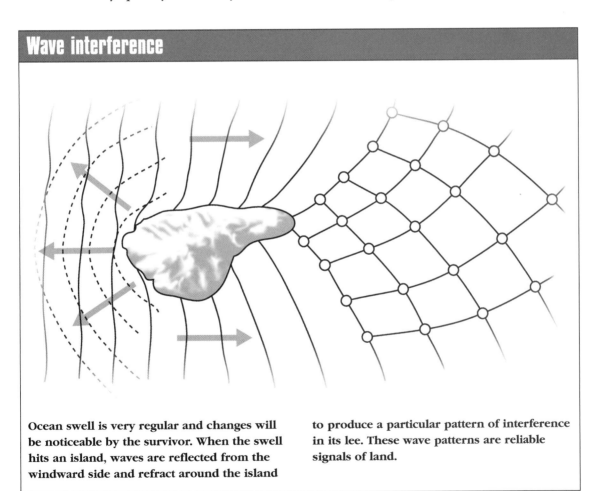

Ocean swell is very regular and changes will be noticeable by the survivor. When the swell hits an island, waves are reflected from the windward side and refract around the island to produce a particular pattern of interference in its lee. These wave patterns are reliable signals of land.

Relationship between wind and waves

In open ocean, wave height is influenced by the strength of the wind, the length of time it has been blowing, and the 'fetch' – the uninterrupted distance over which the wind blows. If the wind picks up steadily over the course of a few hours, but the wave heights remain unaffected, this indicates that there is land to windward, which shelters this area of ocean and reduces the fetch.

Terrestrial odour

Your sense of smell will have become accustomed to the somewhat pungent odour given off by you, your crew and the various stores of fish, seaweed, plankton and oils. Unfamiliar odours will, therefore, be very strong in your nostrils and immediately alert you to something new.

The smell of oil, paint and burned fuel may indicate a passing ship. Coastal swamps, mud flats, city pollution, industry, agriculture, even soil and vegetation will be detectable for many miles downwind. These will be most apparent at night, when the land breeze is blowing offshore. The smell will be unmistakable and the source will be directly upwind.

Sound

Sound carries well over water, especially at night, when hearing improves and you are downwind of the sound's source. Hearing becomes sharper still when the survivor is lacking food or water. Your auditory system will begin to filter out the more familiar sounds generated by your life raft and your crew, allowing you to hear other noises. This could be the throb of a ship's engines, the quiet roar of a major city; the pounding of industry, music from hotels or nightclubs, or, more unsettlingly, the sound of surf crashing over a reef.

Take time to make sure the sound source is definite and distinguishable and locate the direction of the sound.

SECONDARY INDICATORS OF LAND

Without any influence over your direction of travel, you will need to watch out for indicators of land elsewhere, other than to windward.

Air and sea traffic

One of the first indications of a nearby landmass is increased air and sea traffic. As well as converging oceanic traffic, you will find a proliferation of small-scale commercial fishing vessels and leisure craft. Most coastal inhabitants will make a living from the sea and the smaller coastal towns and villages that proliferate on continental shores are generally reliant on the fishing industry. Larger coastal towns will attract short-range cargo traffic in the form of coastal steamers to service small industrial operations, in addition to fishing. Coastal cities will have major, well-established ports frequented by cargo traffic from around the world, and probably an international airport. All these will provide you with indications of nearby land and you will notice a marked increase in VHF traffic.

Orographic cloud

This type of cloud occurs where warm, moist maritime air is driven upwards by mountainous coastal topography. As the air rises, it cools and the moisture condenses into clouds that hang over the coastal feature. Two well-known examples are the 'table cloth' that lies over Cape Town's Table Mountain and the 'Levanter cloud' that hangs above the rock of Gibraltar when the easterly Levanter wind blows through the Straits.

Any mountainous island will tend to be capped with orographic cloud, generally of the stratus type. They can be distinguished from other types because they don't move. The wind sweeping in from the ocean rises, cools and condenses, while the air that sinks behind the mountain warms, vaporizing the moisture once more and dissipating the

Orographic cloud

Mountainous islands are often capped with orographic clouds. These occur when moist air from the sea is driven up by the mountains, cooling with altitude and condensing the moisture. Other clouds move with the wind but these appear stationary.

cloud. The air is moving across the mountain top, but the cloud itself appears stationary.

Lightning

Particularly in the tropics, you should watch for lightning flashing through cloud cover. Lightning is not unusual in mid-ocean, but these storms always move on. If you see lightning that remains active in the same sector of your horizon for some time, it is likely that this is caused by coastal mountain ranges 'earthing' cumulonimbus anvil-headed thunderclouds, acting like conductors for the electricity stored in these clouds.

Birds

The kinds of seabirds that spend weeks on the wing are generally solitary creatures and you will rarely see more than one or two in the same patch of sky. If you see many birds unlike those you have seen at sea, the chances are that you are less than 160 km (100 miles) from land. As a rule of thumb, birds will fly out on fishing trips in the morning and return to their roosts on the island before dusk – their range is seldom more than 160 km (100 miles).

That said, some land birds become lost or blown off course. These will land on your life raft to rest and will probably die of exhaustion later. Such birds tend to be alone, however, and therefore indicate nothing more positive than a small meal for you and your crew.

Rougher ride

If you notice a gradual change from the smoother, longer wavelengths of open ocean to shorter, steeper waves without any increase in wind, this change could be caused by a dramatic reduction in the depth of water – you are now over the continental shelf. Shallower water means shorter wavelengths. In turn, this means that the spare kinetic energy of the wave pattern freed up by the shorter wavelength is used instead to pile up the wave to a greater height, possibly even breaking waves if the reduction in depth is great enough.

Another more obvious indication of a reduction in water depth is a change in water colour. Water at sea is either deep blue or deep green, depending on the cloud cover. If these shades lighten, that is a sure indicator of shallower water. However, it is worth remembering that these wavelength indicators mean only that land is nearby; they do not mean that you are heading for land. Unless and until you have made visual contact with land, you cannot be sure that you are not just passing over an oceanic ridge or across a curve in the continental shelf.

If the water becomes light brown, pale red or some other unusual colour, this indicates that you are near the estuary of a river, and that the discoloration is the result of silt or pollution. The silt washed out by the Amazon colours the water for hundreds of miles beyond its mouth. Bear in mind that water flows out of a river mouth and that, as a consequence, you are probably being swept further out to sea. Attempt to sail with the prevailing wind at right angles to the outflow to avoid the worst of the flood.

Sea and land breezes

If your watchkeepers, or your log, reports that there are regular changes in the breeze – one direction during the day, peaking in strength between 1500 and 1700 local time, and the exact opposite direction at night, peaking at between 0300 and 0500 – this could suggest land. It will certainly frustrate sailing attempts until you recognize, accommodate and use the pattern to your advantage, but it does suggest that land lies in the direction the wind blows during the day.

Land warms and cools more quickly than sea water and in sunny conditions, this sets up convection currents. The land heats during the day, warming the air above it and making it rise and lowering atmospheric pressure over the land. Cooler air above the ocean moves towards land to equalize the pressure differential, and this is a sea breeze. At night, land cools more quickly than the sea. The warmer air over the sea rises and cooler air from the land equalizes the pressure, and this is a land breeze. The presence of both means land is less than 32 km (20 miles) away. In tropical areas, the convection current can influence wind direction beyond that limit.

In the case of larger landmasses in the tropics, you will be able to sail towards land by harnessing the onshore sea breezes that will build throughout the early afternoon, then dropping sail as night falls and deploying your sea anchor over the bow to protect your gains. If you can hold your position in the lee of land, it is simply a matter of time before some traffic passes by and comes to your rescue.

Lagoon glare

The cloud base reflects a degree of the light reflected by the surface beneath it. For this reason, lagoons or icebergs – indeed, any area of a colour markedly different to its surrounding area – show up on the cloud base above the area. Tropical lagoons are pale circles of turquoise in an otherwise deep blue sea and this will be reflected as a slight green tinge on the cloud base above the lagoon. Icebergs will show up on a grey cloud base as an almost luminous area of bright light.

Loom

At night, islands and coastal towns will be illuminated. This light pollution illuminates the cloud or air pollution above the town and can be seen up to 16 km (10 miles) long before the lights themselves can be seen - even further if you are closing on a major coastal city. Some islands have lighthouses, and the loom of their beam can be seen pulsing over the horizon up to 32 km (20 miles) away if atmospheric conditions are right. The direction of any light source will be unmistakable, but make sure the source is genuinely manmade and not a bright star on the horizon.

Mirages

Even though senses are sharper in the undernourished or dehydrated survivor, the sea, like the land, can play tricks on fatigued senses, particularly in the heat of a tropical afternoon. If you believe you have detected an unfamiliar sight, sound or smell indicating a landmass, alter your perspective to see if the source persists. If you are not absolutely sure, ask another survivor to check the source, bearing in mind that they will need to adjust to the ambient sights and sounds before they can confirm or scotch your perceptions.

Your signalling equipment must always be tethered close to the life raft entrance, safe in your grab bag or, in the case of the signal mirror and whistle, attached to your PFD. If you think you have spotted a ship or an aircraft, you will need to operate that equipment immediately before your target moves beyond any reasonable chance of contact.

PREPARING TO LAND

As with every other aspect of survival at sea, preparation is critical to success. Begin preparing as soon as you have spotted land. With accurate navigational tools, you will know where you are likely to land and your

charts will provide you with some detail of the coastal profile. It is unlikely that you will have detailed charts showing reefs, rocks and shoals, but it should show areas sheltered from the prevailing breeze, and these will make your landing easier. Resist the temptation to take to the sturdier dinghy for landing because it will become swamped by the surf and leave you and your crew in the water tethered to the dinghy and extremely vulnerable to injury as the waves roll in. The life raft's buoyancy chambers are much less threatening in the event of a capsize and, even if the life raft disintegrates, the remains of the raft will still provide you and your crew with enough buoyancy to stay afloat.

As you near land, you will be busier than ever. Neither rescue nor landing are assured and you will still need your survival supplies if you land on an uninhabited island - gather them together. Look, too, for potential rescuers and be prepared to signal to them. Rescue at this stage will avoid the treacherous business of trying to land the life raft. Also, you will be taken to a populated area of the island, and this could save you a long walk for which you will be desperately unfit, as well deeply unenthusiastic.

During your survey, look for any signs of civilization inland - radio masts on the hill tops, settlements and roads - and make a mental note of their location relative to your landing zone. Once you have landed, your view of the interior will be limited by the vegetation skirting the beach, and these landmarks will not be visible.

LOOKING FOR TROUBLE

Gauge your approach speed. If it looks like you will arrive at the island during the night, use the devices you have at your disposal - sea anchor, life raft inflation, dinghy, paddles - to make sure you arrive in daylight. This will give you a much better chance of spotting and avoiding potential dangers and

Finding a landing zone

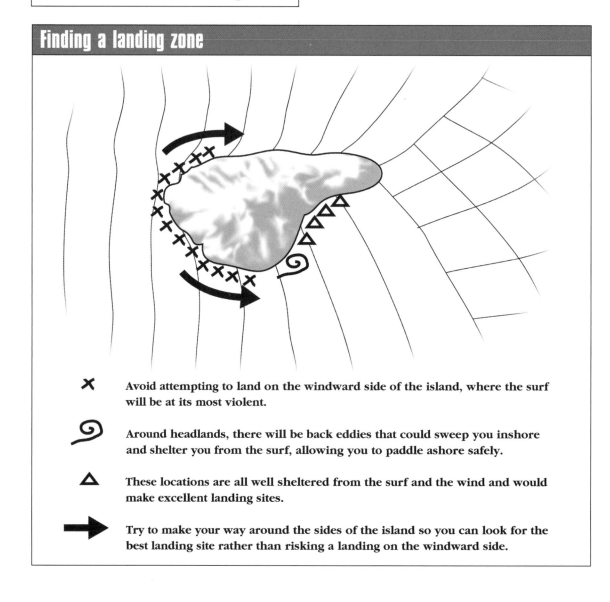

✗   Avoid attempting to land on the windward side of the island, where the surf will be at its most violent.

◯   Around headlands, there will be back eddies that could sweep you inshore and shelter you from the surf, allowing you to paddle ashore safely.

△   These locations are all well sheltered from the surf and the wind and would make excellent landing sites.

➡   Try to make your way around the sides of the island so you can look for the best landing site rather than risking a landing on the windward side.

being rescued. For the same reason, avoid landing when the sun is low and in your eyes.

CHOOSE YOUR LANDING ZONE

Don't head directly for the land nearest to you. If you are heading for an island, do not head for the nearest promontory because the current will drive you ashore, regardless of what lies in wait and your efforts to avoid it. Either side of this promontory, the current will split around the island, taking you with it, and this will allow you to survey the island for suitable landing locations. If you are close enough to the island, this current will eventually bring you to the shore, but you must select a good landing zone and, more importantly, avoid dangerous ones.

If you are heading for a continental landmass, currents will take you along the coast and these will allow you to survey the coastline looking for a good landing zone. Be ready to act when you spot one.

Settlements

The best possible landing location is a port or harbour because its approach will have been dredged (waves rarely break in deep water); it will be free of reefs; and its location will have been chosen with a view to its position, sheltered from the incoming waves. It will also be inhabited and this means there will be regular traffic in and out, which increases your chances of rescue before landing. This means you will not have to forage for food and water once ashore, medical attention will be available, and there will be transport links and communications to spread the news of your epic voyage to those who fear your loss.

Reefs

Listen carefully for the roar of surf. If you appear to be heading directly for the source of that sound, or you can see a barrier of breaking waves some distance away from the shore, make every effort to alter your heading. Most tropical islands are surrounded by reefs. If you are approaching from windward, your life raft will be torn apart on the reef and you will probably suffer a similar fate, regardless of what you are wearing. Strong winds will seal your fate as the waves they generate will pound you on to the reef. Even if you survive the reef's mauling, the blood will attract sharks, you will be too dehydrated to replace lost plasma, and the potential for serious infection from reef cuts is considerable. In short, you should try to avoid reefs.

Most inhabited islands will have cleared a navigable passage through the reef. This channel will be indicated by posts; if not, a break in the surf will indicate its presence. These gaps will never be to windward of the island as they would destroy the shelter of the lagoon, so do not waste time looking for them there. Get around the sides of the island and approach from leeward.

Cliffs

Cliffs generally indicate a rocky shoreline, and this will make for an uncomfortable and dangerous landing if there is any wind. You could also land to find yourself cut off from the rest of the island and be forced to take to the sea again. If you rest below a

Finding a passage

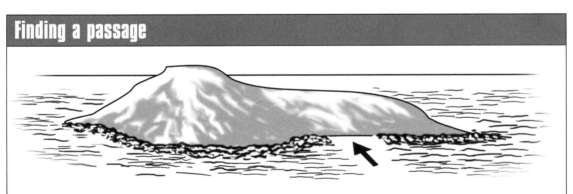

Many islands, particularly in the South Pacific, are in shallow lagoons sheltered by a surrounding reef. If the island is inhabited, there will be a navigable path through the reef into the lagoon and this will be indicated by a gap, possibly marked with posts, in the ring of surf breaking over the reef. Look for this on the leeward side of the island.

Landing in a river mouth

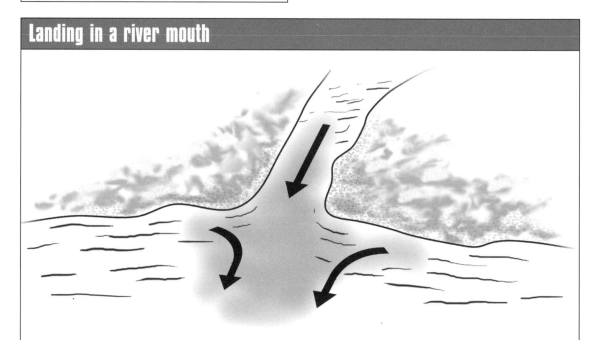

Smaller rivers will always be outward-flowing and coral doesn't grow in fresh water so the area will be free of reefs. Don't try to fight against the current, paddle your raft to one **side and approach the shore. Larger, estuarine river mouths will be tidal, so if you are swept in, make your way to the bank before the tide changes or you may be swept back out again.**

windward cliff too long, the wind may pick up and huge waves will thrash the beach on which you have landed. Obviously, relaunching will not now be an option. For all these reasons, cliffs are best avoided.

Rocks

Unless the sea is flat calm, surf will break on rocks with varying degrees of violence. Most sedimentary rocks on exposed coasts will have been beaten smooth over the aeons, and igneous ones unevenly eroded into a mass of cutting surfaces.

Both present you with little chance of gaining a firm hold on them in the first instance, and a great chance of severe injury, even death, in the second. You could be pulled out to sea again and bounced along the coast. Even an able-bodied strong swimmer would

have trouble coping with this, but you will be weakened by sea survival and even more prone to being knocked unconscious, and your shredded PFD will not prevent you from drowning.

If there is no choice but to land on rocks, choose an area where the waves rush up the rocks smoothly rather than exploding off them in a fountain of spray.

Sand

This is the best possible landing surface, relatively soft and forgiving. Look for long gently sloping beaches with a large expanse of turquoise for some distance beyond the shoreline, or very small waves rolling towards shore, as these indicate a shallow gentle slope.

Avoid steeply shelving beaches, those

with dark water and large waves right up to the shoreline, because the waves will break very suddenly when they reach that shelf, capsizing the life raft and stubbing it into the shelf of rocks or reef.

Such beaches are also swept by strong seaward rip currents once large waves have broken on the shore, and you could be towed out into the breaking surf and bounced off the shore repeatedly.

Surf

Waves will be breaking on the shore right around the island. But there are waves – and there are waves. In a stiff breeze the surf will roll higher and break earlier on a windward shore, dramatically increasing the chances of your life raft capsizing. The sea anchor deployed over the stern should prevent your life raft being flipped over by the surf, but if a breaking wave dumps tons of water on top of your life raft, capsize and serious damage are almost inevitable.

In sheltered locations, or in light winds, you can ride surf to the shore quite safely and with a minimum of effort. However, avoid areas where the surf breaks violently. On the leeward side of the island, the surf will be at its weakest and this will present you with your best chance of a safe landing. Look too for small peninsulas or sandbars topped with scrub. If you position your life raft to pass just beyond the tip of this feature, there will be a back eddy in the lee that will sweep you into safety and shelter behind the feature. This is the best possible landing location as the water will be shallow and sheltered from the surf.

River mouths and estuaries

Smaller river mouths will be constantly outflowing and will take you away from land, but you will not have to travel far along the shoreline to escape their influence, and at that point you will be able to land. One advantage of landing close to the mouth of a river is that reefs do not grow in fresh water. Wherever you see the mouth of a small river, you can be sure that the area immediately surrounding the river mouth is free of coral.

Larger rivers have estuarine mouths – where the water flow is tidal – and discoloured silty water. If you find your life raft being sluiced into the mouth of an estuary, make sure you make it to the bank as soon as possible, otherwise the tide will turn and sweep you back out to sea again.

LANDING WITH A LIFE RAFT

Once you have selected your landing location, specify a prominent rendezvous on the coast so that, should you be separated during landing, you will be able to meet up again. Take down any sailing rig you have erected, as you will need the paddles to assist your landing.

Cut away sections of the life raft canopy to allow your crew to use paddles on either side of the life raft. If your sea anchor is not already deployed, launch it from the stern of the life raft and prepare the spare (improvise a spare if you do not have a purpose-built one) for deployment. If you cannot find a settlement or a sheltered landing location, the sea anchor is your best chance of making a controlled landing.

If you have a towing dinghy, this could be tethered to the life raft stern using the longest line you have available, partially swamped and used as an extra sea anchor.

Secure everything in the life raft so that the already risky process of landing is not further complicated by kit hurtling about inside the life raft. If you land far from civilization, your signalling equipment, water collection gear, fishing kit and first aid kit will be no less necessary once ashore. Having ferried it across an ocean, it would be folly to lose it a short distance from shore. If you salvaged a sail or a tarpaulin, attach its broadest section across the bow of the life raft and stream the cloth below the life raft.

Landing in surf

Even with your sea anchor streamed, you will need to back-paddle as wave crests approach to prevent capsizing in the surf. The stern crew will call the wave pattern and tell the paddlers when to make for shore and when to back-paddle. Everyone should be harnessed to the life raft and use the lanyards to prevent losing their paddles.

(Use soft cloth to protect the buoyancy chambers from chafe by the tethers.) The sail will provide greater protection for the underside of the life raft should you encounter rocks or coral and when you hit the sand.

Make sure you are wearing all your clothing, including boots, foul weather gear and gloves. Put on your PFD and inflate it before the landing approach begins so that if you end up in the water at any stage, you will not drown from exhaustion or by being caught in an undertow. Tether yourself to the grab lines inside the life raft to ensure that you do not end up in the water unless the life raft actually disintegrates.

Delegate landing duties to your crew. You will need one of your crew at the stern to check the waves behind the life raft, warning of any very large, breaking waves, calling the paddling direction and ready to deploy the spare sea anchor if the original fails. Your stern crew should not waste time looking for wave patterns. The popular notion that waves arrive in sets of seven, the first being the smallest and the seventh the largest, is mythical: waves are unpredictable. Another crew member should be deployed at the bow to watch for submerged rocks or small reefs. The rest, the strongest, should be assigned to paddling duties and they should tether the paddles to their harnesses to prevent their loss.

Once you have entered your final approach, you will notice your speed towards shore increases considerably. This is because in deep water, water molecules in a wind-driven wave move in a circular motion, rather than forward with the wave. In shallower water, however, the circle flattens until, nearing shore, the waves reach one-and-a half times their height in deep water and begin to break. On the shore, you can see the water rushing up the beach. It is this progressive speed that makes your sea anchor vital, to brake your approach and gain control.

As a wave crest passes under the life raft, the crew member at the stern will instruct the paddling crew to paddle as hard as possible towards the beach while in the trough of the wave. As the next crest approaches, she will instruct the crew to back-paddle hard, out to sea. This will help the sea anchor to prevent you from surfing uncontrollably and capsizing.

Once the crest has passed, she will call for the team to paddle ashore again. If she spots a large breaking wave, she will alert the paddling crew and everyone should brace themselves for impact by grabbing handholds inside the life raft.

Do not leave the life raft until the bow crew gives the instruction. The life raft may hit the sea bed in advance of a cresting wave while still some distance from the shoreline, indicating a false landing. Once the instruction is given, unharness, exit and haul the raft up the beach beyond the high water mark.

LANDING ON ICE WITH A LIFE RAFT

In Polar regions, you will have little choice but to beach your life raft on an ice floe. You must take particular care when approaching the floe – there will be many small fragments of ice in the water, any one of which could hole your life raft. Approach slowly and use your paddles to fend off any ice. When

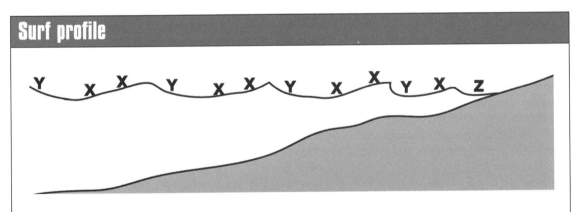

Surf profile

X Paddle as hard as possible towards the beach once the wave crest has passed.

Y When the next crest approaches, back-paddle quickly to prevent capsize.

Z When you are certain you have landed, unclip from the raft and haul it up the beach above the high tide line.

As you approach the beach, you will notice the waves becoming steeper, perhaps even breaking. This depends on the profile of the seabed on the approach to land. Ideally you are looking for shallow waves that roll softly on to shore, indicating a long gentle slope of seabed. Surf indicates a sudden rise in the seabed and potentially a very violent landing.

Avoiding reef and rocks

If your life raft has disintegrated and you are attempting a floating landing, paddle towards the beach once the crests have passed, back-paddle when the next crest approaches (or turn and dive into it if it is large or breaking).

Once in your approach, keep your feet below and ahead of you, paddling with your arms, so that your shoes hit the rock or reef first and your legs absorb the impact. It may be a false landing so keep your legs ahead of you.

looking for a potential landing floe, do not choose one that is unstable or fissured and about to break up. Choose a large floe.

When you approach the floe, use your paddles and fishing gaff to hold the life raft alongside the flow without any contact being made between floe and life raft. If you salvaged any fenders, use them to cushion the life raft while the shore crew leaves the life raft. Once the shore crew has established that the floe is solid and stable, use a salvaged sail or tarpaulin to cover the edge of the floe and protect the life raft as you land

it. Remember, this will take some time because the ballast bags will be full and will need to drain before the life raft becomes light enough to land.

Once ashore, do not deflate the life raft – despite your checks, the floe could disintegrate at any moment and you will need to escape quickly. Look for any shelter the floe might offer from the prevailing wind. Place the salvaged sail or tarpaulin on the ice beneath the life raft for protection and a little extra insulation, then secure the life raft to the floe using line and improvised stakes to ensure the wind does not relaunch you in the worst possible conditions. Your stakes could be large fish bones, knives, paddle handles or gaff fishing hooks. Fish bones are preferable because they are disposable – the rest is valuable kit and you do not want to lose it.

LANDING WITHOUT A LIFE RAFT

If your life raft has disintegrated in the surf, the techniques for landing as a swimmer are similar to those in the life raft, although some adjustments must be made. The first step is to deflate your PFD slightly because it will impede your manoeuvrability. Swimming with it fully inflated will be difficult unless you are on your back, and this is not recommended. Swim using the lifeguard's sidestroke or breaststroke, as these strokes require less energy. Head for the beach in the troughs between the waves. As the crest approaches and you feel yourself begin to rise, dive into the water (unless the waves are large and breaking) and surface once the wave has passed. If you are landing in large waves, turn to face the wave and dive through it as it closes over you. Your partially deflated PFD will make this possible and bring you back to the surface once the crest has passed. If your PFD is fully inflated, you will have trouble diving. Once you have surfaced, turn and swim hard for shore again.

As you enter the final phase of landing, adopt a sitting position facing forwards with your feet braced ahead of and below you. Your boots will protect you from any impact on submerged rocks, coral or the sea bed. Take a very deep breath when you feel yourself rising and hear the next crest approaching. If a crest passes and you have not made contact with land, stay in the sitting position and use your hands only for propulsion.

If you are caught by a large breaking wave, you could find yourself caught in an undertow and held against the sea bed. Push off the floor with your feet as soon as possible because the crest will have passed, and then adopt the sitting position again.

On sandy coasts, get to your feet as soon as possible once you have been bundled ashore by the wave and get up the beach beyond the high water line. If you cannot walk, crawl, but do so quickly because the next wave may pull you back out in its rip current. If landing on rocks, try to hang on to the first one you encounter. This will not be easy and will require all the strength you have, but the option is to be flipped around the rocks like a pinball until the wave subsides, with obvious implications for your health and safety. Once you have a handhold, cling on until the wave subsides, then head inland as fast as possible, but find a handhold on the land side of a rock again when you hear another wave approaching.

Once ashore, make your way to the agreed rendezvous, but inspect the shoreline as the contents of your life raft, such as the floating grab bag, water containers and fishing kit, will probably be washed ashore.

COASTAL SURVIVAL

You will find walking very difficult as your legs will be weak and your balance impaired. So, once ashore with the life raft safe, make sure that you rest and take some fluids and food. Remember, though, that unless you are near civilization, your ordeal is not over. Coastal survival is considerably easier than survival at sea, but markedly different in nature. You will need to maintain rationing while you come to grips with coastal survival techniques.

However, having survived at sea you can be confident that your evolutionary legacy – improvisation, innovation, learning, and the drive to survive – has served you well and will continue to do so. You have exchanged an environment hostile to your survival for one in which you are evolved to prosper – and with confidence in your ability to do so, you certainly will.

Glossary

Buoyancy chambers: These are the inflatable sections of the life raft, or other craft, that allow the vessel to float.

Chemical light stick: A sealed plastic tube of chemicals that luminesce brightly when a reaction is manually started.

Ciguatera: Non-fatal food poisoning caused by eating fish affected with ciguatoxin, picked up from reef-grazing fish in tropical climates.

Dead reckoning: This is approximate navigation, using estimates of speed and direction over a certain period of time to estimate current position based on a known starting position.

Distillation: Distillation involves the use of heat energy to evaporate fresh water from sea water, which is then condensed and collected.

Dye marker: A sachet of powdered dye that colours the water to help the survivor's relocation by raising visibility.

Frostbite: When exposed to extreme cold, blood flow to the body's extremities is cut off to guard against heat loss.

GMDSS: GMDSS (the Global Maritime Distress and Safety System) uses two satellite systems (COSPAS-SARSAT and INMARSAT) to provide distress relay coverage around the world from 76°N to 76°S. When an EPIRB is operated, the owner's distress will be relayed to the nearest Maritime Rescue Coordination Centre (MRCC).

Gorge hook: This is a short wooden or metal bar with a spike at each end and tied around the middle with fishing line. When the fish bites, the spikes catch in the fish's throat.

GPS - Global Positioning System: The GPS unit triangulates its position from satellites and is accurate to within 30 metres (100ft).

Grab lines: These are rope loops attached around the exterior of the life raft.

Growler: These are small chunks of ice, from the size of a box to the size of a house, which split away from icebergs and floes. They are difficult to see but can inflict terminal damage to the hulls of most small craft.

Heat stroke: Sweating reduces the body's fluids and minerals. After continued exposure to heat, the fluid levels drop so far that sweating stops, the blood thickens, causing blood pressure to drop, and the amount of oxygen supplied to vital organs, such as the brain, is reduced. Unconsciousness soon follows.

Heliograph: The heliograph, or signal mirror, aims sunlight to attract attention.

Hypothermia: The body's normal core temperature is 98.4° Fahrenheit (36.8° Celsius). If core temperature drops below 95° Fahrenheit (35° Celsius), the body becomes hypothermic and vasoconstriction occurs, cutting the supply of blood to the extremities to limit heat loss. The body shivers intensely to convert energy into heat, and mental function suffers.

Immersion damage: Continued immersion damages the skin's strength and elasticity, preventing wounds from healing and making the skin prone to tearing.

Land breeze: At night, coastal land loses heat quicker than the sea. The relative heat of the sea warms the air above it and this air rises. The cold air over the land then blows offshore to equalise the low pressure caused by the rising air. This is a land breeze.

Lanyard: To avoid losing equipment overboard, a line is secured to anything being used outside the life raft and then secured around the wrist.

Latitude: An index of north-south position.

Leeboard: An underwater appendage that prevents leeway - a craft's sideways movement caused by the wind.

Logbook: The logbook, filled out by the skipper or watchleader, notes the progress of a craft, the prevailing weather conditions and any other notable factors – any sightings of ships or aircraft, the names and health of those in the craft, water and food stores and details of rationing.

Marlinspike: Pointed steel tool used for ropework, opening shackles and spring clips.

Mayday: From 'M'aidez' (French for 'Help me'), this is recognised internationally as a call for urgent assistance and follows a standard formal procedure broadcast on Channel 16.

MOB: Man Over Board: Should one of the crew fall overboard, there is a standard procedure for their recovery and this should be rehearsed until the entire crew knows the procedure thoroughly.

MRCC: Marine Rescue and Coordination Centre: when you operate your EPIRB, your signal will be received first by the nearest MRCC and its staff will coordinate your recovery.

PLB - Personal Locator Beacon: The PLB is a handheld EPIRB designed to be carried at all times. If equipped with a long-lasting battery, it is a useful backup for your main EPIRB.

Pyrotechnics: Pyrotechnics (handheld, rocket and parachute flares, smoke canisters) are used to attract the attention of passing craft or to help SAR services home in on your position.

Repair clamp: The life raft has a repair kit but it is likely to be inadequate. These clamps are designed to effect an airtight repair on potentially disastrous tears in buoyancy chambers quickly and easily.

Righting strop: If your life raft capsizes before it is loaded, you will need to right it. Attached to the underside of the life raft is a strop. By standing on the edge of the life raft, holding the strop and leaning backwards, the raft will gradually right.

SOLAS - Safety Of Life At Sea: This international safety code was drawn up after the Titanic disaster and has been updated regularly since to ensure that mass produced safety equipment is as effective as possible.

SOS - Save Our Souls: This is an internationally recognised distress signal, generally transmitted in Morse code (. . . - - - . . .) when sending a Mayday is not possible.

Index

Page numbers in *italics*
refer to illustrations

abandon ship bags *see* grab
    bags
abandoning ship 63-7, *79*
    fires 75-6, 77
    fuel accidents 78-9, *85*
    holed vessel 72-3
    preparation *66,* 68-72
aircraft, attracting *167,* 169,
    173-4 *see also* flight
    paths
anchors *see* sea anchors
artificial respiration 55
attitude *see* will to survive
attracting attention 43-4,
    *47,49,51,*57,59
    aircraft *167,* 169, 173-4
    ships 157-9, 165-6,
    173-4
Auralyn 117

Bailey, Maurice 117
bailing 55, 82
ballast bags 105, 106
battery life 163-4
Ben Lomond 37, 40-1
binoculars 36, 159-60
birds
    land indicators 177
    snaring 40, 154-5
body temperature 12, 13,
    14, 128 *see also*
    hypothermia
Bombard, Dr. Alain 131

Callahan, Steve 117, 134
canopy, life raft 125, 127
    landfall 183-4
    sunscreen 130
capsizing 52, 54-5, 64-5, 67
carbohydrates 31, 57, 58,
    128, 131, 133-5
charts 35, 58, 93-4, 101
chemical desalination
    117-18
chemical light sticks 23, 51,
    170-1
cliffs 181-2
clothing
    buoyancy aid 46, 48
    cold weather 20-1, *22,*
    53
    hot weather 21, 130
    sun protection 21, 50-1
    wetsuits 49, 50
clouds 121-4
    land indicators 176-7
coastguards 56, 59
cold *see* hypothermia
compasses 35, 51, 58, 59
    use on a life raft 98, *99,*
    100
condensation 126-7
conservation
    energy 49-50, 55-6
    water 129-31
core body temperature 12,
    13, 14, 128
crew
    rescue 78, *83*
    survival on a life raft 82,
    84-5, 90-1

currents 45, 57
    formation of 103-5
    landfall 180
    monitoring 93, 94, 98

dead reckoning (DR) 96
dehydration 53, 129, 130
    see also sweating; water
desalination 117-20
dew 126-7
Digital Selective Calling
    (DSC) 39, 61, 70, *163,*
    164-6
dinghies *see also* life rafts
    buoyancy 55, 58
    capsizing 52, 54-5
    in emergencies 70, 72
    inflatable 106, 107-10
    righting *56*
    rigid 110-11, *113*
    sailing 52
    sinking 55-6
direction finding 98-100
distances, estimation 94, 96,
    98
distress signals *42,* 43-4,
    *47,49,51,*57,59
    EPIRB *38-9, 160,* 161-4,
    168-9
    flares 35, 36, 56-7, 58,
    60, 61, 167-9
    Personal Locator
    Beacons 51, 88, 164
    smoke canisters 36, 61,
    167, 168
    VHF radio 39, 70, *163,*
    164-6

drinking water *see* water
drowning 11-12, 44
drysuits 49
DSC (Digital Selective
    Calling) 39, 61, 70, *163,*
    164-6
dye markers 23, 36, 51, 168

Ednamair 106
emergencies
    damage to hulls 67, *69,*
    72-3
    fires 73-6, 77
    fuel accidents 78-9, *85*
emergency equipment
    19-36
Emergency Position
    Indicating Radio Beacon
    (EPIRB) *38-9,* 57, 61,
    88, 91, *160,* 161-4, 168-9
emergency rations 70, 90
enemas 125, 129
energy conservation 49-50,
    55-6
EPIRB (Emergency Position
    Indicating Radio Beacon)
    38-9, 57, 61, 88, 91, *160,*
    161-4, 168-9
estimated time of arrival
    (ETA) 94, 102
estuaries, landfall *182,* 183
exposure *see* heat
    exposure; hypothermia

Fastnet Race 1979 63-4
fats 135-6
fear 84-5

fire 73-6, 77
fire extinguishing
equipment 74, *75*, 76
first aid 15, 16, 55, 139, 143
kits 33, *34*, 58, 183
fish
barracuda *142*, 143
crustacea 137-8, 155
dangerous *142*, 143
dorado 134, 138
dressing 148, 150, *152, 153*
edibility 139
flying fish 138
food source 134, 135, 136, 137
jellyfish *141*, 143
poisonous 139, *140*
Portuguese man-of-war *141*, 143
pufferfish 139
sharks 144, 146
stonefish 139, *141*
triggerfish 138, 139, *140*
venomous 139, *141, 143*
fishermen 158-9, 173, 176
fishing 31-3, 143-6, *151*, 160, 183
gaff fishing *145*, 148
line fishing 146-7
spear fishing 147-8, *149*
fishing boats 158-9
flares 35, 36, 56-7, 58, *60*, 61, 167-9
flashlights 36, 170
flight paths 93, 130
floating 45-6, 48
relaxed technique *44*, 48, *50*
foghorns 36, 57, 58, 170
food
carbohydrates 31, 57, 58, 128, 131, 133-5
fats 135-6
human needs 133
minerals 137, 155

proteins 135
ration kit 31, 90
vitamins 136-7, 155
fresh water *see* water
fuel accidents 78, *85*

garbage, land indicators 174-5
gas, fire hazard 74-5
Global Maritime Distress and Safety System (GMDSS) *38-9*, *160-1*, 162, 164
Global Positioning System (GPS) 51, 56, 162, 165
emergency kit 35, 36, 58, 59, 94, 95
grab bags 27-9, *54*, 56, 59, 61, 66, 68, 70
contents 35, 57

harnesses 52, *158*, 159, *184*, 185
heat escape lessening posture (HELP) 49, *50*
heat exhaustion 53-4, 84
heat exposure *13*, 14-17, 21, 50-1, 53-4
heliographs *see* signal mirrors
hulls 64, 67-8, *69*
hunger, effects 19, 133
hypothermia 12-13, 44, 49-50, 53, 84

ice 127-8
floes 185-6
icebergs 128
immersion suits 49
interference wave patterns 175
International Maritime Organization (IMO) 23, 88, 105, 162
International Maritime Satellite Organization

(INMARSAT) 39, 162
islands, landfall 180, 181

land indicators 174-9
landfall 173-4
preparations 179-80
selecting landing zone 180-3
techniques 184-7
lanyards 20, 23, 28, 95
latitude 95, 100, *103 see also* position
lee shore 43, 174
leeboard *108*, 111, 174
L'Heritique 131
life jackets *see* personal flotation devices
life rafts *42*, 60 *see also* dinghies
abandoning ship 65-7
boarding 78, *79, 80-1*
kit 25-36, 85, 88, 90
landfall 179, 183-5
launching *71*, 72-3, 75-6
lookouts 88, 90, 130, *158*, 159, 160-1, 174
maintenance *158*, 160
onboard 82
preparation for launching 68-70, 72
regulations 23-5
rescue quoit, using 78, *83*
righting of 76-7
sailing 105-13
storage of equipment 20
towing *113*, 174
training 168
waiting for rescue 91
lights
flashlights 170
light sticks 23, 51, 170-1
strobe 53, 58, 61
Lindemann, Dr. Hannes 131
logbooks 35, 95
longitude 95, 100-2

lookouts 88, 90, 130, *158*, 159, 160-1, 174
Lucette 105, 106, 117

maintenance
fire prevention 74
life rafts *24*, 27, 90-1
sea anchors 112
man over board (MOB) 51-3, 171
Maritime Rescue and Coordination Centres (MRCC) *38-9*, 88, 91, *160-1*, 162, 168
masts 64, 106-11
Mayday calls 61, 70, 94
mental attitude *see* will to survive
Mobile Maritime Service Identity (MMSI) number 39, *163*, 164-5
mobile phones 56, 58, 59
multitools 21, 23, 51, 55, 57

Napoleon Solo 117
navigation
dead reckoning 96
landfall 174, 179
latitude 95, 100, *103*
longitude 95, 100-2
position, determining 93-6, 174, 179
navigation equipment 33, 35 *see also* compasses; GPS
charts 35, 58, 93-4, 101
sextants *37*, 94-5, *96*, 100, *103*
sight reduction tables *37*, 94-5
watches 95, 99, 100-1
nutrition 134-7

paddles 179, 183
panic 12, 45-6, 85, 91
personal flotation devices

(PFD) 20, *28*, 46, 48, 51-2, 53
abandoning ship 68, 78, *85*
checks 58
landfall 184, 187
lookouts *158*, 159
rescue 171
Personal Locator Beacons (PLBs) 51, 88, 164
plankton *see* seaweed
pocket survival kit 170
Poon Lim 37, 40-1, 154, 158-9
position
determining 93-6, 174, 179
monitoring 48-9, 57, 59
proteins 135
pumps, reverse osmosis 30, 118, *119*

rain 120-4
rainwater *18*, 30, 119-20
collection 124-6
rations
carbohydrate 31, 57, 58, 128, 131, 133-5
water 25, 70, 90, 117, 128-9, 131
reefs 181
repair kits 25-7
rescue kits 36
rescue quoits 25, 78, *83*, 96
reverse osmosis pumps 30, 118, *119*
rigging, dinghies 108-11
river mouths, landfall *182*, 183
Robertson family 105, 106, 117
rudders, dinghies *108*, 111, 174
Safety Of Life At Sea (SOLAS) regulations 23, 105, 167

sails 70, 174
salt
depletion 14, 19
in seawater 115-16, 119, 125-6, 131
tablets 14, 53
saltwater *see* seawater
salvage 79
sea anchors 26, 27, *35*, 36, 109-10
estimating direction 98
landfall 179, 183
life rafts 73, 78, 82, 112-13, *160*
seabirds 154-5
seasickness 17, 82, 84, 129
seawater *see also* water
composition 115-16, 131
desalination *30*, 117-20
sores 16, *120*, 130
seaweed, as food 135, 136, 137, 155
sextants *37*, 94-5, *96*, 100, *103*
sharks 9-10, 17, 49, *80*, *86-7*, *89*, 150
shipping lanes 93, 130
ships 157-9, 165-6, 173-4, 176
shock 84
sight reduction tables *37*, 94-5
signal mirrors 35, 36, *167*, 169-70, 179
signals *see* distress signals
smoke canisters 36, 61, 167, 168
snow 127-8
solar distillation 119, *125*
SOLAS regulations 23, 105, 167
sores from seawater 16, *120*, 130
speed, estimation 94, 96
stars, direction finding 99-100, *102*

static lines, in life rafts 68, 70, *71*, 72, 73, 76
streaming markers 168
strobe lights 53, 58, 61
sun
direction finding 99, 101
exposure to *13*, 14-15, 21, 53-4
sunblindness 15-16, 20
water distillation 119, *125*
sunburn 14-16, 50-1
sunglasses 20, 21
sunscreen 14, 21, 23, 50, 51
survival blankets *169*, 171
survival kits 66, 68, *71*, 72, 85, 88, 90 *see also* emergency equipment
pocket 170
survival suits 49
sweating *13*, 14, 17-18, 53, *120*, 130
swell, land indicators 175, 177-8
swimming
bad weather 48
landfall *186*, 187
precautions 57

tenders 70, 72, 106
thirst 17-18, 19
toolkits 36
toxins, from fish 139, 143
training, sea safety 168
transits 48-9, 57
turtles 152-3, *154*

ultraviolet (UV) radiation 14, 15, 21
Unique Identification Number (UIN) *160-1*, 162
vectors 93, 94
VHF radio 35, 36, 39, 56, 58, 59, 90
distress signals *163*, 164-6

DSC 39, 70, *163*, 164-6
emergency channels 39, 61, 70, 164-5, 166
Mayday calls 61, 70, 94
visibility 171
vitamins 136-7, 155

watch system *see* lookouts
watches 95, 99, 100-1
water *see also* seawater
bottled 53, 56, 57, 58, 116-17
collecting *18*, 19, 29-31, 125-6, 160-1 183
conservation 116, *120*, 129-31
emergency supplies 70, 72, 90
for survival 18, 19, 29
rations 25, 70, 90, 117, 128-9, 131
solar distillation 30,119, *125*
wave patterns 175, 177-8
weather
clouds 121-4
low pressure systems 124
rain 120-4
weather forecasts 58
wetsuits 49, 50
whales 73, 106
whistles 23, 36, 49, 51, 53, 57, 170, 179
will to survive 37, 40-1, 84-5, 91, 113, 130
wind
formation of 102-3
global *104-5*
monitoring 93, 94, 98